Theology in Folk Culture

STUDIEN ZUR INTERKULTURELLEN GESCHICHTE DES CHRISTENTUMS
ETUDES D' HISTOIRE INTERCULTURELLE DU CHRISTIANISME
STUDIES IN THE INTERCULTURAL HISTORY OF CHRISTIANITY
Herausgegeben von/edité par/edited by

Richard Friedli   Walter J. Hollenweger   Hans Jochen Margull
Université de Fribourg   University of Birmingham   Universität Hamburg

Band 33

Verlag Peter Lang
Frankfurt am Main · Bern · New York · Nancy

George MacDonald Mulrain

THEOLOGY IN FOLK CULTURE

The Theological Significance of Haitian Folk Religion

Verlag Peter Lang

Frankfurt am Main · Bern · New York · Nancy

CIP-Kurztitelaufnahme der Deutschen Bibliothek

Mulrain, George MacDonald:

Theology in folk culture : the theol. significance
of Haitian folk religion / George MacDonald Mulrain. -
Frankfurt am Main ; Bern ; New York ; Nancy : Lang,
1984.
 (Studies in the intercultural history of
 christianity ; Vol. 33)
 ISBN 3-8204-7467-6
NE: Studien zur interkulturellen Geschichte des
Christentums

ISSN 0170-9240
ISBN 3-8204-7467-6
© Verlag Peter Lang GmbH, Frankfurt am Main 1984

Druck und Bindung: Weihert-Druck GmbH, Darmstadt

SYNOPSIS

The theology which has for long monopolized the world scene is
a reflection of God-talk by people of the rich western nations.
By contrast, the religious experiences of people within the
poorer countries have often been regarded as having little
or nothing worthwhile to contribute to the mainstream of theological scholarship.

Today African, Asian, Caribbean and Latin American theologians
are constantly reminding the rest of the world that God also
reveals Himself in their cultures through varied channels.
Western theological thinking does not constitute the ensemble
of objective, universal truths about God's activity in the
world. Theology in its totality acknowledges the uniqueness of
divine revelation from culture to culture.

This thesis attempts to continue the process of sensitizing
people to the value of theology emanating from folk cultures
around the world. The Caribbean Republic of Haiti is one
country which has retained most of the facets of its original
oral culture. The Vaudou religion, based on the veneration of
spirits or 'loas', is sometimes regarded as superstitious nonsense. Yet within it, people have some unique spiritual
experiences which have serious implications, not just for
Caribbean theology, but indeed for a truly multi-cultural
approach to theology.

ACKNOWLEDGEMENTS

The production of this work has been a team effort. I owe deep
gratitude to so many people who shared in it that to list them
all would be impossible.

Professor Walter J. Hollenweger, in supervising the research, has
been of tremendous help. His scholarly advice and sound criticism have enhanced my theological thinking.

I am grateful to Mr. John Eaton and Dr. Frances Young of the
University of Birmingham's Theology Department, and to Dr.
Sigvard von Sicard and Dr. and Mrs. Frank Pearce of Selly Oak,
all of whom provided me with helpful suggestions for specific
sections of the thesis.

I learned a tremendous lot from my own students within the
Selly Oak Colleges. Fellow members of staff always gave
assistance when called upon.

I am aware how much I owe to all those with whom I worked in
Haiti. Without their help, I could not have received all these
insights which I have attempted to share in the pages of this
work.

Thanks are also due to Miss Yvonne Taylor and Miss Sally Parker
for typing the final manuscript.

Last, but not least, I am indebted to my immediate family - Elaine, my wife, who has given full support and encouragement throughout the research; my daughters Karla-Lee and Heidi who have had grudgingly to take second place to my typewriter as the study progressed.

CONTENTS

5

INTRODUCTION

Aim and Scope

This research is entitled "Theology in Folk Culture" because it
is meant to be a theological treatise which will stimulate
general interest in the theological perspectives emanating from
within the context of folk culture. Its sphere of observation
will be the Caribbean region where there are several indigenous
religious expressions, for example Vaudou (or Voodoo) of Haiti,
Cumina, Pocomania and Rastafarianism of Jamaica, Shango of
Trinidad, Santeria of Cuba, the Big Drum Dance of Grenada and
Carriacou, and Kele of St. Lucia.[1] We have not the time to deal
with more than just one within the scope of this research. Our
major concern will be Vaudou, which, until now, has hardly
featured in any serious reflections by theologians of the Caribbean, even though it is an integral part of the culture. Vaudou
is undoubtedly the most developed of all these religious expressions. But let us, in the first instance, focus our
attention upon the Caribbean republic of Haiti wherein the drama
of Vaudou unfolds itself.

Haiti

Someone once made the remark that the republic of Haiti is "like
nowhere else on earth."[2] Indeed there are many distinguishing
features which help to make this a rather unique place. It is a
mountainous country[3] occupying the western portion of the
Caribbean island of the Greater Antilles[4] known as Hispaniola.[5]

The eastern section of the island is known as the Dominican
Republic. The island of Cuba is north-west of Haiti, whereas
Jamaica is in a south-westerly direction. Haiti prides herself
on being the Pearl of the Antilles[6] but there are other Caribbean islands which make similar claims for themselves. However,
Haiti has the distinction of being the first black republic of
the New World. She started off as a colony of Spain towards the
end of the fifteenth century. By the end of the seventeenth
century she was numbered among the possessions of France. One
century later, her political status was undergoing drastic
changes with the result that in January 1804 she had emerged as
a free nation, independent of France's political control. Among
the popular heroes who featured in the panorama of Haitian
political history were Toussaint L'Ouverture and King Henri
Christophe, whose stories will be treated in more detail in
our first chapter.

French is the official language, but most of the five and a
half million people speak a French-based créole.[7] Today the
country is ruled by a young man approaching the age of thirty.
Shortly before his death in 1971, 'Papa Doc' François Duvalier[8] had named his teenaged son, Jean-Claude, to succeed
him as President and had given him a mandate to rule the
country for life (président à vie).

Haiti is a land of paradoxes. It is rich in natural beauty,
with lovely beaches and warm sunshine contributing to a charm

beyond compare. But is is poor in natural resources. The
presence of bauxite has not succeeded in making the national
economy sufficiently viable. Agriculture and farming are
major pursuits. Most people struggle to eke out an existence
from the land. Evidence of the gravity of the country's economic situation is the hundreds of men, women and children who
daily risk their lives in tiny little boats and flee the country in the hope of finding refuge in the United States of
America. It is understood that there are some 700,000 Haitian
refugees scattered in places like Florida, the Dominican Republic, the Bahamas, New York, Montreal, Guadeloupe, French
Saint Martin, Cayenne, Suriname, Venezuela and France.[9] In
Florida, for example, the arrival of refugees in 1981 was
estimated at over 300 a week.[10] Unfortunately many of these
boat-people do not complete the journey, but perish at sea.

However, despite the rigours of life's experience - poverty,
illiteracy, malnutrition, hunger, sickness, intense suffering,
inadequate housing, death - Haitians are a warm, friendly and
deeply religious people. Although the country is reputed
economically to be the poorest in the Western Hemisphere, and
certainly one of the most destitute in the entire world, it is,
in terms of painting, sculpture and various other artistic
pursuits, one of the wealthiest in the world.

The Negative Approach

When I mentioned the subject of my research to a friend, the

question which he asked me was: "What has vaudou got to do with
the Christian gospel?" As far as he was concerned, there was no
point in any follower of Christ, let alone a Christian minister,
spending time reflecting on what he thought was sheer nonsense.
I daresay that what my friend expressed was a typical reaction
to the negative image which is conjured up in people's minds
at the sound of the word "Vaudou" (or "Voodoo"). The tendency
has always been to describe it as black magic, or obeah[11] or
anything which involves sticking pins into rag dolls and thereby causing pain and suffering to other individuals.

It is interesting to note how anything in our world which is
classified as being inferior in quality, or undesirable, is
given a black label - blackmail, black sheep of the family,
black market prices, and now, in reference to vaudou, black
magic. Just as women are today waging a campaign against what
they see in the English language to be sexist, male chauvinis-
tic words and expressions, e.g. mankind, to man the stalls, so
too there is a move afoot by black people to change the image
of blackness. It is the feeling that since whiteness has
always symbolized rightness, wholeness, cleanliness and purity,
it must now be brought to the attention of the world that blackness is also indicative of beauty.[12] The problem with vaudou
is that it has always been described as the art of 'black'
magic, performed mainly by 'black' people, hence its constant
association with all that is evil.

In a sense, black people are themselves responsible for perpet-
uating the idea of the evil connotations of vaudou. In the
republic of Haiti for example, the air of mystery in which vaudou is shrouded, has been exploited as a tourist attraction.
Hence, the first thing which may be asked by visitors to Haiti
is, "Where can I go to see a vaudou ceremony?" No tourist,
upon leaving the country, would feel that the visit had been
worthwhile if there had been no opportunity provided to see a
houmfort.[13] In fact, Haiti has become so well known as the
Caribbean's major centre for the practice of black magic, that
vaudou priests often receive invitations from countries abroad
to visit and conduct courses on the subject.[14]

The Positive Approach

The first impression about Vaudou which needs to be corrected
is that it is entirely evil. In all honesty, there are some
frightening things about, not the least of which is the
question of zombies.[15] Much of the prejudice against vaudou
has come from the novelists and film producers who have exploited it to create stories of bloodshed and violence. Two
New English Library novels illustrate this point aptly. Voodoo Queen[16] deals with a young mulatto beauty who, during the
years of Haiti's struggle for independence, prostitutes herself
in order that she and her baby might survive. Throughout the
narrative there is the unmistakeable element of terror which
lurks in the background. Zombie[17] portrays vaudou as a
religion associated with blood, human sacrifice, zombies,

graves and evil spirits. This seems to be the sum total of it. Nothing positive is inherent in it.

But there is a positive side to vaudou, which has attracted my attention as a Christian minister, and which I hope will be fairly evident throughout this research. When I arrived in Haiti in September, 1973, I had been numbered among those who thought of vaudou as something which had no earthly good in it. In August, 1977, at the end of my period of service as a Methodist pastor, attached to the Methodist Conference in the Caribbean and the Americas (MCCA),[18] I had an entirely new concept of vaudou. It was not just something to be dismissed lightly as superstitious nonsense. Rather, I saw in it a religion which, although not claiming to be an expression of Christianity, embraced certain theological stances[19] that warrant further enquiry into the nature of the created order and of divine revelation. This I consider to be the second impression which needs to be corrected, namely that vaudou is sheer superstition.

Vaudou, like Christianity, is a system of beliefs and practices involving the worship of a Supreme Being. Christianity is a religion, and so too is vaudou. According to Eugene Nida,

> "It is too easy to miss some important contrast
> or resemblance by passing off other people's be-
> liefs as 'superstitious' and regarding one's own
> beliefs as 'doctrines'. In the same way that we
> avoid 'savage' and 'native' when talking of
> social and material culture, we do well to avoid
> the word 'superstition' in talking of religion."[20]

This brings me to the point about orthography. Throughout this study, I will use the French spelling of 'vaudou' because of the negative connotations attached to the English 'voodoo' which conjures up the 'black magic or obeah' image.[21] The vaudou which is my concern in this research is not 'black' in the sense of being 'evil' or inferior in quality. It is black because of its affinity with the black culture of Haiti.[22] It is not 'magic' in the sense of being entirely a matter of pretence. Belief in magic is a part of its system, and it must be stressed 'only a part'. It is something real which, because of the inability of western culture to fully comprehend it, has been given the inappropriate title of 'magic'.[23]

Vaudou must be accepted for what it is worth, namely as a religion. It is not just a cult. A cult refers to a transient feature, some passing fancy or fad which may soon die out.[24] A religion is more permanent. It is true to say that several religions of the world, Christianity being no exception, began as cults, but have persisted until this day. From the eighteenth century down to the present, vaudou has existed as a true religion on Haitian soil. The Haitian writer, Jean Price-Mars, maintains that vaudou is a religion:[25]

- All its followers believe in the existence of spiritual beings which live somewhere in the universe in close association with human beings over whose activities they exercise control.

- Chief among these spiritual rulers is the Great Master, whom
  we may call God.
- It depends upon a hierarchical priesthood, a company of
  believers, temples, altars, ceremonies, and an oral tradition
  which, in spite of the modifications which it has undergone
  throughout the years, still displays the essential characteristics of a religion.
- It contains a theology or a system whereby the descendants
  of ancient Africans could explain natural phenomena.

Given that what is done within vaudou qualifies as worship,
not superstition, and that magic is but a part of vaudou, not
the be-all and end-all of it, the question often posed relates
to education. What is the relationship of a belief in vaudou
and education? Does education erase beliefs in vaudou? In
answer, let us look at the following case studies.

Case No. 1

Claude was a teenager attending a secondary school in Port-au-
Prince, the capital of Haiti. He was the eldest of a fairly
large family. Academic records at school supported the fact
of this young man's intelligence. In June 1975 he was sitting
the Baccalaureat examination, a very demanding exercise.[26]
On the last day of exams, he became very ill and had to be
confined to bed. Doctors were called in, but none could cure
him. A medical diagnosis was not forthcoming either. He just
lay there for several days, speaking to no-one, eating nothing,

as if in a trance-like state. It so happened that when his aunt
had called at the house, she diagnosed her nephew's illness as
having a spiritual causation. According to her, someone had
been jealous of the boy's outstanding academic progress and had
cast a spell upon him. A vaudou priest was summoned. He lifted
the spell and Claude was well again.[27]

The question which this incident would immediately evoke is as
follows: Was Claude actually the victim of a spell, or was his
mysterious illness really caused by sheer mental exhaustion
after his exams? If the answer is the latter, then we are bound
to pose another question. Why did medical expertise fail to
bring about a cure? We can hardly regard it as purely coinci-
dental that Claude's restoration to health came at the time
when the vaudou priest entered the picture. Whatever explanation we may deem satisfactory, it is noticeable that vaudou
did, through its priest, play a positive role in this highly
intelligent young man's life. It is foolhardy to suppose that
if the masses of vaudou worshippers become highly educated
overnight they would cease believing.

Education cannot eradicate the beliefs in vaudou because vaudou
is itself based upon a specialized form of education, namely a
deeper knowledge of the complexity of factors, physical and
spiritual, which are involved in human existence. It is significant that in the healing of Claude, the vaudou priest, not
the medical doctor, displayed superior knowledge. So that

vaudou is not just a question of 'black magic'. It involves
a healing ministry as well.[28] But let us look at the other
case.

Case No. 2

Denis was a lad of thirteen when he began suffering from continuous bouts of sickness. He was the eldest of five children.
The family lived on the outskirts of the northern coastal town
of Cap-Haitien. Most of his father's scanty earnings were
used up in paying doctors' fees, yet the boy's condition, instead of improving, grew progressively worse. While under the
influence of one of these bouts of illness, he would run around
in circles, lift heavy physical objects which his father would
have extreme difficulty in removing, and sometimes storm out
of the house and come to a halt only when he had fainted upon
somebody's doorstep.

At school one day, he had a brainwave. It was as though a
voice was advising him to follow an alternative route home.
Like any thirteen-year old, he soon forgot this sudden impulse.
That afternoon, he walked, as usual, with his friends who,
one by one, stopped off at their homes. Then he was alone when
suddenly a strange man accosted him. It was as though the
boy's spirit were transported to the top of a mountain. He
could hardly see the man's face, but he could certainly sense
his anger. Ripping off a protective charm from the boy's neck,
the man boomed: "It's that Catholic mass you said in school

today that has saved you. But one of these days, I'll get you!"
With that, the man vanished, and Denis was back on the street,
all alone.

Denis' parents used to be adherents to the vaudou religion,
but through their son's illness, they came into contact with a
circle of friends who were Christians. They heeded these
friends' advice and decided to link themselves to a Protestant
Church.[29] Members of the Methodist Church, to which they became
attached, paid constant visits to their home and prayed fer-
vently for the healing of the boy. Their prayers proved to be
effective, for Denis was completely restored to health.

In this second incident, we may find much upon which to speculate. What of Denis' healing? Was he facing, at the age of
thirteen, an identity crisis which only resolved itself when
the entire family made him the focal point of its concern?
Did the prayers of the church members merely coincide with
this stage in his development, or was this a fine example of
the effectual prayer leading to healing, as mentioned in the
letter of James?[30] And what of the root cause of his illness?
Was Denis demon possessed? And what of the strange meeting
on the way from school? Did this literally take place? Was
it a vision of some sort? It may be difficult to arrive at
completely satisfactory answers to these questions. But
then, these are some of the complicated cases which do arise
within folk cultures across the world. Within highly

industrialized societies, incidents of the kind as described
in the two case studies might be rare. Yet they are commonplace in Haiti, in other parts of the Caribbean, and indeed
throughout Africa.

Apart from my desire to illustrate the point that education
does not erase beliefs in vaudou, I deliberately selected for
my introductory case studies two young persons. Usually with
adults who are supposedly under spells, or demon-possessed,
one cannot be too sure that one is not simply witnessing a
splendid acting performance. But with younger, less mature
subjects, it is easier to detect fraud. In any case, these
younger subjects have very little, if any, to gain by deception or pretence over a protracted period.

Methodology

As mentioned at the very beginning, my interest in Vaudou is
theological. The presupposition under which this work has been
conceived is twofold:
i)   God has revealed Himself in Haitian Folk religion.
ii) God has spoken in a unique and normative way through Jesus
     Christ although that revelation is in contextual forms.

Most of the research carried out on Haitian Folk religion has
been done from a sociological point of view.[31] I want to
explore the phenomenon of vaudou in order to have my understanding of God broadened, and to have some of my doctrinal

stances challenged. It shall become evident, as we go along
in this study, that I identify with much of what is being said
by African theologians. This is to be attributed to similarities in cultural and religious insights. The thinking of
Laennec Hurbon[32] is also worthy of mention. His book is one
of the very few works which have attempted to look at vaudou
from a theological standpoint. The work of Jean-Marie
Salgado[33] is also theologically stimulating, though his is
not as intense a study as Hurbon's. Although most of the
written material, viz. books, essays, pamphlets and articles,
which I have used in putting together this thesis, have been
published, I have had access to a fair amount of unpublished
works by Haitian writers who have provided me with many valuable insights. An indication of sources used will appear in
the numbered footnotes after each chapter. A bibliography in
alphabetical sequence of authors and editors, will follow the
final chapter.

Because of the recurrence, throughout the seven chapters, of
certain unfamiliar words, a glossary appears after the bibliography. Of course when such unfamiliar words appear in the
first instance, a definition or some form of explanation will
be made available. The glossary is designed to facilitate
quick reference.

The greatest resource in helping me to understand and appreciate Haitian folk culture and folk religion was the orally

transmitted information which came to me either directly or
through my wife, as a result of conversations with Haitian
people. There could be no substitute for this constant interaction which we had every day for a period of four years with
people from all walks of life, drawn from different strata of
society. We met them in varying situations, in the urban and
rural areas, listening to them and conversing freely with
them in their mother-tongue, Créole. The settings for such
dialogue were mostly informal. However sometimes discussions
were of a formal nature, as for example, at youth camps, conferences for rural teachers, seminars for lay preachers,
community meetings and classroom discussions with teenagers
attending secondary school.

Naturally my work as a pastor facilitated my research on the
field. I had a fairly good general knowledge of the six
parishes in which the Methodist Church operates.[34] These cover
both urban and rural communities. I had an intimate knowledge
of the two parishes wherein I served. These two parishes -
Port-au-Prince and Cap-Haitian - list a total of twenty-one
congregations. Of these, two could be classified as urban,
six as sub-urban and the remaining thirteen as rural. It was
in these areas that I encountered men and women, boys and
girls, for whom Vaudou offered a genuine religious experience.
Some of the persons I interviewed had bizarre tales to tell,
the authenticity of which was questionable in some cases, in
other verifiable through the testimony of others whose word I

trusted. A few of them will appear during the course of the presentation. The vast majority have been omitted, seeing that our purpose in this thesis is not to strive towards the sensational, but rather to engage in a quest for theological truth. Obviously, information of a highly confidential nature would also be omitted, but purely upon ethical (not sensational) grounds. Needless to say, some of the vaudou worshippers interviewed were priests of the religion. In one or two exceptional instances, I encountered priests who had been converted from vaudou and were seeking to follow Christianity.

Often a distinction can be made between vaudou ceremonies held in the rural areas and those held in the towns with tourists in mind. In researching these ceremonies, I have come to the conclusion that tourist oriented ceremonies can also be genuine. This is the case when those involved are not professional actors playing a part, but persons who in their daily life are practising vaudou worshippers. What therefore may commence as a performance designed for an audience soon develops into something authentic and on a par with any other ceremony with no spectators.

Chapter 1 will give a description of the major features of folk culture as it exists in Haiti, as well as a rapid historical overview of how this culture developed. Chapter 2 will, in the first instance, describe the main aspects of vaudou and in so doing will raise some theological questions. One of these questions, pertaining to revelation in the presence of syncretism, will be treated in the second part of this chapter. The others will be dealt with in subsequent chapters. Chapter 3 represents the theological struggle to come to terms with 'spirit' as a functional entity within folk culture, and 'spirit' as a variegated concept within the Bible. In Chapter 4 we are to decide what sort of effect folk religion in Haiti has had upon people's understanding of and response to God. Chapter 5 will examine the various responses of Christianity and Vaudou to the needs of the Haitian community, and will highlight some ways whereby vaudou represents a challenge for the rethinking of the church's mission. In this respect, attitudes to women and to the ministry of healing will be discussed. In Chapter 6 we will survey the major influences upon theological reflection within the Caribbean and show how, in at least two areas, folk religion and culture can be a tremendous asset. Chapter 7 will examine the major theological perspectives arising from the study. In so doing it will spell out at least five steps which may be considered as constituting the way forward for theology.

My hope is that what appears in the pages of this study will awaken the interest, not only of Afro-Caribbean and other Third World theologians, but also that of theologians from the rich industrialized nations across the world. I am convinced that they too can benefit greatly from exposure to theological perspectives from outside their immediate range of vision, for it seems fairly obvious that the Church in Europe has lost contact with the oral people of this age. Western Christianity identifies mainly with written culture. This is a form of sectarianism, that one has changed from an oral stance to a completely written one. In such a situation, dialogue is of vital necessity, and will be of benefit both to the industrialized nations and to the Third World countries. Just as Caribbean theologians must read Barth, Brunner, or strive to appreciate the thought patterns of European anthropologists, so too must European theologians seek to cultivate what is so badly lacking, namely the ability to communicate with the Third World. These theologians must be encouraged to refrain from trying to justify the literary and western captivity of the Church and theology, but to break out of this, for these attempts at justification have deprived them of the possibility of intercultural growth.

INTRODUCTION - NOTES

1. A Brief overview of these religions is provided by George Eaton Simpson, "Religions of the Caribbean".

2. This slogan was seen on a tourist brochure about Haiti.

3. Haiti is derived from an Arawak word meaning very mountainous land.

4. The Greater Antilles are the larger Caribbean islands found towards the north-west comprising Cuba, Jamaica, Hispaniola and Puerto Rico.

5. Columbus, in 1492, called it Hispaniola or Little Spain.

6. Inhabitants of some of the Lesser Antilles, or smaller, easterly Caribbean islands have claimed that theirs is the 'pearl of the Antilles'. In Haiti, the number-plate of every vehicle proudly displays the words, 'Haiti - Perle des Antilles'.

7. More will be said about Créole in Chapter 1.

8. François Duvalier was a country doctor who, for fourteen years, had been in charge of a public health project. He was also an ethnologist by training, who soon became Under Secretary of State for Labour. He succeeded to the Presidency in 1957.

9. "Colonies of Haitian refugees in need of help" in Caribbean Contact, Vol. 9, no. 3, Barbados, July 1981, p. 17.

10. "Dumping of Haitians on Puerto Rico" in Caribbean Contact, Vol. 9, no. 5, Barbados, September 1981, p. 20.

11. Obeah comes "from two Ashanti words oba - 'a child' and yi - 'to take'. The idea of taking a child was the final test of a sorcerer, a deed giving the status of PhD in witchcraft". - Leonard E. Barrett, The Rastafarians - The Dreadlocks of Jamaica, Kingston, Jamaica and London, Sangster's Book Stores Ltd., in association with Heinemann, 1979, p. 18. Obeah is a commonly used Caribbean expression for harmful magic. "To work obeah upon someone" signifies that superhuman powers are being invoked in order to hurt an opponent.

12. This theme on the worth of blackness, in so far as it relates to theology will be dealt with in the sixth chapter.

13. __Houmfort__ is the name given to the hut or 'temple' where vaudou ceremonies are usually conducted. It will be described in greater detail in Chapter 2.

14. This fact is not commonly known. It was a friend of mine who works in a Port-au-Prince travel agency shared this piece of information with me. Apparently contacts in Martinique, Guadeloupe and countries outside the Caribbean region send prepaid airline tickets to his office. These are designated for well-known vaudou-priests.

15. __Zombies__ or 'living dead' are human beings who have been raised from the grave soon after burial and become slaves to vaudou sorcerers. A full treatment of this will appear in Chapter 2.

16. Adam Turner, __Voodoo Queen__.

17. Errol Lecale, __Zombie__.

18. The Methodist Conference in the Caribbean and the Americas (MCCA) comprises a total of eight districts: Bahamas, Haiti, Jamaica, Leeward Islands, South Caribbean, Guyana, Panama/Costa Rica and Belize. Formerly attached to the Methodist Church in Great Britain, it is now an autonomous conference.

19. These theological stances will be spelt out in Chapter 2, under the section entitled 'God and Revelation in Vaudou'.

20. Eugene A. Nida, __Customs and Cultures__, California, William Carey Library, 1976, p. 140.

21. This is how one English dictionary defines __voodoo__: 1. n. use of, belief in, religious witchcraft as practised among W. Ind, etc, Negroes. 2. v. t. Affect by voodoo, bewitch. (Dahomey). - __The Popular Oxford Dictionary of Current English__, London, Oxford Univ. Press, 1978, p. 1019. By contrast, the French dictionaries do not refer to __vaudou__ as witchcraft, thought they see it as something which has to do with magic. At least, they see it as a form of worship. __vaudou__ - m. culte secret, animiste et magique, introduit aux Antilles par les esclaves africains et qui s'est surtout développé à Haiti. - Maurice Davau, __Dictionnaire Du Français Vivant__, London, Harrap, 1973, p. 1241. __vaudou__ n. m. culte africain importé par les Noirs dans les Antilles. - __Nouveau Larousse Elémentaire__, Paris, Librarie Larousse, 1968, p. 725.

22. In Chapter 1, we will examine more fully the nature of the culture of Haiti.

23. One writer on vaudou suggests that the magic which is associated with the religion is not entirely black, in the sense of being wholly an African import. On the contrary, the French have made a significant contribution in this regard: "... les Haitiens ont pris des colons français des XVIIe et VIIIe siècles ce qu'ils avaient de mal, aux yeux sévères de la morale du moins: leur magie. Bien sûr, je ne prétendrai pas que les Français ont, seuls, initié les Haitiens à la magie. Cependant, ils les y ont initiés, c'est certain, comme on le verra, et, du moins, ils ont réactivé ce qui somnolait de tendance magique au coeur des Haitiens. Un legs colonial, un cadeau empoisonné que les maîtres blancs ont fait à leurs esclaves et à leurs fils". - Jean Kerboull, Vaudou et Pratiques Magiques, Paris, Pierre Belfond, 1977, p. 16.

24. I am aware that popular usage of the word cult suggests either an inferior religion or a sub-section within a larger religious entity. My working definition is: cult - a religious worship esp. as expressed in ceremonies; study and pursuit of worship of (esp. derog. of transient fad). The Popular Oxford Dictionary of Current English, London, Oxford University Press, 1978, p. 200.

25. "Le Vaudou est une religion parce que tous les adeptes croient à l'existence des êtres spirituels, qui vivent quelque part dans l'univers en étroite intimité avec les humains dont ils dominent l'activité.

"Ces êtres invisibles constituent un Olympe innombrable formé de dieux dont les plus grands d'entre eux portent le titre de Papa ou Grand Maître et ont droit à des hommages particuliers.

"Le Vaudou est un religion parce que le culte dévolu à ses dieux réclame un corps sacerdotal hiérarchisé, une société de fidèles, des temples, des autels, des cérémonies et, enfin, toute une tradition orale qui n'est certes pas parvenue jusqu'à nous sans altération, mais grâce à laquelle se transmettent les parties essentielles de ce culte.

"Le Vaudou est une religion parce que, à travers le fatras des légendes et la corruption des fables, on peut démêler une théologie, un système de représentation grâce auquel, primitivement, nos ancêtres africains s'expliquaient les phénomènes naturels ... " Jean Price-Mars, Ainsi Parla L'Oncle, Ottawa, LEMEAC, 1973, pp. 82, 83.

26. The Baccalaureat would correspond to GCE Ordinary Level examinations.

27. I will never forget how his borther, also a teenager at secondary school, upon relating to me how effective the vaudou priest's treatment had been said: "Immediately my brother got out of bed and began to eat like a cow!" - referring to the amount, rather than style of eating.

28. More will be said about the ministry of healing within vaudou in the second and fifth chapters.

29. I met this family while serving as pastor to a Methodist congregation in Haiti.

30. James 5:15, 16.

31. Examples of this are: James G. Leyburn, <u>The Haitian People</u>; George Eaton Simpson, <u>Religious Cults of the Caribbean: Trinidad, Jamaica and Haiti</u>; Melville J. Herskovits, <u>Life in a Haitian Valley</u>.

32. Laënnec Hurbon, <u>Dieu dans le Vaudou haitien</u>.

33. Jean-Marie Salgado, <u>Le Culte Africain Du Vodou et Les Baptisés en Haiti</u> - <u>Essai de Pastorale</u>.

34. The areas covered by the Methodist Church are Port-au-Prince, Cap-Haitien, Jérémie, Les Cayes, Petit-Goave and La Gonave island.

CHAPTER 1

HAITIAN FOLK CULTURE

In a recent report on Haiti, it was revealed that eighty percent of the population of school-going age lives in the countryside, but that seventy-five percent of the education system is
in the towns.[1] These findings reflect two general truths about
Haiti. The first is that more than eighty percent of the republic's five and a half million inhabitants are rural dwellers.
In fact, the majority of Haitians, whether they will consider
themselves as peasant farmers or not, do admit that agriculture exerts a tremendous influence upon their lives. The
second truth, which we will take up more fully in Chapter 5,
is that the pattern of industrial growth has always been confined to urban centres. The very few industries which do
exist are located in and around the capital city of Port-au-
Prince. And yet, there is no decided advantage in migrating
and becoming a member of the urban working class as opposed to
the rural working class. Wage earning in both areas is generally low. "The minimum annual wage established by the
government in December 1979 of G650 (650 Gourdes) is reached
only by five percent"[2] of the population. It would be more
realistic, then, instead of talking about two distinct working
classes, viz. urban and rural, to refer to the one working
class in the entire country.

Throughout Haiti, whether in town or village, working class

folk stick together, encouraging and mutually supporting one another. Whereas in other parts of the world, chiefly the industrialized nations, people are lamenting the individualistic lifestyles of their conurbations, and the breakdown of kinship ties, due to the mobility of urban society, Haiti, in almost every corner, displays the characteristics of rural organisation. The mule-drawn cart, for example, which many modern communities associate with the rural milieu, is quite commonplace in the busy streets of Port-au-Prince. It is not without significance that Haitian culture, or the way of life of this particular people, is dominated by the thoughts, language and customs of the masses of rural-oriented working class folk. The rich and educated elite may not want to admit it, but the wealth of the country's cultural expression is not to their credit. Rather it is to the grass-roots, the level of simple ordinary farming people. The official language of the country may be French, as had been decreed during the days of French colonial rule, but Haiti is by no means a replica of Parisian culture. Seen in its true perspective, Haiti is a country whose lifestyle has been made all the more attractive through the invaluable contributions which are forever being made by the unsophisticated majority. The fact that the agrarian sector is so strikingly reflected in the overall picture makes it justifiable to describe the Haitian way of life as folk culture.

The term 'folk culture' is sometimes referred to as 'oral'

culture, 'living' culture, or 'popular' culture. It is an apt description of the way of life of Haiti, as well as that of other countries in the Caribbean. This predominantly 'folk', 'oral', 'living' or 'popular' culture, as descriptive of the Caribbean islands, is agreed upon by scholars with an intimate knowledge of the region.[3] It is equally adequate for describing the culture of Brazil and several other Latin American countries. It is interesting to note that many of the European nations, e.g. France, Switzerland and Germany, are discovering how very much they too are affected by folk culture.[4] Of particular relevance to this thesis, the world of the Bible was heavily influenced by oral culture, a theme which we will reserve for discussion in our final chapter.

Let us take a look at some of the dominant facets of folk culture in the Haitian context. We can recognize them as being (i) oral literature, (ii) Creole language, (iii) Family patterns, (iv) Grass-roots' socialism, (v) Indigenous medicine, (vi) Indigenous art forms, and (vii) Popular belief.

(i)   Oral Literature

The report referred to earlier on estimates the illiteracy rate in Haiti to be about eighty-five percent. In such a situation, the majority of people will be geared towards oral expressions. Consequently, oral literature is the source of almost every aspect of the country's life. What do we understand by the term 'oral literature'?

> "Oral literature is merely literature which has
> come into existence in an oral culture or group
> without the use of writing. Sometimes such
> literature is called folklore. A popular mis-
> understanding of this last term might lead to the
> conclusion that literature created orally is of
> much inferior quality when compared to written
> literature. To think of oral literature as being
> limited to snatches of poetry, a few tales and
> some legends is to underestimate its range and
> quality. Oral literature comprehends both prose
> and poetry including both historical records,
> genealogies, and didactic material as well as
> panegyrics, elegies, hymns, prayers and ritual
> poetry."[5]

A pamplhlet on Haiti, though employing the often misunderstood

term 'folklore', suggests that the oral expression for which

the country is famous, penetrates very deep into the culture:

> "Haiti's social, artistic and literary life, to a
> certain extent architecture and fashion, all
> painting and sculpture, education, furniture,
> cooking and leisure activities nowadays corres-
> pond broadly to a national tradition whose
> source is folklore - a folklore of exceptional
> beauty and richness."[6]

Many scholars of outstanding ability, including a former vice-

Chancellor of the University of the West Indies, have suggested

that Africa was a main stream of influence for the oral

literature of the Caribbean region.[7] The Haitian writer,

Jean Price-Mars[8] is of equal certainty that oral tradition on

the whole has its roots in Africa. He speaks, for example, of

the custom of story-telling in the open air during the night

and recalls that in one part of the African continent, there

used to be the belief that a gourd would fall on the head of

any narrator who told a story during the day. Another belief

cited by Price-Mars is that the narrator's mother would be

changed into a zebra.[9] Just as Anansi[10] stories receive
popular acclaim in Jamaica, so too the famous legends of
l'Oncle Bouqui and Ti Malice[11] excite today's audiences just
as they have done in the past. The custom of night-time entertainment, so preciously preserved by the Haitians, continues to reveal a pageantry of oral literature - legends,
stories, songs, riddles, proverbs, jokes and the voicing of
popular beliefs.

Two observations should be made at this point. First of all,
oral literature is no longer confined to the night. On the
contrary, it continues during the daytime, providing, as it
does, a pleasant background to the humdrum of everyday life.
We may, for example, refer to the use of proverbs. It is
amazing the number of proverbs one can learn merely by
listening to conversations, whether out in the fields, or on
the streets of towns and villages. The writer always received
an education in this direction whenever he visited the hill
community of Duplan, overlooking Pétionville. Frère Bertin
Cazeau, Methodist local preacher and community leader, is
one of those Haitians whose usage of Créole proverbs serves to
enliven many a conversation. Another Haitian community leader,
also a Methodist local preacher, to whom I am indebted for my
knowledge of Haitian proverbs is Frère Alberto Jean-Baptiste,
from the village of Lévêque near Duvalierville. The second
observation is that Oral Literature is increasingly being preserved in written form. Haiti can justifiably boast of

numerous novelists and poets. The names of Jacques Roumain, Jean Fouchard, Emmanuel Paul, Henock Trouillot, François Duvalier, Dantès Bellegarde, Jean Price-Mars and Jean-Joseph Vilaire are to be numbered among those who helped to transform into written form the wealth of Haitian literature.

Haitian proverbs are now making their way onto the printed page. Pasteur Pauris Jean-Baptiste, director of the Centre Pédagogique Rural Protestant[12] has collected many well-known proverbs and condensed them in book form.[13] Some of the proverbs listed in his work are as follows:

> "Ravèt pa janm gin rézon dévan poul" - A cockroach is never in the right when it is up against a hen.

> "Avan ou ri moun bouété, gadé si ou maché douat" - Before you laugh at a lame person, examine yourself to see whether you are walking upright.

> "Tandé ak ouè sé dé" - Hearing about something and actually seeing it are two different things.

> "Soulié konnin si chosèt gin trou" - The shoe knows if the socks have holes.

The one drawback of this concerted effort to transform oral literature into the category of written literature lies in the inability of the printed page to represent some of the facial expressions which are so characteristic of the narrator of l'Oncle Bouqui and Ti Malice stories, or the reciter of poems, or the speaker of proverbs.

(ii) Créole Language

Oral literature is expressed in the language spoken by the

masses, Créole. There was a time when Haitian Créole was regarded as a language inferior to French, spoken by the poor illiterates who could not successfully cope with the complicated grammar and syntax of the official language. To a certain extent this prejudice against Créole still obtains when one considers that some parents insist that nothing but pure French must be spoken by their children. However, Rev. H. Ormonde McConnell insists

> "that Créole is not just a debased form of French. Some experts suggest with plausibility that the syntax and grammar of Créole resemble certain African languages while its vocabulary is drawn from old French, especially the dialects of Normandy and Picardy, about the 16th and 17th centuries, with the addition of some African, Spanish and English words.

> "It is significant that Créole developed independently in several different countries (e.g. Louisiana, Martinique, St. Lucia, etc., as well as Haiti) and the resulting language is so similar in all these places that it is claimed that a person from any one of them can understand and be understood in the others. This suggests that the formation of Créole followed certain specific principles."[14]

Other writers have stressed the uniqueness of Créole, born as it was as the collective creation of the necessity for both slaves and masters to communicate their thoughts.[15] The presence in Saint Domingue of peoples belonging to various scattered tribes from all parts of the African continent had precipitated the necessity of a compromise between the languages of France, England and Spain and those of African nations. Although Créole may have been hybrid in its embryonic stages, it is today widely

regarded as a language in its own right. No longer must it be
considered a 'patois', or broken French. It is that medium of
communication which holds the distinction of being true folk
talk on the one hand and preserver of folk culture on the other.
It is becoming increasingly recognized alongside French as the
language of the mass-media, though this is more true of radio
than it is of the press. Whereas broadcasting stations such
as Radio Métropole and Radio Lumière in Port-au-Prince, and
Radio Citadelle and Radio 4VEH in Cap-Haitien transmit over
their sound waves programmes in both French and Créole, national
newspapers such as Le Nouvelliste and Le Nouveau Monde are
printed in French.

Apart from radio emissions, another formalized setting wherein
Créole is orally employed is in discussion groups and seminars
designed for the simple, unsophisticated folk. It is used as
the vehicle of instruction in adult literacy classes (cours
d'alphabétisation) or in agricultural seminars, to give just
two examples. The main reason for its non-use in many written
extracts is the fact that there is yet no consistent and standard orthography.[16] It should be pointed out that despite this
setback, translations of the New Testament in Créole continue
to appear on the market. Two such versions are Nouvo Téstaman
Avèk Som Yo[17] and Bon Nouvèl Pou Tout Moun.[18] The longer
Créole exists strictly as a spoken language, the more difficult
it will be to get rid of the false impression that it is not
suitable for anything learned, scholarly or worthwhile. In

general terms, we run the risk of forgetting the value of the
oral just as well as the written, of forgetting that the one
complements the other. For this reason, Arlindo Stefani,
writing about Brazil, but with implications for elsewhere, has
said:

> "we ought not to separate oral culture and written
> culture as if some people were swimming in oral
> culture like fish in water while others were
> swimming in the water of written culture. We all
> have an oral culture, even the learned and the
> scientific."(19)

One of the useful things about Créole is its picturesque nature.
It expresses itself through descriptions rather than using
abstract terms. This is what makes it easier to be memorized.
Indeed the Bible itself, orginating with oral tradition, is
written in a style which is easily memorized,[20] a point which
we will be looking at in our final chapter.

As a language, then, Créole has an amazing potential. In fact,
as one writer puts it, Créole may be regarded as an instrument
of reconciliation among the divided factions within society.[21]
It is important that this potential be recognized by the
majority.

(iii) Family Patterns

In Haiti, as elsewhere in the Caribbean, it is generally
accepted that a family must not begin until two persons concerned go through the formality of a legal marriage ceremony.
In order to do this, they must each have an 'acte de naissance'

(birth certificate), a 'carte d'identité' (identification card) and a 'certificat prenuptial' (or medical certificate attesting their fitness to contract marriage). Among people of the lower socio-economic group, fulfilling the legal requirements is a luxury they can ill afford. On the one hand, the mere thought of exposing themselves to the insecurity of the sophisticated atmosphere which is generated by government offices, is frightening. On the other hand, marriage is an expensive proposition. Even though the State relaxes some of its requirements to facilitate the very poor who wish to become married, most Haitians dream of celebrating with their friends on their wedding day. Hence it is unlikely that any Haitian would treat their marriage as a private affair. Consequently, rather than spend money, which they do not have, to finance a wedding reception, most poor Haitians prefer not to get married. But the family instinct is so strong that people do set up house together in defiance of the accepted "marriage ceremony" norm. This sexual union, corresponding to a state of faithful concubinage, is the system of <u>plaçage</u> or <u>common-law marriage</u>. The two persons involved usually live in the hope that one day they may have sufficient money to finance a proper wedding. But for the vast majority, that day never arrives.

Another family pattern may emerge from a <u>visiting union</u>. With this sort of arrangement, the young man visits the home of the girl on a regular basis. There is a mutual rendering of services, only there is no cohabitation. This is not the same thing as promiscuity, for usually the two persons involved in a visiting union remain faithful to each other. They eventually graduate into a common-law relationship which involves cohabitation, and share the widespread dream of one day contracting a socially acceptable marriage.

The other point to be made about family patterns in Haitian folk culture is that it is never limited to the nuclear family. The ideal is to consider as family a wider network of relationships, including not just father, mother and offsprings, but grandparents, uncles, aunts and cousins. It is this tremendous emphasis placed upon kinship which has helped to shield Haiti, and particularly the urban centres, from the individualistic and impersonal lifestyles which were alluded to at the beginning of this chapter.

(iv) Grass Roots' Socialism

By the term "grass roots' socialism" I am referring to a type of social organisation which the Haitian peasants employ to help them resolve some of their economic needs. It is not the scientific socialism with which we are accustomed, "the political and economic theory of social organisation advocating State ownership and control of commercial activities."[22] This brand of socialism has not been based on theory, but rather it grew out of the practice of living with deprivation. It is not a question of the State taking the initiative. Here, the people themselves operate collectively, sorting out their priorities

and the ways of resolving problems as a group. Let us see how
the system operates. There is the "coumbite" on the one hand,
and the "sou-sou" on the other.

In rural areas where there is always a shortage of money to hire
labour, the farmers have devised the system of "coumbite" or
"koumbite"[23] which guarantees that the job will be done never-
theless. The "coumbite" is the pooling of human resources into
a band of workers who put themselves at the disposal of members
within the community who are desirous of help. This is help
in realising specific projects, such as preparing the land for
the planting season. While the men work, the women might be
busy preparing a meal. Usually the men sing as they work and
the relaxed atmosphere so created is conducive to healthy
community spirit.

One way of tackling the money shortage problem and ensuring that
help is given when an individual is in need of a considerable
sum of money for a particular cause is for farmers to form a
rotating credit association, known as a "sou-sou" or "susu".
The sou-sou, as a savings device was commonly employed by the
Yoruba, who were among the ancestors of Haiti:

> "Basically the idea is for one individual to act
> as the 'banker'. A group of individuals contri-
> butes a set amount of money each week which is held
> by the banker. It may be as much as ten dollars or
> a smaller amount. The group may be just a few
> individuals or run to thirty or forty people.
> Each week, one individual is entitled to a
> 'partner-hand' and he collects the total invest-
> ment of all members for that week. In a hand

of thirty members contributing five dollars a hand, each individual will collect 150 dollars when his turn comes round. After each individual has gone through in rotation, the order is reversed. There- fore, once in every thirty hands each member will get the last hand in the last round plus the first hand of the next round. This doubles his share to 300 dollars. This system can give a sizeable sum of money to each member at fairly regular intervals. Often, of course, the 'hands' will be much smaller because the membership is lower or weekly payments less.

"This system relies on a high level of mutual trust and, consequently, the banker is usually a person with a high degree of prestige within the household or kinship network. These associations are often restricted to family networks or close friends for this very reason."[24]

The idea of grass roots' socialism is one worth further en-

quiry. We will, in Chapter 6, devote some more time to con-

sider its effectiveness. Suffice it to say, this form of

socialism may well provide the alternative to the models of

capitalism, Marxist-Leninist socialism and communism which

have so far constituted the range of choice considered by

Caribbean politicians and economists.

(v) Indigenous Medicine

In the field of medicine, there is a marked absence, within

the Haitian rural milieu, of sophisticated drugs. The chemi-

cal and drug companies of western nations may be essential

to the day to day running of town hospitals and clinics.

But the ordinary farmer in the rural area is geographically

located far away from the reach of western medical care. In

order to get to the nearest hospital, he must travel several

miles, on foot, or on muleback. Usually the journey into town
will take several hours. Indeed Haiti, 'the land of many
mountains' encounters serious problems of internal communications.

Since he is located so far away from urban life, the farmer
has learnt that there is healing for illness to be had from
the plants and herbs which form part of his natural environment.
In fact, it is true to say that this medical knowledge is something which has been retained from the African ancestors. The
rural housewife knows that a certain bush can produce a suitable remedy for the common cold, or another for high blood
pressure and still another for high temperatures.

The person, though, who has a superior knowledge of all the
secrets of plants, which ones are of medicinal value and which
ones are poisonous is the vaudou priest.[25] In him we discern
a definite link with the African continent whose traditional
priests are generally numbered among the native healers.

The subject of indigenous medicine will be dealt with more fully
in chapter 5.

(vi) <u>Indigenous Art Forms</u>
Vaudou is also bound up with the artistic expressions of Haitian
folk culture. Haitian art, which is so popular as a tourist
attraction, has its origins rightly or wrongly traced to the

vêver, a symbolic drawing used in the context of a vaudou
ritual. More will be said about the vêver in the next chapter.
However, this view is supported by Selden Rodman,[26] eminent
Haitian poet, biographer and art critic. He it was who initiated and directed the famous mural paintings by Haitian primitive painters in the Cathedral Sainte Trinité in Port-au-Prince.

It is equally argued that handicraft, which includes the making
of carpets, bags, shoes, sisal mats, baskets, pottery and wood
carving, owes its inspiration to the vaudou religion. In fact,
the role of vaudou is evident in just about every form of art
expression, allowing as it does for the continued influence of
Africa. Vaudou has affected music and dance.[27] Perhaps the
grand climax of music and dance is on the two days of Carnival
- the Monday and Tuesday preceding Ash Wednesday. Thousands
of folk literally take over the streets of main towns, as they
sing popular folk songs and dance to the rhythm of orchestras.
Carnival parades constitute a creditable display of Haitian
genius for all forms of artistic expression. Also popular in
haiti are Ra-Ra bands which parade for the three days and three
nights preceding Good Friday, holding kerosene lanterns and
blowing bamboos. These bands are more frequently seen in the
countryside than in the towns, and they are more stately in
procession, quite unlike the wild revelry which is associated
with Carnival.

(vii) Popular Belief

Popular belief is another rather strong element in Haitian culture. It is a belief pertaining largely to the dead and to the world of spirits. To sweep a house after dark is regarded as a bad sign, for such an act is supposed to disturb the spirits of those who are dead. The same restriction is placed upon throwing water out of a window at night. The influence of the Vaudou religion can be seen here, for vaudou views the cosmos as one in which there exist numerous spirits, some of which are good, some of which are evil. As mortals, we are at the mercy of these spiritual beings who are continually at work to shape the course of history.

One belief which is again traceable to Vaudou is that concerning the existence of zombies. Zombies are persons who have been raised out of their graves and are now walking among the mindless undead as prisoners of vaudou chiefs. Their daily routine consists of performing slavish tasks required by their masters. Although on the surface zombies may appear to be the superstitions of a rural people, they do in effect constitute a reality and cannot be lightly dismissed. We will therefore give a full treatment of zombification in the next chapter when we describe and comment upon Haitian Folk Religion.

Before we can describe Haitian vaudou, let us in the next section give an historical overview of the culture we have just presented as folk culture.

Historical Background to the Culture

Haiti covers an area of 10,800 square miles. It was discovered on December 5, 1492 by Christopher Columbus who colonised it in the name of the Spanish Crown. The original inhabitants, the Arawak Indians, were a gentle people:

> "They bear no arms, nor know thereof; for I showed them swords and they grasped them by the blade and cut themselves through ignorance; they have no iron. Their darts are a kind of rod without iron, and some have at the end a fish's tooth and others, other things. They are generally fairly tall and good looking, well made. I saw some who had marks of wounds on their bodies, and made signs to them to ask what it was, and they showed me how people of other islands which are near came there and wished to capture them, and they defended themselves. And I believed that people do come here from the mainland to take them as slaves. They ought to be good servants and of good skill, for I see that they repeat very quickly all that is said to them; and I believe that they would easily be made Christians, because it seemed to me that they belonged to no religion." - Journal of Columbus, 1492.[28]

These Indians, though, did not last very long, for they were eventually exterminated through repression, sickness and massacre by the Spaniards. Just as they suffered in Haiti, so too did they meet a terrible fate in other parts of the Spanish Empire. Hence the Catholic missionary, Bartolome de las Casas, in an Account of the First Voyages and Discoveries made by the Spaniards in America, 1540, has written:

> "We shall make it evidently appear to your Majesty, that the Spaniards in about eight and thirty or forty years have unjustly put to death above twelve millions of your subjects; and what an incredible damage must your Majesty have further sustained by these massacres, as they have hindered all these people from multiplying ... And how unjust soever these wars have been which they

> have made upon the Indians, if the poor creatures
> put themselves in a posture of defence, they
> cruelly cut their throats without any distinction
> of quality, sex or age; such as escaped their fury
> they reserved for slaves, many of whom they condemn
> to the gold or silver mines, others they yoke
> together like beasts to make them carry vast
> burdens. They don't much concern themselves
> whether the Indians live or die, provided they
> reap some advantage by their labour."[29]

Las Casas was like a voice crying in the wilderness, a loner

challenging the Spanish-imposed policy of having the Indians

voluntarily submit to the Christian faith or face extermination.

Las Casas, Apostle to the Indians, condemned the Spanish use

of force and even refused to invoke divine blessing upon the

wars supposedly fought in God's name. "We are not surprised

to learn that people reviled Las Casas as a heretic, anti-

christ and a Lutheran."[30] But such outbursts against the

cruel treatment of Indians in the New World eventually led

to the start of a new enterprise, namely the Slave Trade. The

Spanisards saw that the best possible way of solving their

colonies' labour shortage was to introduce slaves from the

African continent. The first slave-ship landed its human

cargo in 1503. These Africans had belonged to various tribes

- Bantus, Sudanese, Congolese, Senegalese, Mandingoes, Ibos,

Dahomeans - though there are many Haitians today who cite

Guinea as the land from which they had been uprooted.

Spanish domination of the whole of Hispaniola lasted for almost

two centuries. In fact, from as early as 1625 both French

and English landed simultaneously. Wrangling among European powers continued until 1697 when, by the Treaty of Ryswick, "Spain confirmed French occupation of its long established settlement in Hispaniola."[31] So France held on to the western part of the island, which came to be known as Saint Domingue, but which we now know as Haiti.

The period of slavery had a decisive effect upon the culture that was to emerge on Haitian soil. Slavery meant a series of atrocities[32] - whippings, chains, human-beings being treated as beasts of burden - which conditions created the desire for freedom amongst a defenceless people. Revolts were many, and they were often suppressed by the powerful planters. The cruelty suffered by the early African settlers in Haiti constituted a disgrace to humanity. The French fully exploited the country. In 1749 they founded Port-au-Prince, which was to become the country's capital in 1806. Towards the close of the eighteenth century, Saint Domingue was the pride and joy of France, so prosperous a country it had become:

> The progress of Saint-Domingue from 1783 (the year of the independence of the United States of America) to 1789 (the year of the outbreak of the French Revolution) is one of the most astonishing phenomena in the history of imperialism. Its exports in 1788 amounted to 31,350 tons of clayed sugar, 41,607 tons of brown sugar, 2,806 tons of cotton, 30,425 tons of coffee, 415 tons of indigo; the value amounted to 193 million livres or nearly eight million pounds sterling. The colony contained 800 sugar plantations, 3,000 coffee, nearly 800 cotton, and 2,950 indigo. Saint Domingue supplied half of Europe with tropical produce. Its exports were one-third more than those of all the

British West Indies combined; its commerce employed
1,000 ships and 15,000 French sailors. Saint
Domingue was the world's premier sugar producer,
the gem of the Caribbean."33

But the glamour which Saint Domingue, under French rule, enjoyed

had been at the expense of hundreds of lives. In 1758 for

example the name of François Makandal (also spelt 'Macandal')

came to the fore. He was a Muslim from Guinea, who had been a

slave in the district of Limbé. C.L.R. James says this of him:

"Mackandal was an orator, in the opinion of a white
contemporary equal in eloquence to the European
orators of the day, and different only in his
superior strength and vigour. He was fearless and,
though one-handed from an accident, had a fortitude
of spirit which he knew how to preserve in the
midst of the most cruel tortures. He claimed to
predict the future; like Mahomet he had revelations;
he persuaded his followers that he was immortal and
exercised such a hold over them that they considered
it an honour to serve him on their knees ... "34

Makandal and his companions had terrorised the plantations

guerilla-style, in a bid to gain the much sought after free-

dom from bondage. But Makandal was arrested and burned alive.

He is somewhat of a legendary figure who has undoubtedly made

a tremendous impression upon Haitian folklore. It is reported

that while being burnt, he miraculously escaped from the fire

and had to be rebound before being thrown a second time into

the furnace. His heroism in the face of death continues to

live, particularly because slaves of succeeding generations

had seen in him an intercessor who gave them hope that they

would one day be delivered from their misery.

So the lives of thousands were lost, but the cause for freedom lived on. Then in 1789, it happened. This year saw the outbreak of the French Revolution. In the words of Eric Williams,

> "The French Revolution struck this society like a thunderclap. Its immediate consequences in France were the convening of a National Assembly for the first time in centuries, the power of the Third Estate or bourgeoisie, the limitation of the King's power, the declaration of the rights of man, and the abolition of the feudal system and the ancient privileges of the landed aristocracy. Three questions were immediately posed for Saint Domingue: first, the rights of the planters; second, the effect of the rights of man on the mulattoes and the slaves; third, the colony's loyalty to the revolutionary regime."[35]

The French Revolution marked the beginnings of a new era in the history of Saint Domingue. The suffering masses took this as inspiration enough to successfully bring about their liberation. It was during this period of time that two other legendary figures sparkled in Haitian annals.

The first was the famous Boukman, a man of outstanding leadership qualities. Boukman's followers had "caught the whisper of the watchwords of the revolution"[36] and were fully determined to rid themselves of the French yoke. On the night of August 14, 1791 Boukman conducted an African ceremony in the north that started a massive slave revolt. This ceremony, known to posterity as the 'Bois Caiman' was of a religious nature and included the sacrifice of an animal and the drinking of its blood. All pledged allegiance to the cause of the revolt which indeed furthered the move towards the abolition of slavery in Haiti. Historians have maintained that the Bois

Caiman ceremony was instrumental in starting the Vaudou
religion. This point will be discussed more fully in the next
chapter. Consequently the claim has been made that Haitian
independence is closely intertwined with the origins of
Haitian Folk Religion.

The other legendary character who featured prominently at this
time was Toussaint L'Ouverture. C. L. R. James has given a
possible reason why this man, Toussaint Breda, came to be
known as L'Ouverture.

> "L'Ouverture means 'the opening'. One of the
> French generals, hearing of news of another
> victory by Toussaint said: 'This man makes an
> opening everywhere.'"[37]

Another theory is that L'Ouverture could have been a nickname
given to him by other slaves because of the gap in his teeth.

Born in 1743 as Pierre-Dominique Toussaint, he was the son of
Gaou-Guinou, African King of Aradas. He lived in slavery on
the Breda plantation for more than forty years before he
was freed. At the age of fifty, he could not read nor write.

> "To the end of his days he could hardly speak
> French, he literally could not write three words
> without the grossest errors in spelling and grammar."[38]

But he was interersted in education, and through his initiative
schools were built. He organised the plantations, punished
laziness and tried to emphasize the dignity of labour. He
was somewhat of a bush-doctor who knew a great deal about the
healing properties of plants. He was determined that complete
liberation for all would be a reality during his lifetime. He

was well respected. The fact that his troops comprised blacks, whites and mulattoes is a testimony to his greatness. It was Toussaint who proclaimed general freedom for the slaves in 1793. He soon became General and then following the drafting of his famous Constitution in 1801, he became Governor for life.

The dramatic events which took place in Haiti towards the close of the eighteenth century were viewed with disfavour by Napoleon Bonaparte (1769-1821), the great conqueror of Europe. According to Napoleon, the Haitian proclamation of Independence which he saw as forthcoming, would seriously undermine the authority which he had built up for himself and for France on the Continent. He was therefore determined to restore slavery in Saint Domingue, by first of all crushing Toussaint whom he considered to be an upstart. This was to be understood, because Napoleon had equally been an upstart, when one follows his biography carefully.[39] Upon the death of his father in 1785, he had been chosen above his elder brother to be the head of the family. These responsibilities drove him deep into poverty, but he seemed destined to enjoy a swift rise to political power. The 1789 upheaval in France gave him the opening he wanted. He joined the Jacobins. In 1792 he had been made a captain; in 1793 the general of the brigade; in 1794 he had been placed in command of the artillery of the army of Italy; in 1795, following his success in putting down a royalist insurrection and thereby saving the republic, he had been named commander in chief of the army of Italy. Soon after he had been elected Consul and eventually voted Consul for life. Such steps were to lead him to the position of emperor in 1804. Given such an amazing record of unlimited power, one can well appreciate why Napoleon did not wish to tolerate a slave from overseas whose career threatened to develop into a successful pattern like his own. In fact, he is reported to have said,

> "Centuries will pass before the unique combination of events which led to my career recur in another."[40]

In order to ensure that his prophecy was not falsified while he lived, Napoleon placed Toussaint on his death list.

At Napoleon's direction, an expedition set sail on December 14, 1801. It was his brother-in-law, General Leclerc, husband of the beautiful Pauline, who was in command. . Leclerc negotiated with Toussaint and a general amnesty was eventually agreed to. So Toussaint retired to his home on the west coast. On June 7, 1802, Leclerc acted in breach of his promise. He arrested Toussaint by night and deported him. The struggle was renewed by Toussaint's followers.

> "In spite of the fact that large reinforcements arrived from France it was impossible to inflict a decisive defeat on the Negro forces, and the French were now faced by a more terrible enemy than the Negro army as a frightful epidemic of yellow fever swept through their ranks. By the end of November, 1802, less than eleven months since the first French troops had landed in Hispaniola, some 40,000 men had died, including Leclerc himself and many of his senior officers."[41]

Toussaint himself met his death in one of Napoleon's prisons on April 7, 1803, but not before he had uttered his famous words:

> "In overthrowing me, they have merely cut down
> in Saint Domingue the trunk of the tree of black
> liberation: it will again sprout at the roots for
> they are deep and numerous."[42]

Indeed, Toussaint's prediction came true, for seven months after his death, on November 18, 1803, the Haitian army gained a decisive victory over the French under Rochambeau at the Battle of Vertières. The victorious Haitian General-in-chief, Jean-Jacques Dessalines, who had also won the battle of La Butte Charrier, led the country to its independence.[43] Like Toussaint, Dessalines had been a former farm slave. He was one of Toussaint's guides. He is described as

> "Unable to read and write, his body scarred with
> strokes from the whip, but a born soldier, soon
> to hold high command."[44]

So on January 1, 1804 Jean-Jacques Dessalines proclaimed Independence. He tore up the French flag, and to his troops assembled in the town of Gonaïves he thundered forth the frightening command: "Burn houses, cut off heads!" Despite this proclamation, the black population did not molest the whites. It was two months later when the news of the presence of a French squadron in the harbour at Gonaïves reached the people's ears, that they acted swiftly and violently. Dessalines became Governor-General for life. On September 22, 1804, he was crowned Emperor under the name of Jacques I.

> "Private merchants of Philadelphia presented him with
> the crown, brought on the American boat the 'Con-
> necticut', his coronation robes reached Haiti from
> Jamaica on an English frigate from London. He made
> his solemn entry into Le Cap in a six-horse
> carriage brought for him by the English agent, Ogden,
> on board the 'Samson'. Thus the Negro monarch entered

into his inheritance, tailored and valeted by
English and American capitalists, supported on
the one side by the King of England and on the
other by the President of the United States."[45]

Less than four years later, Dessalines was assassinated at
Pont-Rouge near Port-au-Prince.

The Independence of Haiti from France was complete. Bonaparte,
humiliated because some slaves in Haiti had succeeded in
bringing France to her knees, still hoped to reintroduce
slavery in that country. History has it that he appointed
General de la Pailleterie (1762§1806) for the mission. The
general, whose mother had been a slave in Saint Domingue,
proudly refused to act in any way which he considered a be-
trayal of the people of his mother's race. Napoleon never
forgave him for this. But if General de la Pailleterie was
one obstacle, there was an even greater stumbling-block in the
person of Henri Christophe, the Civiliser. Himself a former
slave, he was president of the northern part of Haiti from
January 1807 to March 1811, following which he assumed the
title of King Henri I and ruled the North until October 1820.[46]
About that same time Christophe was ruling the North, Alexandre
Pétion, a mulatto was President of the west department (March
1807 § March 1818), and he was followed by President Boyer.
King Henri had been well aware of the aspirations of Napoleon
and had decided that at all costs, should he return, Napoleon
must suffer defeat at his hands. He therefore built the
famous Citadelle Laferrière on the top of a mountain, the

Bonnet à l'Evêque, which was so well fortified with cannons and so advantageously placed overlooking much of the countryside, that it is almost certain that should Napoleon's forces have returned, their mission would have been catastrophic. The citadelle, renowned as the eighth wonder of the world, took almost fourteen years (1804-1817) to build. To complete this fortress, along with his famous Sans-Souci castle, located at the foot of the hill containing the citadelle, Christophe used the sweat and blood of his people. A tyrant in the eyes of many, he obliged his people to work extremely hard and had them severely punished if they were not as industrious as he thought they should be. Small wonder it is that at the end of his reign, he was despised by thousands. He committed suicide, by shooting himself with a golden bullet.

As we peruse the pages of Haiti's history, we cannot help but observe how filled it was with bloodshed - the blood shed by the original Arawak Indians at the hands of the Spaniards, the blood shed by the African slaves under the oppression of their overlords, the blood which was spilled as slaves sought desperately to gain their freedom, and towards the close of the eighteenth century, the blood of the defeated Europeans, being crushed by victorious Haitian generals. The Independence of which the country is proud today, came as a result of endless suffering on the part of the masses. The outcome of the revolution was a victory won by the people themselves. It gave to them a tremendous sense of worth that they could

defeat a country such as France, which country, under Napoleon
Bonaparte as Emperor, had been feared by other European powers.
Indeed from that time onwards, Haitians have been determined
to shape their lifestyle along lines which they approved for
themselves. But how successful have they been?

In the early 1840s Haiti was ruled by President Riché. Between
1844 and 1847 there were four presidents. Then followed
Faustin Soulouque (1847-1859), reputed to have been a strong
believer in Haitian folk religion, and General Geffrard in
the 1860s. These rulers were not willing to let foreign powers
dictate to them. But then, from the 1860s Haiti was again
slipping out of the hands of the indigenous people, and as we
shall see in the next chapter, during this time, Vaudou
suffered terribly. The result was that in 1915 there was an
American intervention.[47] The Americans had occupied the country after the Haitian ruler, General Leconte, had been assassinated in 1912. His death had ushered in a period of political
chaos, and in July 1915, Admiral Capperton ordered the marines
ashore. During 1915 to 1934, American money poured into the
country, as the country's potential in sugar and sisal
production was exploited to the full. It was during this era
that there emerged Jean Price-Mars (1876-1969), the young
black intellectual who became more and more disturbed that
Haitian values were becoming European, American and elitist.
He made one of the most significant contributions to the
development of folk culture in Haiti. Author of Ainsi Parla

<u>L'Oncle</u>, he called upon Haitians to put away any inferiority feelings about their culture, and in so doing founded a movement for the appreciation of it. This was about the year 1928.

The withdrawal of the American presence from Haiti had been authorised by President Roosevelt in 1934. This saved the day for Haiti. For it meant that the threat of Haitian culture being swamped by the industrialised culture of the United States was removed. It paved the way for Haitian culture to be shaped, not by foreigners, not by the rich, sophisticated elite, but by Haitians themselves, the simple, unsophisticated folk who may be found at the grass roots' level.

The historical background to Haitian folk culture will not be complete if no mention is made of current challenges to it. The basic problem lies in the fact that although Haiti has been independent since 1804 she is still very much dependent upon outside help. In a sense, she has not really severed her ties with the United States. This fact is dramatised by the eternal link of the Haitian Gourde to the American Dollar. The Gourde is always the value of twenty American cents. Any fluctuation of American currency automatically brings about a fluctuation in the Haitian monetary system. In addition to this, many of the industries which have cropped up in Haiti are American controlled and geared towards the American market, for example, the baseball-making industry, and the handicraft

of soft toys for Disney World. And yet, for the survival of
the country, such ties are indispensable. Haiti is often
obliged to offer tax-free incentives to the United States. It
is the goodwill of the latter which determines the country's
industrial and economic expansion. The United States is without doubt a powerful factor in the life of Haiti, and can, at
will, hold the country to ransom. In August 1981, for example,
the Director of the U.S. Agency for International Development
(AID) revealed that there would be a cut of 1.5 million
dollars from the economic development assistance programme to
Haiti because the money is not being effectively spent.[48] The
country can ill afford such losses in financial assistance.
One may well ask, "Is it possible to shake off these shackles?"
The honest answer to that question is "No", for those who
understand the situation in Haiti know only too well that
open revolution is not possible. The only revolution which
can succeed must be a silent revolution, one which begins
with the mental liberation of the people.

At the very beginning of this chapter, we referred to a recent
report on Haiti. We return to that same report[49] to highlight
a couple more statistics. The partial and total unemployment
rate is about eighty percent. Because of the chronic unemployment situation, there are about eighty-five percent of
Haitian intellectuals, professionals, technicians and skilled
workers who live abroad. Of course, many of those who live
abroad are refugees, as we pointed out in the Introduction.

The development of the country has been open to much influence from foreigners, in which category must come the Church. In Chapter 5 we will say more about what denominational bodies comprise the Church in Haiti and how development work is carried out by them. It suffices to state here that the Church poses serious challenges to the folk culture of Haiti, sometimes misunderstanding it, sometimes upsetting it, while still appreciating it. The theological implications of all this will emerge as the study develops.

In the final analysis, it must be said that the one domain in which the independence of Haiti lies unchallenged is in folk religion. Vaudou is the most powerful sustainer of this country's folk culture. In our next chapter, we will spend some more time examining some of the major features of this religion which is so crucial to the country's survival.

CHAPTER 1 - NOTES

1. "The Hell That's Haiti" in <u>Caribbean Contact</u>, Vol. 9, No. 7, Barbados, November 1981, p. 4.

2. Ibid, p. 4.

3. In support of this see Julie Pearn, <u>West Indian Popular Culture: Is Fe We Own</u>.

4. A fine collection of essays in this regard is found in G. Poujol et R. Labourie, <u>Les Cultes Populaires</u>.

5. R. C. Culley, "An Approach to the problem of oral tradition" in <u>Vetus Testamentum</u>, Vol. XIII, no. 2, Leiden, E. J. Brill, 1963, p. 118.

6. <u>English Texts and Captions</u>, Port-au-Prince, National Tourist Bureau.

7. Philip Sherlock, <u>West Indies</u>, London, Thames and Hudson, 1966, p. 137.

8. Jean Price-Mars, <u>Ainsi Parla L'Oncle</u>.

9. Ibid, p. 54.

10. "Anansi" is also spent "Anancy". He is "an Ashanti spider-god and has magical powers. He can change himself into whatever and whoever he wishes at certain times, and his stories make it quite plain that he is able to get away with tricks which ordinary mortals can't. He is a rascal but lovable, and every existing custom is said to have been started by Anancy." - Louise Bennett, <u>Anancy and Miss Lou</u>, Kingston, Jamaica, Sangster's Book Stores Ltd., 1979, p. xi.

11. "It is rightly said that these two inseparable heroes are the personifications, the one of the good beast, of an unintelligent and friendly nature, the other of trickery." - Jean Price-Mars, op. cit., p. 57.

12. The Centre is a rural teacher-training college, located at Frères, in the Pétionville area.

13. Pauris Jean-Baptiste, <u>Kout Flach Sou 250 Provèb Dayiti</u>.

14. H. Ormonde McConnell, "A Note on Créole and the Literacy Campaign undertaken by the Haitian Government for the Teaching of Adults to read and write Créole" in H. Ormonde McConnell and Eugene Swan, Jr. <u>You Can Learn Créole</u>, Port-au-Prince, Haiti, 4th Edition, 1960, p. 7.

15. See Jean-Joseph Vilaire, "Notre Créole" in Maurice Vil-
    aire, ed., 4 Causeries, Haiti, Imprimerie du Séminaire
    Adventiste, 1974, pp. 47-66. Also cf. Jean Price-Mars,
    op. cit., pp. 65, 66.

16. This need for standardised Créole formed the basis of a
    seminar in May 1981 organised by the Caribbean Research
    Centre and the Folk Research Centre of St. Lucia.
    c.f. Pearlette Louisy, "Giving Caribbean Creole a Face
    Lift" in Caribbean Contact Vol. 9, no. 4, Bridgetown,
    Barbados, August 1981, p. 2. cf. also Norman Faria,
    "Creole alphabet for Dominica" in Caribbean Contact,
    Vol. 9, no. 10, Bridgetown, Barbados, February 1982, p. 2.

17. The New Testament With Psalms.

18. Good News for Modern Man.

19. "... nous ne devons pas séparer culture orale et culture
    écrite comme s'il y avait des populations nageant dans
    la culture orale comme des poissons dans l'eau et
    d'autres nageant dans l'eau de la culture écrite.
    Nous avons tous une culture orale, même les savants et
    les scientifiques." - Arlindo Stefani, "Cultures Orales
    et Media" in G. Poujol et R. Labourie, op. cit., p. 120.

20. See Walter J. Hollenweger, "Le livre oral. Portées
    sociale, politique et théologique des religions orales"
    in G. Poujol et R. Labourie, op. cit., pp. 123-134.

21. "C'est grâce au Créole que nos traditions orales existent,
    se perpétuent et se transforment, et c'est par son inter-
    médiaire que nous pouvons espérer combler un jour le
    fossé qui fait de nous et du peuple deux entités appare-
    mment distinctes et souvent antagonistes." - Jean Price-
    Mars, op. cit., p. 66.

22. The Popular Oxford Dictionary of Current English, London,
    Oxford University Press, 1978, p. 866.

23. "The word probably derives from the Spanish 'convite'
    meaning 'invitation', but the institution is an old one
    common to many West African peoples." - H. Courlander
    and R. Bastien, Religion and Politics in Haiti - 2 essays,
    Washington D.C., Institute for Cross-Cultural Research,
    1966, p. 7. Another writer sees koumbite as "a continu-
    ation of the 'Dokpwe' in Dahomean tradition". - Laënnec
    Hurbon, Dieu dans le Vaudou Haitien, Paris, Payot, 1972,
    p. 83.

24. David G. Pearson, Race, Class and Political Activism - A
    Study of West Indians in Britain - England, Gower, 1981,
    p. 33.

25. This factor is borne out in a popular Haitian ballad in which a mother prays to the spirit Timilo, asking him to save her from the misery caused by her sick child. She is confident that if she visits the priest (houngan) he can effect the healing which her child so desperately needs:
"Feuille, oh - sové la vi mouin nan misè mouin yé - oh
Pitit mouin malade, mouin pralé kay Houngan Timilo
Si ou gnou bon houngan oua sové la vi mouin nan misè
   mouin yé - oh."

26. Selden Rodman, The Miracle of Haitian Art, New York, Doubleday and Company, Inc., 1965, p. 18.

27. "Enfin, le rôle du vaudou est indéniable dans le champ de l'expression artistique. C'est lui qui a permis à la paysannerie haitienne de maintenir l'héritage afri-cain dans deux domaines où il avait atteint un haut de-gré d'excellence: la musique et la danse." - Alfred Métraux, Le Vaudou Haitien, Paris, Gallimard, 1958, p. 323.

28. F. R. Augier and S. C. Gordon, Sources of West Indian History, London, Longmans, Green and Co. Ltd., 1962, p. 1.

29. Ibid, p. 3.

30. Walter J. Hollenweger, Pentecost Between Black and White, Belfast, Christian Journals Limited, 1974, p. 38.

31. Eric Williams, From Columbus to Castro: The History of the Caribbean 1492-1969, London, André Deutsch Limited, 1970, p. 81.

32. For a vividly moving account of some of the atrocities suffered by Africans who had been brought from the West Coast to Saint Domingue, see C.L.R. James, The Black Jacobins, New York, Vintage Books, 1963. James has a very interesting chapter entitled "The Property", pp. 6-26, in which he has made good use of French and Afri-can historical sources to produce this most memorable narrative.

33. Eric Williams, op. cit., pp. 237, 238.

34. C. L. R. James, op. cit., p. 21.

35. Eric Williams, op. cit., p. 246.

36. J. H. Parry and P. M. Sherlock, A Short History of the West Indies, Second Edition, London, Macmillan & Co. Ltd., 1963, p. 185.

37. C. L. R. James, op. cit., p. 126 (footnote).

38. Ibid, p. 104.

39. The Encyclopaedia Britannica, Vol. 16, Fourteenth Edition, London, 1929, Chapter on Napoleon, pp. 84-95.

40. The Encyclopaedia Britannica, Vol. 16, Fourteenth Edition, London, 1929, Chapter on Napoleon I, p. 85.

41. Sir Alan Burns, History of the British West Indies, London, George Allen and Unwin Ltd., 1965, p. 581.

42. "En me renversant, on n'a abbatu à Saint Domingue que le tronc de l'arbre de la liberté des noirs; il repoussera par les racines parce qu'elles sont profondes et nombreuses." C.L.R. James suggests that as Toussaint stepped on board the boat, after his arrest, he spoke these words to Savary, the Captain. - C. L. R. James, op. cit., p. 334.

43. For a good description of the politics of the period 1804-1971, see David Nicholls, From Dessalines to Duvalier. This book gives an in-depth study of race, colour and national independence in Haiti. Dr. Nicholls describes how race and colour feature prominently in post-colonial politics, to the extent where foreign intervention is the direct outcome of deliberate moves by one colour group to overcome the other.

44. C. L. R. James, op. cit., p. 130.

45. Ibid, p. 370.

46. The Life of Henri Christophe who rose from the status of slave to that of king is contained in John V. Vandercook, Black Majesty.

47. A full treatment of this is contained in Arthur Chester Millspaugh, Haiti Under American Control, 1915-30. It describes the paternalism of the United States in trying to solve the social, political and economic problems of Haiti. See also Ludwell Lee Montague, Haiti and the United States 1714-1938, and Hans Schmidt, The United States Occupation of Haiti 1915-34.

48. "USAID New Policy Cuts US$28 M. off 11 Caribbean - Latin American Countries" in Caribbean Contact, Vol. 9, no. 5, Bridgetown, Barbados, September 1981, p. 16.

49. "The Hell That's Haiti" in Caribbean Contact, Vol. 9, No. 7, Bridgetown, Barbados, November 1981, p. 4.

CHAPTER 2

HAITIAN FOLK RELIGION

Part I - General Description

Vaudou - Living Religion of the Masses

Vaudou is rightly to be regarded as the sustainer of folk culture in Haiti. Louis Maximilien, in a profound study of this religion, concludes that in spite of the fact that the Haitian elite looks upon it with scorn and fear, vaudou is a force to be reckoned with.[1] Another writer on Haiti, James G. Leyburn, contends that vaudou is

> "the second religion in Haiti.........the living religion of the masses."[2]

When one considers that the educated upper and middle classes are a minority group, confined to the urban areas, and that the vast majority of Haitians are rural dwellers whose style of living may be aptly described by the term "grass-roots' level", then can one begin to appreciate the seemingly excessive claims being made for vaudou. Statistics in favour of vaudou tend to be rather conservative. When it is claimed that there are about twenty percent of the population who are vaudouisants[3], this figure includes only those who admit their religion, but it does not reflect the vast numbers of people who bear the label 'Catholic' but are in practice vaudou worshippers.

Vaudou is by no means a new phenomenon in Haiti. It has made

its presence felt for over a century and a half. The word
vaudou is derived from the Dahomean term, vodun meaning
spirit. (Dahomey, used throughout this research, will refer
to the ancient West African kingdom, present-day Benin.) As
a religion, vaudou reflects elements of West African religions,
French Catholicism and the religions of the Amerindian tribes
which were the original inhabitants of Haiti. We mentioned,
in Chapter 1, the description of these Indians as a gentle
people. The Africans, who were brought to the West Indies as
slaves, maintained a lively interest in their various types of
worship. But upon arrival in Saint Domingue, they faced a
rather difficult situation because according to the French
Code Noir,[4] every slave should be baptized into the Roman
Catholic faith. Consequently there developed in Haiti a type
of religion wherein elements of religious life as practised
in Dahomey, Congo, Sudan, Senegal and Cameroun, combined with
that of Rome. Some writers suggest that Masonry has contributed greatly towards the evolution of vaudou.[5] We will
return to the influence of masonry later on in the chapter.
So too we will discuss the matter of revelation and examine
the extent to which the term "syncretistic religion" may be
applied to vaudou. But first, let us delve into the history
of the religion.

Vaudou and the Political Order

From the very beginning, vaudou had strong affinities with
politics. Certainly in its initial stages, it helped to make

possible the successful Haitian rebellion of 1791. In defiance of the Code Noir, the Africans held many secret nocturnal gatherings. Such ceremonies included frenzied excitement, shouting, singing, drumming and dancing. These were the occasions when support was whipped up against the whites of the land. Leyburn[6] has mentioned four distinctive periods in the life of vaudou. Firstly, 1730-1790 was the time of its emergence, when the importation of slaves was steadily increasing, and there was a gradual ascendancy of Dahomean ideas. Secondly, 1790-1800 saw its practical testing in the fires of revolt when, out of apparent innocence and enforced secrecy, vaudou effectively united the slaves in their action for freedom. We may note here that oral tradition in Haiti cites Boukman, the organiser of the slave revolt of La Plaine du Nord, Hallou, Hyacinthe, Lafortune and other such heads of revolutionary bands as vaudou priests.[7] Thirdly, 1800-1815 saw the suppression of the religion under the black rulers. This was indeed significant. Toussaint L'Ouverture, for example, when he became Governor in 1801 refused to tolerate vaudou because he knew only too well how powerful a force it had been for uniting the slaves. He was now anxious lest its revolutionary nature should be turned in his direction. Fourthly, 1815-1850 witnessed the quiet diffusion to all the people and the assumption of the form which it today displays.

With regards to Leyburn's fourth period, we may here affirm that the tremendous growth of vaudou had been, in some way, due to the weakness of the Roman Catholic Church. Some of the

country's leaders were sympathetic to vaudou, as for example
Faustin Soulouque (1847-1859).

> "It was not until 1860, after the death of the Emperor
> Soulouque, that Haiti signed a concordat with the
> Roman Church. Thus it can be seen that for the first
> sixty or more years of Haitian Independence Catholic
> influence was weak and sporadic. Those years were
> crucial in perserving, crystallizing, and hardening
> the form of vodoun."[8]

The coming of General Geffrard in the 1860s[9] with whom the
Roman Catholic Church had signed the concordat on March 28,
1860, marked the start of a period of severe testing for vaudou.

There had been a period of political instability in Haiti during
the latter part of the nineteenth century and early part of the
twentieth century.[10] This coincided with a campaign launched
against vaudou. The campaign got underway in 1896, and by the
start of the twentieth century, the religion was on the brink
of destruction. Perhaps the rule of Antoine Simon (1906-1911)
who believed in vaudou, did something to save the religion
from complete extinction. However, subsequent rulers - Leconte
(1911-1912), Sudre Dartiguenave (1915-1922), Louis Borno (1922-
1930), Sténio Vincent (1930-1941), Elie Lescot (1941-1946) -
were incapable of anything but propagating attacks against
vaudou. In 1913 there had been a serious anti-vaudou campaign.
During the American occupation (1915-1934) vaudou had been
prohibited on the grounds that it was a backward religion,
unworthy of a civilized people. The campaign was intensified
in 1939-1940 as both the Roman Catholic Church and the State
engaged themselves in a wave of religious intolerance.

According to Laënnec Hurbon,[11] this campaign was, in fact, a failure for the Catholic Church. Although it succeeded in getting rid of several sacred objects within vaudou, and in making some believers renounce idolatry and Satan, very soon, vaudou regained its fervour. Still, it must be admitted that vaudou did change on account of persecution, and had incorporated into its system candles, rites of all sorts, the sign of the cross and other evidence of Catholic pomp and splendour. These additions could only be explainable as a conscious attempt to make the religion more acceptable in the eyes of the political order. This point will be elaborated in the later section entitled "The God Revealed in Vaudou".

It would appear that during the second half of the present century, vaudou is being meted out with more tolerance on the part of rulers - President Estimé (1946-1950), President Magloire (1950-1956), President 'Papa Doc' François Duvalier (1957-1971) and the current Président à Vie, Jean-Claude Duvalier.

The Loas

Vaudou is more of an informal religion of action than a formal one of dogma. In Christian worship, it is possible for a person to be merely touched spiritually and nothing more. This is not the case with vaudou worship, for here the total participation of the individual, the physical self and the spiritual self, are, in the words of Dr. Pierre Mabille, vitally necessary.[12] This is so because apart from respecting God, either as the Great (or Grand) Master,[13] vaudou acknowledges a number of <u>loas</u>[14] or <u>spirits</u> who wield tremendous authority in the universe. They make the land fertile or sterile, bring rain or cause drought, make seeds grow or destroy them, cause the harvests to ripen or bring them to ruin. They afford protection against invisible evil spirits, which are forever present; they keep people away from the evil spells cast by magicians.[15] Indeed we have, in Vaudou, the reflection of a Dahomean idea that there are, in the universe, certain beings which are superior to men but inferior to the all powerful God.[16] One school of thought traces the origins of loas[17] to the rebellious spirits cast out of heaven by God. But there are clearly numerous categories of loas. There are the loas of historical heroes like Toussaint L'Ouverture, Henri Christophe, or Jean-Jacques Dessalines, of prominent ancestors, of powerful priests, in fact of any of the distinguished dead. The understanding of ancestral spirits comes from African traditional religion, and this will be more fully outlined in our next chapter.

Writers on Haiti make the point that vaudou varies from place to place.[18] There are countless numbers of loas, each one preferring different geographical localities, having peculiar characteristics, favourite foods and favourite colours. In this, vaudou resembles <u>macumba</u>, the spirit religion of Brazil, where each spirit "has his own distinctive color, necktie, favorite food, and special drinks."[19] Sometimes a loa may have certain attributes in one part of the country and different

attributes altogether in another area. There is therefore no
uniformity in belief about loas.

Among the more prominent loas are old African gods including
Damballah, Legba, Obatala, Erzulie, Ogoun and Shango, many of
whom are related particularly to Dahomey.

Damballah is regarded as the most powerful of spirits. He
dwells in springs, rivers, the sun, the stars, and the rainbow.
His wife is referred to as Aida Woedo. In Dahomey, Dangbé
referred to a snake cult,[20] and it is quite likely that the
name Damballah has there its origins. The snake was taken over
in vaudou, not as representing the Supreme Being, but as the
symbol of an ancestral spirit. Alongside the African links
with Damballah, we have also to reckon with the possibility
of Indian influence. In an Indian myth, there is a serpent
deity among an Andean tribe which is associated with the rainbow.[21] In the Mexican-Aztecan legends he is the plumed serpent
or double serpent[22] or double-headed serpent.[23] All this gives
a neat parallel with the double snake and the rainbow which,
in vaudou, symbolize Damballah and Aida Woedo, his female
counterpart. Damballah is sometimes equated with Saint Patrick[24]
who is supposed to have rid Ireland of its snakes. In vaudou,
he is ugly and strong, likes much food, especially pork and
goat meat and is specially addicted to alchohol. His favourite
colour is red.

Legba[25] is a well-known Yoruba deity worshipped also in Dahomey particularly where his statue appeared on all main roads and crossroads.[26] In Dahomey he was the first manifestation of divine creative power, the means whereby life - male and female - began. In vaudou, his status is that of the gatekeeper, and he is always invoked at the start of a worship ceremony, in the hope that he will open the door and allow the spirits to enter into communication with the worshippers. Jesus Christ Himself cannot enter unless Legba allows it. This loa corresponds to Saint Anthony the Hermit and Saint Peter, but more popularly the former.[27] He is aged, with flowing beard, handsome, lives under banana trees, or at the crossroads and autoroutes, and likes an abundance of meats and alcoholic drinks. He is symbolic of fertility. He protects those who worship him from evil spirits. His favourite colours are black and yellow.

Erzulie corresponding somewhat to Mater Dolorosa, but also linked with Saint Anne[28] is a young brown woman, a mulattress, beautiful, very amorous, and among delicate foods she likes white chicken, fine cakes, desserts and fine non-alcoholic liqueurs. Her colours are pink and white.

Ogoun is the protector against firearms. His origin is Dahomean, where he was the blacksmith among the gods.[29] He corresponds to Saint Joseph[30] and Saint Jacques.[31] His favourite colour is red.

Although most of the loas whom we have cited originate in Africa, or in Indian tradition, and have a parallel in Catholic hagiography, there are certain loas which are distinctively Haitian. A good example would be the "loas of death".[32] Baron Samedi, master of death, is so named because he is worshipped on Saturdays. (French 'Samedi' = Saturday.) He must be consulted before anyone may be permitted to engage in enterprises against the lives of others. He lives near the cross in the cemetery and is portrayed as wearing a black coat, hat and cane.[33] His chief helpers are the Guédés and they love fish. They also relish the taste of black chicken and fried plantains.[34] Black is the favourite colour of these loas of death.

Loas which are of Dahomean and Yoruba origin have been classified as Rada. They include such names as Legbas-Atibon, Damballah-Woedo, Agouet-Arroyo, Ogoun Ferraille and Ibo Lellé. Loas of Haitian origin, as well as those from other African countries are known as Petro. The latter, considered to be the more violent of the two,[35] include loas like Carrefour, Grand-Bois d'Ilet, Baron Lacroix, Ti Jean Pétro and Marinette. One writer explains the hostility of Petro loas as follows:

> "It is the raging revolt of the slaves against the Napoleonic forces. And it is the delirium of their triumph. For it was the Petro cult, born in the hills, nurtured in secret, which gave both the moral force and the actual organisation to the escaped slaves who plotted and trained, swooped down upon the plantations and led the rest of the slaves in the revolt that, by 1804, had made of Haiti the second free colony in the western hemisphere, following the United States."[36]

At this point, it is fair to say that it is the Petro rite, rather than the Rada, which has caused onlookers to view vaudou as black-magic, or devil worship.

The Participants

A key figure in the vaudou religion is the houngan[37] or priest.
He occupies a position of prestige in the rural Haitian communities, because he is spiritual leader, healer, magician and
exorcist. His ministry of exorcism often succeeds where western
oriented doctors and clergymen may have failed. His rise to the
position of houngan may have come about through being selected
by the community, or he may have inherited the post from his
father. But before he can be ordained he must undergo a
period of training for at least six months. Training for a
houngan must include a study of leaves, plants and their
medicinal properties. The houngan must also be familiar with
the use of holy water, anointing with oil and the part which
they play in the healing process.[38] He must be able to distinguish between natural or physical ailments requiring herbal
treatment, and unnatural or spiritual ailments which warrant
ritual treatment. His training makes him aware that within his
milieu, illness is very often associated with offending a loa.
Because of his superior knowledge, yet complete identification
with the real live situation of the people whom he serves, he
commands from them a tremendous amount of respect.

The houngan is the one who usually chairs a worship ceremony.
But of equal importance is the mambo[39] or priestess, who may
be his wife.

In any ceremony there are a number of persons assisting the houngan or mambo. These are the hounsils[40] who may be priests in training. During their training period of approximately two months, they familiarise themselves with the general running of the sacred house, the ceremonies, dances and songs.[41] Then there is the hougenikon, usually a woman who is aspiring to be a mambo. She directs the choir. In the course of a ceremony, she voices the salutary words "Aie Bobo"[42] directed to the officiants, which are echoed in chant by the choir, accompanied by the musicians. Apart from the hougenikon, another person who helps the houngan is the la-place,[43] the one who takes care of the physical arrangements for a ceremony. At times the la-place may have to deputise for the houngan if the latter becomes possessed by a loa while worship is in progress. Persons who do become possessed are described as serviteurs (servants), whereas the believers in general, hitherto referred to as vaudouisants, may also be referred to as fidèles (the faithful). Spirit possession is of an ecstatic nature, as obtains for example in macumba[44] of Brazil. In another section of the next chapter, we will be examining the phenomenon of spirit possession in greater detail. We simply make the point here that worship services are held in honour of the loas, and many of them are aimed at invoking their advice and help to supplement the inadequacy of human resources.

The Ceremony

The worship ceremonies are many and varied.[45] Some ceremonies are centred upon agricultural rites, such as the offering of first fruits. A typical ceremony of this kind is the manger-gname[46] in which offerings of yams are presented to the spirits and eventually eaten by the fidèles. ("Manger-gname" literally means "to eat yams.") They eat as a sign of thanksgiving for the harvest which has been bestowed upon the land.

The nature of vaudou worship is such that it may be held anywhere - under a tree, in the hills, within a cave, near a waterfall - since nature in general is regarded as sacred. However, a houmfort or hut is constructed for the purpose.[47] The ideal houmfort is said to be modelled after Solomon's temple, in that it contains a peristyle, or area whereon the ritual dances take place, and a holy of holies, restricted in its use to members of the priesthood. The focal point in any houmfort is the poteau-mitan[48] or sacred pole which extends from the ground level right up to the ceiling. Vaudouisants regard it as the link between the world of spirits and the world of humankind. It is at the poteau-mitan that celestial and terrestrial beings meet. As to the origin of the sacred pole, certain exponents of vaudou suggest the influence of the Amerindian totem, particularly that which the ancient Mexican merchants employed when leaving on their business trips.[49]

Within the ideal houmfort there are numerous ritual objects.[50] The decorated altars with their lithographs of saints may be taken as a clue to Roman Catholic influence. There is a batterie of three drums. These drums must have been initially baptized.[51] The small drum is used to beat a fixed rhythm, the middle sized drum adds variations to the regular beat of the little drum, whereas the large drum bears the distinction of being able to produce what is referred to as the rhythm "of the blood" or "of the true human self". Rada drums are tuned by hammering pegs which stretch the skin. During Rada rites the dancing is "on the beat". Petro drums are laced with rope, which when tightened with pegs, stretches the skin. During Petro rites, the drumming and dancing are "off-beat".[52]

There is the asson[53] or sacred rattle of the houngan, regarded too as a magic stick. It is made from a calabash into which small seeds or the vertebrae of serpents have been placed. It is supposed to represent astral powers and powers of the ances-tors. The asson is useless in anyone's hands, but powerful in the houngan's hands. Of course it must be emphasized that although he would feel somewhat handicapped without it, the houngan's power does not depend upon the asson. The govi is a clay jar in which the spirits of the dead are stored. It calls to mind the zemi[54] or fetish objects of Indian tribes. Among the Taino, for example, such sacred objects served much the same purpose as they do in vaudou, namely, as oracles which give advice. This is in fact the nearest thing to the practice of divination rites. Divination is not as developed as it is in Africa. Some houmforts contain a serpent in cast iron, symbol of Damballah. This is known as the assen. Other objects used during the course of a ceremony include the flags of the loas, clairin or native rum, leaves and herb mixtures. If a sacrifice is to take place, then a live chicken, pigeons, a goat, pig or bull would be available in the houmfort.

In a worship ceremony held in honour of one of the loas, the first thing to be done is to invoke the spirit's presence. At the foot of the poteau-mitan, a symbolic drawing is done.[55] This is called a vêver[56] and is skilfully done by the houngan, or la-place, using cornmeal or cornflour. The houngan takes the flour in small quantities between the thumb and the index finger and allows it to fall on the ground, making a drawing which, when completed, will represent the symbol of the loa to be called upon during the ceremony. The symbol of the cross-roads and walking-stick are associated with Legba, that of the snake with Damballah and Aida-Woedo, the heart with Erzulie, and the cross in the cemetery with Baron Samedi. Indian religious tradition as well as medieval European magic made use of symbolic drawings, so it is quite likely that these have exercised some influence on vaudou.[57]

To ensure that the spirits invoked do come, the air must be purified of evil or malevolent spirits. Symbolically, this may be done by striking the atmosphere around the poteau-mitan with a machete or cutlass. Libations have got to be offered, the usual form being for the houngan to take some clairin in the mouth and spray the liquid into the air.

Respect must be paid to Legba who, as we said earlier on, has power to open the door so that the spirits may enter into communication with the fidèles. Homage is also due to the Marassa[58] or divine twins who are regarded as being the first children of God. We may note here that in Haiti, people who have twins are often filled with great joy and a sense of pride since twins are "considered to be endowed with powers of divination and magic."[59]

As a ceremony develops, the keen observer notices distinctively Roman Catholic practices emerging as well as those which have obviously been borrowed from Amerindian and West African religions. Prayers offered during worship may include the recitation of the "Hail Mary" and other known Roman Catholic prayers. The flags of the loas are presented by the flag-bearers who at the same time perform a snake-like dance, in that the neck and body move back and forth in the manner of a snake. Such movements are peculiar to Amerindians of Latin America as well as to Indians of the Asian sub-continent. The singing, dancing, hand-clapping, drumming and spirit-possession which follow are akin to African religious ceremonies. When during the performance of an elaborate ritual, an animal's throat is slashed or the neck veins bitten into by a possessed person and the blood drunk, we identify yet another typically African religious trait.[60] Indeed, many of the ancestors of present day rural dwellers in Haiti came from Dahomey, a land where offerings and sacrifices to the gods was a matter of great importance.

The Dahomey situation resembled somewhat that of the people of Israel who had been expected to bring their first-fruits to Yahweh.[61]

Sacrifice is to be understood in the context of the vaudouisant's belief in the communication which exists between the physical world and that of the spirits. Jean Price-Mars lists a number of reasons for sacrifice in vaudou:[62]

- thanksgiving for favours bestowed by the loas upon individuals and groups.
- expiation for having invoked, wilfully or unconsciously, the divine wrath.
- obedience to an annual traditional act of homage, neglect of which could have serious consequences for the individual or group as a whole.
- a communal meal symbolizing human participation in mysterious, supernatural powers.
- a pact with the invisible world, the terms of which bring blessing and satisfaction.
- a duty towards the dead which ensures them peaceful existence in the supra terrestrial world, the neglect of which could bring upon the living the wrath of these departed spirits.

Whatever the reason for the sacrifice, it is done with food, drink or with live animals. No support for the claim of human sacrifice can be given[63] nor for the suggestion that vaudouisants are cannibals.[64]

Before leaving this description of the ceremony, it is important to note that there are quite a few rites associated with death. Indeed, death is a common theme in vaudou. The fact that loas

include the spirits of persons who have died attests to the
power which is associated with death. The dead are believed to
be both protectors and persecutors of family members, and it is
important for ceremonies to be given in their honour.[65] Immediately after a vaudouisant dies, the dessounin rite must be
performed. In it, the houngan ceremoniously removes the spirit
from the corpse and allows it to lodge in a surviving member of
the family or a close friend. If it is not possible for the
ceremony to be performed immediately after death, then it had
better be done later on, even in the cemetery. A dead vaudouisant
can become extremely dangerous if this has been neglected, for
as a ritual, dessounin symbolises a new birth into a new life.[66]
If it has to take place in the cemetery, then the ceremony is
know as the voyé mort, the literal Créole meaning being the
'sending of death'. Nine nights after the death of a vaudouisant,
there is usually a service held in honour of the family ancestors.

We now switch from our survey of general features within Haitian
vaudou. In Part II, we will be looking at particular issues
of theological import. These will relate to eschatology,
syncretism and divine revelation.

Part II - Theological Issues

Eschatology

Vaudou eschatology is not preoccupied with matters about judgment, heaven and hell. This is to be understood, since in
life, one is not seemingly engaged in the ethical and moral
struggles of right and wrong. The important thing is survival
at whatever cost. As far as the vaudouisant is concerned,
life does not end at death. There is the belief in continued
existence beyond the grave. In some circles when a burial is
performed, the relatives may place in the grave some of the
earthly possessions of the departed. These may sometimes include
food and a change of clothing for the journey into the unknown.
Although from this we may deduce that vaudouisants expect some
form of physical existence in the after-life, it would be
more true to say that this is the exception rather than the
general rule. The vast majority of fidèles aspire to a spiritual form of life after burial.

No clear statement of dogma is given about the soul. On the one
hand, it is believed that in natural death, the soul is in a
state of suffering, reminiscent of the credal statement, "He
descended into hell."[67] After this the soul returns to God.
On the other hand, it is also stated that the soul may rest
in water for one year where it serves as an oracle to be
consulted.[68] In the case of houngans and mambos, their souls
can be transferred immediately after death into the govi, by
virtue of their having undergone during their lifetime the

second degree of initiation. Of course, this idea of the power inherent in the important dead is nothing new. In fact, when we study the history of the Christian Church, we note that in the western Mediterranean during the third and right on through the sixth centuries, there had been developed the cult of saints owing to the power which had been associated with relics of Christian saints and martyrs.[69] Healing and exorcism were among the marvellous works which were an integral part of their shrines' activities.

A soul which is left to suffer in water becomes an evil spirit which will inflict terrible illnesses upon people.[70] There are some types of evil spirits which have been produced because children have died un-baptized. These are ghosts known as lutins. Female evil spirits, diablesses, are generally feared for the evil which they may inflict upon unsuspecting persons. The loup-garou, or Haitian version of the vampire, is usually a woman.

What complicates the doctrine about the soul is the fact that in vaudou there are two. The Gros Bon Ange is that part of the human being which controls the intellect. It is

> "the metaphysical double of the physical being, and since
> it does not exist in the world of matter, it is the
> immortal twin which survives the mortal man."[71]

It may separate from the body during sleep or under possession. The Ti Bon Ange is that part of the human being which controls the conscience. It never separates from the body until death.

We may inject here that such a concept offers an explanation
of what is meant when people, who have survived states resembling
death, claim they were actually looking down on their bodies.

It may be that the soul being referred to as experiencing a
state of suffering at death is the ti bon ange, whereas the soul
which may be eventually consulted as an oracle is the gros bon
ange. In fact, the complication arising from an understanding
of which soul is being referred to is not a problem unique to
vaudou. Paul the apostle, Christian as he was, never gave a
clear-cut distinction of what he was referring to when he used
the terms soul and spirit. On the one hand, he could have
been referring to ideas as interpreted by Gnostics. The
Gnostics thought of the soul ($\psi \nu \chi \eta$) as the spiritual or divine
substance which combined with matter to comprise human beings.
This spiritual substance was in a state of imprisonment and was
waiting to be released. Or Paul could have been employing
typically Jewish ideas, wherein the spirit was seen as the
divine self to be distinguished from the soul, which was the
earthly self.[72]

The idea of resurrection has found its way into vaudou eschatology. However this is definitely a bodily resurrection, as
opposed to a spiritual one. The other thing about it is that
it is a state to be feared rather than to be desired. To explain
this belief we must turn to the controversial issue of zombification.

Zombification

A _zombie_ is a person who had been buried and raised from the grave by some mystical formula which makes him or her a total slave to a _bocor_[73] or _sorcerer_. We interject here that the _houngan_ himself may be a _bocor_ if indeed he uses his knowledge and powers to nefarious ends. Laënnec Hurbon regards _houngan_ as the one who acts for good, _bocor_ as acting sometimes for evil, sometimes for good, and _sorcerer_ as serving purely evil interests.[74] Sometimes when sudden death occurs, and there is an aura of suspicion, the surviving relatives do all in their power to ensure that the corpse is spared the degradation of zombie's slavery.[75] There have been cases where a knife is plunged into the heart so that the apparent corpse becomes a real one, thereby ensuring freedom from possible zombification.

During my stay in Haiti, I would hear the reports by people that they had seen certain individuals whom they had known to be dead, actually walking as living persons in some other parts of the country. They were not describing some spiritual apparition. My first impulse was usually to dismiss this as mistaken identity. Evenutally my opinion was changed. Indeed I now have information, which proves that the claim of vaudou regarding a form of resurrection is actually true.

Today, more and more information is being revealed about the nature and process of zombification. A Haitian psychiatrist, Dr. Lamarque Douyon, has for over ten years been carrying out

research on a drug made from certain species of a plant and a
type of small fish found in Haiti, which is no doubt being used
to zombify people. We may here recall that by virtue of
training for the priesthood every houngan has an intimate
knowledge of the Haitian flora. The drug, which is several times
more powerful than cocaine, has lasting effects upon the will
and self determination of individuals, and can induce a state
resembling death. Associated with Dr. Douyon in his research
are a psychiatry professor from McGill University, Montreal,
a world authority on the biochemistry of the mind and a
psychiatrist and physician, who twice won the American equivalent
of a Nobel Prize for his research into new drugs.[76]

The research carried out in Haiti included the examination of
subjects who had been zombified. They had actually been
buried. Death certificates attest to this. They had been
exhumed and revived by bocors and put to do slavish work on
secluded plantations. Two such zombies are Francine and
Clervius.[77]

Francine had been zombified by a bocor as a punishment for
unfaithfulness to her husband. She had been given the secret
drug and two days later was pronounced dead. This was in
1976. Shortly after burial she was exhumed and made to work
for three years as a slave. She was found wandering around
the countryside and eventually placed in the care of psychiatrists who now describe her as a diminished person, making slow

progress.   During Francine's absence, her husband remarried.

Clervius Narcisse had been zombified following a dispute over
some land.   He died on the 2nd May, 1962, following an illness
lasting twenty-two days.   He was then forty-three years old.
Two doctors at the Albert Schweitzer Hospital near Gonaives,
one American, the other Haitian, certified the cause of death
as "malignant hypertension and oedema".   According to Narcisse,
he actually heard when he had been pronounced dead, and at the
time of his burial he could hear his sisters Angelina and
Marie-Claire weeping, though he could not talk.   A scar on the
face which he now bears is attributed to a flesh wound occasioned
by a nail in his coffin.   He had been raised from the grave,
taken into the bocor's house, re-animated, then set to work
as a slave where, for two years, he planted corn, yams, bananas,
sweet potatoes and coffee, alongside one hundred and fifty-one
other zombies.   Following the murder of the bocor by one of
the zombies, they all gained their freedom but when they re-
entered the world as live human beings, they were thrown in
prison.   In 1979, Narcisse reappeared and presented himself
at the market-place to his sister Angelina, in whose arms he
had died some seventeen years ago.   He introduced himself by
using a boyhood nickname known only to the family.   The shock
of seeing her brother alive caused her to faint.   Now, the
psychiatrists in whose care he has been entrusted, are satisfied with the recovery he has made so far.

Medical scientists are finding out more about this drug which, for long, has been a closely guarded secret among the vaudou houngans and bocors. It is said that the drug may be administered as a powder, sprinkled in the victim's food, or as a skin acting liquid poison which can be absorbed through the soles of bare feet. The drug acts within a day or two, and the victim coughs blood and develops symptoms of respiratory failure. Body metabolism is reduced and the person appears to be clinically dead. Western researchers would welcome more knowledge of the vaudou drug because of the potential which it has for open heart surgery and brain surgery, apart from other areas of medical care. Meanwhile, Haitians live in fear of becoming zombies.

In the light of recent evidence, therefore, zombification is something real. It is more than 'good fairy-tale stuff', ideal for a fictitious horror film. Scientists are now searching for answers to their questions. But zombification is not just a scientific issue. It is a legal issue, as well as one pertaining to social ethics. Is it right to deny human beings the enjoyment of life and to create slaves of them? Certainly in English law, the writ of Habeas Corpus (lit. you must produce the body) is designed to protect against the violation of human freedom. A prisoner is, by this writ, brought before a judge to decide whether he or she is being held lawfully. Yet such legal and ethical implications are hardly ever alluded to in Haiti.

A prominent houngan, Max Beauvoir[78] suggested that zombification
is less cruel than certain methods of punishment which are
employed by western society, e.g. beheading, hanging, the
electric chair. His opinion is that by turning people into
zombies, they are not actually put to death, therefore they
receive a more humane punishment. Beauvoir may be right that
the guillotine, the hangman's rope, the gas chamber and electric
chair are indicative of human barbarism. In fact, several
countries have abolished these methods of capital punishment
and have opted for long term prison sentences for very serious
crimes. But to make a virtue of zombification merely because
there are other seemingly more cruel methods of punishment is
going a bit too far. It ought to be remembered, too, that
hundreds of persons may well have gone to their actual deaths
through first being zombified for no crime except that they had
offended some spiteful person. Just as the question has been
asked, "Is it right for society or for one individual to
decide whose life is no longer worth living?", and this in
relation to forms of capital punishment, so too the moral issue
must be raised with regards to zombification. Is it fair that
some persons, in a free society, should be allowed to suffer
the degradation of slavery? Answers to such issues must be
in the negative, for only God has the legitimate and moral
right to take away life and to deny persons their freedom.

Naturally there will still be those who want to make out a
theological case to justify zombification, or any form of

slavery for that matter. They may cite Pauline passages which suggest that it is the duty of the slave to obey[79] ergo, the Bible recognizes slavery as a noble institution within society. But Christian thinking has evolved over the centuries and today it is widely accepted that in the light of the tremendous value which Jesus placed upon the human personality[80] in his recognition of people as being made in the image and likeness of God, it is downright immoral to rob men and women of their basic human rights, uppermost among which is the right to be free. We cannot help but conclude that the system of zombification is not only so puzzling as to warrant further scientific enquiry, but so immoral and criminal as to require the intervention of legal machinery to bring it to an end.

Syncretism

At the beginning of this chapter, we noted that vaudou reflects elements of West African religious traditions, French Catholicism and Amerindian tribal customs. As such, vaudou may be regarded as a syncretistic religion, since it has attempted to reconcile at least three main influences or schools of thought. West African religious traditions are reflected in the idea of the spirits who are present as a force to be reckoned with in the universe; in some of the Rada loas; in the houngan who combines the roles of religious leader, healer, magician and exorcist; in the pattern of religious ceremony, viz. singing, drumming, dancing, spirit-possession, and the offering of sacrifices. The influence of French Catholicism

is evident in the inclusion of Catholic liturgical prayers;
in the inclusion of Catholic saints among the loas; in the
presence of altars; in the practice of consecrating objects
for sacred use. Amerindian tribal influence appears chiefly
in the presence of ritual objects such as the poteau-mitan,
the asson, the govi and the vêvers.

Apart from these three main syncretistic strands, there is
free-masonry which, as we said earlier on, must have contributed
somewhat to the shaping of Haitian folk religion. The question
to which we ought now to address ourselves is, How far is it
justifiable to describe vaudou as the masonry of the masses?

Vaudou - Masonry of the Masses?

The first thing to be said is that Freemasonry is not a religion
although it strongly supports religion. We may speak, for
example, of the "Christian degrees" which, though accepted by
most Masons, are under separate jurisdictions than the basic
ecumenical Freemasonry.[81] Its true origin is uncertain and
there are many conflicting theories going back to Noah, to King
Solomon and others. A widely held view is that Ancient Masonry
dates back, firstly to the Egyptians and then to the ancient
Assyrians whose Semitic root word "mag", apart from meaning
"mason" referred to "magician" and to "imagination". It is
therefore held that the first masons were among the wisest and
holiest of men. They were astrologers, like the Magi of Egypt.
They carefully studied the zodiacal signs, convinced as they

were that energies flowed from planets and influenced human
destiny. They also investigated the spirit zones, or homes of
the dead, because of a conviction that

> "the soul survives physical death and sometimes communicates
> with those still in the flesh."[82]

The more they knew about the human soul, the more chance they
would have of making spiritual progress and attaining the
highest existence possible.

The ancient Masons made use of the language of universal symbolism. The lodgeroom is supposed to represent the ground plan of
King Solomon's Temple, itself a masterpiece of masonry and
architecture and attesting not to the glory of man but rather
to the glory of God, the Great Architect. It is

> "asserted that there are three columns, or pillars, that
> support the lodge. These are the equinoctial colure, the
> solstitial colure and the meridian. They are the support
> of the lodge because the lodge is the vault of heaven
> and all calculations relating to it are referred to one
> or more of these three lines, or pillars."[83]

In masonic lodges, the windows are concealed, so that none from
outside may look in at the ceremonies.

Old Testament personalities, apart from Noah and King Solomon,
who inspire Masons, include King Hiram of Tyre, Moses and
Zedekiah. Varying degrees or stages in masonic achievement
are based on such personalities. These degrees are of importance, because not all masons are party to the whole ceremony.
Some have to leave at particular points in the ceremony.
Because of the symbolism, masonry is shrouded in mystery. It

is associated with magic, occult power and an accompanying veil
of secrecy. Those steeped in masonry are supposed to journey
through the physical realm, the astral plane and the spiritual
world. The symbolism is found in the manner of walking, shaking
of hands, signs and gestures. It is found in tools. The gavel
is

> "the symbol of the Universal Creative Principle: the
> supreme attribute of Deity."[84]

The 12-inch gauge symbolises the twelve zodiacal signs. The
24-inch rule refers to

> "the 24-hour day during which the signs of the zodiac,
> bearing with them all the planets, rise and set."[85]

Trowel, compass, square and sword all add to the symbolic
functions of planets, sun, moon, stars and seasons. In modern
masonry, though, the zodiac is not a strong idea. Of greater
concern is the universal goal of masonry, which includes the
attempt to create a universal brotherhood of humanity.

According to historical records, modern freemasonry was first
organized in England in 1717 when the Grand Lodge came into
being. It took roots in France by 1725, and it is during that
time there were developed the "Christian degrees" alluded to
earlier on. By 1737, Freemasonry had spread to Germany.
Understandably, overseas French colonies would have had branches
of the lodge set up there. In Haiti, the first lodge was
founded at Cap Haitien in 1740.[86] Dr. Pierre Mabille states
that Masonic lodges were flourishing in Saint Domingue towards
the end of the eighteenth century, and that these lodges

included freed slaves. He contends that in the drawing of some

of the vêvers, in the hierarchical structure and in certain

parts of the ritual, the influence of Masonry is evident.[87]

There are many parallels between Masonry and Vaudou. It is not

without significance that the masonic terminology "Grand Master"

is used by vaudouisants, who refer to God as 'Gran Met-la'

(Grand Master). Masonry also acknowledges that there are non-

human influences exerted upon individuals. Vaudou ceremonies

dramatize this truth through loa possession, whereby personality

changes are effected in individuals.

Just as the masonic lodgeroom is a symbolic rather than a

factual representation of the ground plan of Solomon's temple,

and includes the sanctum sanctorum, so too the houmfort is

modelled after it. In both systems, there is a defined area

of the 'temple' where ceremonies take place. But what is more,

houngans are very much attracted to masonry, as Maya Deren

points out:

> "It is also significant that most of the houngans who
> claim the patronage of Ogoun belong to the Masonic
> Order. It is a logical association. As ironsmith,
> upon whose craftsmanship much depends, as moral authority,
> as the respected 'influential' citizen much involved in
> civic affairs and welfare, as a natural leader and
> organizer of men, and certainly as a believer in ritual,
> initiations, hierarchy, etc., Ogoun might very well have
> been a leading member of a local Masonic Lodge. Moreover,
> since Vodoun is not a centralized religion, the Masonic
> order has come to serve, curiously enough, as a kind of
> unifying meeting ground for houngans, even to the point
> where the Masonic handshake has become a standard part
> of the ritual Vodoun salutation between houngans. It is
> possible that other Masonic symbols have been introduced
> into Vodoun ceremonial, but it would require an advanced

member of the Order to recognize the actual degree to
which this is so."[88]

Masonry is veiled in mystery. Vaudou is associated with magic
and secrecy. The journey into the spiritual world as undertaken by the person who becomes possessed will continue to
baffle many who are but spectators to this religion. Both
Masonry and Vaudou are concerned with exploring beyond the
physical world in search for the truth about human destiny.
In so doing, they both impose upon their followers certain
strict initiation rites and a rigorous discipline. We may
justifiably state that vaudou is the masonry of the masses,
not in the sense that vaudouisants copied from the Masonic
Order so as to bring their religion to a level comparable to
the elites. Granted there are some happy coincidences found
in both systems, which may even be due to direct borrowing
by the vaudouisant from Masonry. But the real sense in which
vaudou is the masonry of the masses is in its function. The
complicated, formalised structure of Masonry, with its wealth
of symbolism, serves to conduct the educated upper and middle
classes along the journey from the physical world to the astral
plane. And this is what vaudou does, in a less sophisticated,
less complicated, less intellectual manner for the masses of
rural folk. It is the means whereby their spiritual journey
to the astral realm is made possible.

That Vaudou is a syncretistic religion, there can be no doubt.
However, there is a very real fear that if we attribute every-

thing to syncretism, we do so at the risk of undermining the uniqueness of religious insights which had been revealed to the early Haitian people, descendants as they were from various parts of the African continent. The authenticity of divine revelation within vaudou is defended by Laënnec Hurbon, who charges that the Christian faith in its western cultural garb has been paraded as superior to vaudou. Vaudou is classified by western culture as a second rate religion. Vaudou is not a simple borrowing from Roman Catholicism, but in it

> "we are confronted with an authentic religious experience, a cultural language which is just as valuable as any other language, and which satisfies the Haitian vaudouisant in his search for an understanding of the things of this world and of a purpose to human existence."[89]

Hurbon continues,

> "in reality, the use of the concept of syncretism conceals a negation of vaudou as an original culture and a living religion."[90]

Let us take up the question of revelation, following which we will examine the concept of God within vaudou.

Revelation

Human nature varies with individuals. No two persons, not even 'identical twins' or persons produced through the genetic engineering of cloning are exactly alike. There are bound to be differences between individuals, families, tribes and nations because people do have experiences which are unique to them. Thus the notion of culture indicates a way of life which has been conditioned by certain specific experiences. Such

differences suggest that people's awareness, or non-awareness
of God, would be the direct outcome of the type of experiences
they have in life. To speak therefore of divine revelation,
we must be prepared to accept that the manner of God's revelation to the peoples of Africa has differed from that in which
His truth has been communicated to the peoples of Europe.[91]
This is not to deny that there are aspects of God's revelation
which might be accepted as authentic by both Africans and
Europeans. Obviously, certain aspects of God's revelation
have been regarded as universal. There is, for example, the
notion that nature reveals the activity of a creative God.
This, of course, is not the same thing as to deify certain
elements within nature. It is rather the expression of a
conviction that when one contemplates the wonder of nature, one
might be led to an awareness of God's presence. But there have
been other aspects of His revelation which are not universal,
but certain groups of people believe that they are. This is
Hurbon's point. He accuses western culture of positing the
Christian faith as the one, true revelation of God. The
Christian faith acknowledges God as revealed through nature,
Holy Scriptures, salvation history, Jesus Christ, the Holy
Spirit, the Church and Christian tradition. Karl Barth concen-
trates upon God who reveals Himself in Scripture as the Tri-une
God, the Three-In-One and One-In-Three; God the Creator and
Eternal Father; God the Reconciler and Eternal Son; God the
Redeemer and Eternal Spirit.[92] Barth's stress is upon
Scriptural Revelation. In one section of his dogmatics, he

treats "Scripture as a witness to Divine Revelation".[93] Very
few theologians would disagree that Scripture is a powerful
medium of divine revelation. Those who have been influenced by
the thinking of Rudolf Bultmann, for example, would suggest
that revelation comes alive today through the preached Word.
However, religions like vaudou which are outside the realm of
Christianity, are staking a claim for the authenticity of the
revelation which is unique to their particular culture. I
daresay this body of opinion is a rather strong one.

Paul Tillich, like Barth, is sold on the idea of Scriptural
Revelation. But Tillich appears to be more concerned about
developing the Biblical idea of the social conditioning of
revelation. He writes:

> "There is no revelation 'in general' (Offenbarung ueber-
> haupt.) Revelation grasps an individual or a group,
> usually a group through an individual; it has revealing
> power only in this correlation. Revelations received
> outside the concrete situation can be apprehended only
> as reports about revelations which other groups assert
> that they have received. The knowledge of such reports,
> and even a keen understanding of them, does not make
> them revelatory for anyone who does not belong to the
> group which is grasped by the revelation. There is no
> revelation if there is no one who receives it as his
> ultimate concern."[94]

That Scriptual Revelation is conditioned by social, economic and
political realities comes across vividly in the writings of
Hugo Assmann, liberation theologian speaking out of the context
of Latin America:

> "The 'word of God' is no longer some perduring, unchanging
> absolute, some eternal proposition that we accept as
> such before analyzing social conflicts and committing
> ourselves to the transformation of historical reality.

God's summons to us - God's word today - arises out of
communal analysis of historical data and historical
happenings as praxis. The Bible and Christian tradition
as a whole do not address themselves 'directly' to us
in our present situation; instead they stand as a basic
point of reference for us, indicating how God speaks to
human beings in widely divergent contexts. Thus they
can help us to see how God might be speaking to us in our
present context...
....
"The basic reference points of traditional theology, the
Bible and tradition (however the latter term may be
understood), do not suffice for doing theology because
they are not directly accessible. Our approach to these
touchstones of the Christian faith is affected and conditioned by blocks set up in the past. We must take note
of these blocks in our present context and try to remove
them in our own analysis and praxis."[95]

H. Richard Niebuhr, in stressing that there are certain univer-

sal truths about the Christ, admits that the revelation of God

in Christ is socially conditioned:

"Interpreted by a monk, he may take on monastic characteristics; delineated by a socialist, he may show the features
of a radical reformer; portrayed by a Hoffman, he may
appear as a mild gentleman. But there always remain the
original portraits with which all later pictures may be
compared and by which all caricatures may be corrected.
And in these original portraits He is recognizably one
and the same. Whatever roles he plays in the varieties
of Christian experience, it is the same Christ who exer-
cises these various offices. The founder of the church
is the same Christ who gives the new law; the teacher of
truths about God is the same Christ who is in himself
the revelation of the truth."[96]

In arguing his case in support of an alternative revelation of

God to be found in Haitian vaudou, Hurbon suggests that

attention should be paid, not only to the universality of

Christianity, but also to its particularity.[97] In the Old

Testament, the Israelite people have a special role assigned

to them by Yahweh. The God of Abraham, Isaac and Jacob, who

revealed Himself to be their God, had entered into a Covenant relationship with them, whereby they had a duty to obey and remain faithful to Him, in return for which He would protect them. Through the Exodus event and other saving acts in their history, the Israelites observed that God was keeping His side of the bargain. But it was only up to a point that Israel kept its side of the Covenant. Certain traditions, such as the keeping of the Sabbath and practising the rite of circumcision, were rigorously adhered to. These signs were very dear to the Israelites, so much so that they classified all people who did not subject themselves to the demands of the Mosaic Law as people who were outside the range of Yahweh's care and concern.

It became fairly obvious that the Covenant relationship had created in the people of Israel a false pride. They held an exaggerated opinion of their own worth. The point at which this covenant broke down was in their failure to remain faithful to the responsibility which it demanded of them. To be special in God's sight meant that they were to be faithful to him and maintain a high ethical standard of living. But they were not to suppose, as they had been doing all along, that they were the only nation under God that mattered. Israel was one nation among many. This idea was progressively revealed to them through the mouths of the prophets. Amos, Hosea and Micah echoed in their prophecies the need for ethical living.[98] Amos announced that Yahweh is the One true God who controls the

destinies of all peoples. He could employ other nations to
execute His will, even if that will involved suffering on the
part of those who considered themselves chosen by Him:

> "For behold, I will raise up
> against you a nation,
> O house of Israel," says the
> Lord, the God of hosts;
> "and they shall oppress you ...."[99]

A similar warning was sounded by the prophet Jeremiah.[100] The
prophet Isaiah taught that God's plan of salvation was not for
the benefit of Israel only, but rather for the entire world.
Thanks to God, Israel had a role to play in this plan.[101]

When one looks at the person of Jesus, one also gets the impression that His concern is not for one nation only, but for all.
The God whose Sonship His personality proclaimed was the father
of all people, hence Jesus' desire to effect a reconciliation
among all of humankind. Naturally for the Incarnation to become
possible, Jesus could not be born everywhere. He had to be
limited to one culture, and it was within the Jewish set-up
that he appeared. This is why He ordered the disciples to
begin their mission first among the "lost sheep of the house
of Israel".[102] Just as the prophets of old spoke out against
Israel for having forgotten her responsibility and becoming
complacent in her righteousness, so too did Jesus attack the
chief priests, Scribes and Pharisees for having failed God.
Sometimes He warned that the kingdom of God would be taken away
from them and given to a nation producing the fruits of it.[103]
He warned, too, that people would come from the east and west

and sit at table with Abraham, Isaac and Jacob in the kingdom of heaven, while they who had all along considered themselves to be sons of the kingdom would inherit utter darkness.[104] Throughout His ministry He mixed with those whom the "righteous" religious leaders had scorned as outcasts and sinners, namely prostitutes and tax-collectors.

Jesus proclaimed that God had selected Israel, but that salvation was a universal feature and an eschatological hope. From what the Old and New testaments teach about the special role which Christianity may today claim to have in God's plan for universal salvation, we cannot deny that there are other religions under God which do matter. Hurbon's point is that Christianity has been accepted in the west as the framework wherein God has chosen to reveal Himself to the world. But western religion and culture must not parade Christianity as universal, when in fact it is not. What Hurbon notices about Christianity is that in it God has been the white man's God, and that for the indigenous people of Haiti, God's power has signified economic oppression, cultural alienation and political alienation.[105] Now just as in Christianity God has revealed Himself to the rich, western cultures, so too in vaudou He has disclosed Himself to the poor folk of Haiti.

We may sympathize with Hurbon's view of revelation, especially if we consider the work wrought by the Spirit of God. In Joel, God had promised to reveal Himself in the world through the

Spirit. This was to be the Spirit of prophecy whereby people

"will have insight into Divine truth, and will be moved to express it, in the manner which is at present confined to such as specially bear the name of prophets."[106]

His Spirit, says the prophet Joel, will be poured out on all flesh.[107] Sometimes the use of the term all flesh could, in a very wide sense, refer to human beings and animals.[108] At other times its use could be restricted to humankind.[109] Israel believed that the term, as employed in Joel's prophecy, was pointing to the pouring out of God's Spirit on all Israelite flesh. However when this prophecy was eventually fulfilled on the Day of Pentecost, an amazing thing happened. The Spirit had been poured out, not only upon Israelites, but also upon representatives from several other nations of the earth.[110] No cultural superiority could therefore be claimed by Israel. Notice the testimony of Peter before Cornelius, that

"God shows no partiality, but in every nation any one who fears him and does what is right is acceptable to him."[111]

Notice also the shock when, following this particular incident, the Jews realised that the gift of the Holy Spirit was poured out even on Gentiles.[112] The challenge presented by all this is that the Church is called upon, in humility, to accept that God reveals Himself and pours out His Spirit not only upon Christian flesh, but indeed upon all flesh.

Throughout the Bible, then, God has progressively revealed Himself. First thought of as special to Israel, He eventually became known as the God of all the nations. The Israelites had been misguided into thinking that salvation was theirs

alone, until it had been revealed to them that salvation was
universal in scope.

Following what has been said, what must be the attitude of the
Church? Must the Church preach Christ as the only revelation,
or must it be accepted that non-Christian religions also have
authentic revelations of God? We may not agree with Professor
Hick that the Incarnation is purely a myth and not literally
true.[113] Yet it is important to this discussion that we bear
in mind his words:

> "When we see the Incarnation as a mythological idea applied
> to Jesus to express the experienced fact that he is our
> sufficient, effective and saving point of contact with
> God, we no longer have to draw the negative conclusion
> that he is man's one and only effective point of contact
> with God. We can revere Christ as the one through whom
> we have found salvation, without having to deny other
> points of reported saving contact between God and man.
> We can commend the way of Christian faith without having
> to discommend other ways of faith. We can say that
> there is salvation in Christ without having to say that
> there is no salvation other than in Christ."[114]

Paul's letter to the Romans contains support for Professor
Hick's line of reasoning. Paul, for example, develops the
idea that God has no favourites.[115] If there is no partiality
with God, then it cannot be true that non-Christians who have
been born within their God-given cultures, and have invariably
adopted the religion of those cultures, have been denied divine
revelation, and are doomed to damnation. If there is no
favouritism with God, then Christianity must not claim special
privileges. Indeed, judgment will not be to the Christian's
advantage and to others' disadvantage, because knowledge of

God is not the monpoly of the Christian. Commenting on the
same Pauline passage, Anders Nygren writes:

> "The Jew's advantage is that he has the law, while the
> heathen does not have it. Paul does not deny that
> difference. He speaks of him who sins with the law
> and of him who sins without it. But he reduces this one
> difference to its proper significance. Though the heathen
> does not have the law, he is not without knowledge of
> God's will."[116]

The dilemma faced in Haiti is that the Europeans who imposed
Catholicism had tried to suppress vaudou because they felt
that western culture was the only acceptable framework for God's
revelation to take place. Yet in spite of this, knowledge of
God within vaudou is unique for although some of His attributes
are definitely compatible with Christian theology, there are
some which are alien to it.

The God Revealed in Vaudou

Vaudou is a montheistic religion. The God revealed to the
Haitian people is the Creator, the all powerful and invisible
lord of life. Vaudouisants refer to Him as Gran-Met-la (Great
or Grand Master) because that is what He is. He controls the
entire universe. As mentioned above, there are certain aspects
of God in Haitian vaudou which make it difficult sometimes to
reconcile Him with the God revered within the Christian tradition. The Supreme Being in vaudou tends to be an impersonal
power, an abstraction, far removed from the grasp of ordinary
individuals. This is to the Christian an unacceptable concept,
when considered that the God of the Christian faith is very

near, very personal. He is addressed in familiar terms, such
as "father". He is the very ground of all being, hence the
psalmist could say to Him:

> "O Lord, thou hast searched me and known me!
> Thou knowest when I sit down and when I rise up;
> thou discernest my thoughts from afar.
> Thou searchest out my path and my lying down,
> and art acquainted with all my ways."[117]

With certainty, the Christian preacher proclaims a God who is
intimately involved with His creation, a God whose love and
warmth are very real to the faithful.

It must be made clear, though, that although Christian eyes
may discern a cold and impersonal God within Haitian folk
religion, the vaudouisant's view of God is not like this. For
the fidèle, Gran-Met-la only appears to be far away. But He
is intimately concerned about each and every individual so
much so that He constantly intervenes in human affairs. He is
approached, not directly, but through the spirits. This idea
of approaching an important being, not directly, but through
someone else is part and parcel of Haitian culture. If a simple,
uneducated farmer wants an audience with a person in civil
authority, he may seek out a friend who knows someone who may
know someone else who can transmit to the one in authority the
content of the farmer's message. In a similar fashion, the loas
in vaudou facilitate communication between the fidèles and
Gran-Met-la.

The idea of loas in Haitian vaudou says something about God's

created order. These loas are not, as psychologists and
psychoanalysts may conclude, figments of the imagination.
They are part of the order of supernatural beings who are
below God. They are to be numbered in the same category as
angels whom we encounter in the Bible, and who are classified
as the messengers of God who execute His commands.[118] They
exist as objective realities and become incarnate in people.
Perhaps what is disturbing to the Christian mind is the fact
that these loas seem to be gods in themselves. The vaudouisants
believe that God is in control, but the He has delegated some
power to the loas, hence their importance. Still, this does
not take away from the fact that loas appear to be on an equal
footing with God, because the worship ceremonies are held
entirely in their honour. Vaudou seems therefore to have done
a disservice to Christian theology in that the Supreme Being
is forced to share the adoration which is due to Him alone, with
spirits who are personal to the extent of actually investing
the worshippers with a large portion of themselves.

The impression which one gets of God from an understanding of
loas is an Old Testament, jealous and vengeful God. Sacrifices
must be offered in order to appease the wrath of the spirits,
and, as has already been mentioned, neglect of this could
have some catastrophic consequences. Christian theology maintains that the God who revealed Himself in Christ does not
require sacrifices:

> "What to me is the mutititude of your sacrifices?
> says the Lord;

> I have had enough of burnt offerings of rams
> and the fat of fed beasts;
> I do not delight in the blood of bulls, or of
> lambs, or of he-goats."[119]

These are the sentiments echoed by the prophets[120] who emphasize that what God really requires of the individual is a life of justice, mercy and humility. The Christian God is loving and forgiving.

The ethical living required of the Christian suggests that the God revered in Christianity is basically good. There seems, however, to be a problem with the God of Haitian Folk religion. Gran-Met-la is also good. In fact, sometimes He is addressed as Bon-Dieu (the good God) and He may even be described as Providence.[121] But what is significant is that not all of the loas, who are subordinate to Him, are ethically good. The Petro loas are a case in point. They are the malevolent, violent spirits, responsible for what is often described as 'black magic'. Indeed, some vaudouisants are more interested in this unethical type of God rather than the good God concept. An onlooker at a particular vaudou ceremony had been told in a very threatening manner by a female fidèle, "Pinga ou rélé nom Bon Dieu isit!" (You'd better be careful not to call the name of the good God here!) Perhaps for many, the idea of an ethically good God is threatening in a situation of abject poverty. For people are more inclined to live off their wits, than by any strict moral code of conduct. It is so often mouthed, in that situation, "Dégagé pa péché!" In other words, the use of unfair methods to achieve certain ends is no sin. James Leyburn has summed up the situation quite adequately when he said:

> "By conceiving his spirits as in manner and desires resembling himself, the Haitian can understand his little universe without subjecting himself to the bewilderment which faces a simple Christian trying to reconcile an all-loving father with the obvious evil He allows on earth."[122]

There is an obvious difficulty which we face in deciding whether, in the context of the Haitian situation, the God worshipped by the majority of vaudouisants is moral or amoral. However, there is one thing which can be said in general. He is always on the side of His people. He may be jealous, requiring sacrifices and vengeful. But He sides with the poor and oppressed. When one looks at Haitian history, one gets the impression of a sort of salvation history with God, the liberator, or saviour, acting deliberately in favour of the oppressed. He it was who allowed the oppressed slaves to gain victories over the French, which brought about their freedom and the independence of their country in 1804. Clearly, in this high point in the country's history, God was decidedly working against the capitalists and colonialists from France.[123]

From what we have said, it is evident that there were marked differences in the concept of God between the descendants of Africans who settled on Haitian soil and the French who at one time exercised political power over the country. It is a known fact that

> "when two religions come into contact, the result will be either religious stratification, with one of them being considered the only true religion and the other relegated

to the realm of mysterious cults or black magic, or an
attempt to establish equivalences between the gods and
place them on a common value level. But the two religions
will always tend to persist as entities."[124]

In Haiti, Roman Catholicism had the advantage by virtue of its

official nature. As a result of persecution by the State and

the Roman Catholic Church during the nineteenth and early

twentieth centuries, the Haitian masses believed that the only

way for their religion to survive was for them to introduce into

vaudou worship elements resembling the official religion. This

would, they had hoped, give an aura of authenticity about vaudou.

So that, there were Catholic prayers, the saints, the cross and

other elements grafted into vaudou. The result of this sort of

exercise is fairly evident today, with vaudou acknowledging not

only an endless number of loas, but also including in it systems

the names of Jesus, the Virgin Mary and many Roman Catholic

saints. In some circles, Jesus is thought of as a mediator

between the loas and God. He it is who imparts courage for

people to perform religious duties. There are some adherents

who regard loas and saints as one and the same thing. Indeed

several feast days of the Catholic Church are set aside in the

vaudou calender as special days:

Epiphany	-	Feast of Damballah
Easter	-	Sacred to Legba
Pentecost	-	Initiation ceremonies
All Souls' Day	-	Feast of the Guédés
Christmas	-	Feast of the Marassa (Divine Twins).

Then too, it is quite common for followers of vaudou to attend

Catholic masses and not to experience any contradiction with their general commitment to that religion. In fact, before a person can be initiated into vaudou, he or she must go to the nearby Roman Catholic Church, pray, confess and be in a state of peace.[125] Just as Roman Catholics in Haiti speak of their protective saint or guardian angel, so too vaudouisants may have one or two loas who are more important to them, and one principal "loa protecteur" or "protective spirit".

Earlier on we referred to Laënnec Hurbon's contention that the concept of syncretism undermines the originality which is inherent in vaudou. But Hurbon is not alone in his opinion. Jean-Marie Salgado would like to qualify the nature of syncretism found in vaudou.[126] He contends that there is ritual syncretism, not doctrinal syncretism. When, for example, the vaudouisants were faced with the saints of Roman Catholicism, they did not abandon a belief in loas and reinterpret their doctrines to make them coincide with those of Roman Catholicism. Instead, they began to establish similarities between the loas and the saints and make equations. What they did in Haiti was similar to what was done in Brazilian folk religion. The Brazilians, too, examined their spirits and sought for them counterparts in Catholic hagiography.[127] It is therefore more correct to speak of ritual syncretism, of Catholic elements being juxtaposed or added to what already existed within vaudou, e.g. hierarchical structure of priesthood, initiation, baptism of sacred objects. The doctrine of God remained the same. He is not the God of the Trinity, but He is the One who reveals Himself through the spiritual beings which are part of His creation. Hence Hurbon's warning that

> "the God whom the vaudouisants worship is not a pure and simple borrowing of the Christian God"[128]

and Salgado's point that despite the similarities which exist between Catholicism and Vaudou, there are two vastly differing concepts of God's revelation which are operative.[129]

Finally a word about Protestantism. One has to agree with Hurbon that Protestantism, more than Roman Catholicism, is a complete reversal of the vaudou universe.[130] Whereas Catholicism, by virtue of its hagiography, may be regarded as acknowledging divine revelation which is paralleled in vaudou loas, Protestantism holds on doggedly to a Trinitarian revelation. There can be no authentic revelation without God as Father, without the central Christian concept of the Incarnation, without emphasis on the centrality of Christ, and without a doctrine of the Holy Spirit. In the fight against vaudou, this may be Protestantism's strength, namely its refusal to entertain suggestions that God discloses Himself through ways other than those traditionally accepted. But this approach of expelling from its system whatever cannot easily be accepted could quite likely be Protestantism's weakness. If God is to make use of the Church for continued revelations of Himself, then part of that Church's responsibility is to remain open to the possibility of new truths, and not simply engage in a process of expulsion. Expulsion, rejection, excommunication, denial of existence - these may be the least difficult ways which the

Church adopts when dealing with difficult problems, whether these problems be persons or issues. But just as they are the least difficult methods, they are equally the least creative.

It may be that the vaudou idea of spiritual beings, or loas, is an amorphous concept. It may not match the systematically worked out Christian doctrines pertaining to a God who has revealed Himself as a Trinity of Father, Son and Spirit. Yet in our search for theological truth, we are duty bound to explore further the concept of spirits as a possible revelation of God. Hence in our next chapter, we will look in greater detail at spirits, firstly within the culture of Africa, from which the Haitians have undoubtedly shared this aspect of divine revelation, then secondly from the context of the Bible. Such an enquiry should help us to form a more reasoned opinion about the vaudou loas and about the possiblity of spirits being authentic as a tool of divine revelation.

CHAPTER 2 - NOTES

1. "Il perpétue de très belles traditions communes à tous les peuples de la terre, qui devaient être en majeure partie du folklore plutôt que matières de croyances religieuses. Son inflence sur les populations haitiennes est énorme, et par la conviction de ses adeptes, il constitue une force qui le rend considérable. L'élite haitienne vis-à-vis de lui garde une attitude de profond mépris et de crainte à cause du diabolisme qui lui est accordé gratuitement. Cette dernière position s'explique par le recul de certains membres de cette élite habitués à s'adresser, dans leur cupidité, au magicien plutôt qu'au grand-prêtre." - Louis Maximilien, Le Vodou Haitien: Rite Radas-Canzo, Port-au-Prince, Haiti, Imprimerie de L'Etat, 1945, p. 223.

2. James G. Leyburn, The Haitian People.

3. Vaudouisant is the term we will use for adherents to the vaudou religion.

4. Article 2 of the Code Noir, 1685 - "All slaves in our islands shall be baptized and instructed in the Catholic religion, Apostolic and Roman. We instruct the colonists buying newly arrived slaves that they should inform the Governor and Intendant of it within one week at the latest, on pain of a summary fine, and they shall give the necessary orders to have them instructed and baptized in due course." - F.R. Augier and S.C. Gordon, Sources of West Indian History, London, Longmans, Green & Co. Ltd, 1962, p. 145.

5. Pierre Mabille, "Preface" in Louis Maximilien, op. cit. p. xix.

6. James G. Leyburn, op. cit.

7. Hyacinthe, for example, is described as a slave who "went from plantation to plantation claiming, as most leaders of agricultural revolts, that he was divinely inspired." - C.L.R. James, The Black Jacobins, New York, Vintage Books, 1963, p. 108.

8. Harold Courlander and Rémy Bastien, Religion and Politics in Haiti, Washington D.C., Institute for Cross-Cultural Research, 1966, pp. 16, 17.

9. General Geffrard ruled from 1860-1867. He was followed by Salnave (1867-1870), Nissage Laget (1870-1874), then three presidents (1874-1878) and Saloman (1878-1888).

10. The period 1889-1908 saw three presidents, and that between 1908-1915 eight presidents.

11. "Cette campagne fut, à la verité, un echec pour l'Eglise Catholique. Elle réussit à détruire plusieurs objects de culte du Vaudou, elle obtint même de la part des fidèles des serments de renonciation aux idoles et à Satan. Mais très tôt, le Vaudou retrouva sa faveur, sauf, bien sûr, dans certaines localités où la campagne fut particulièrement sévère et où la peur s'empara des esprits eux-mêmes." - Laënnec Hurbon, Dieu dans le Vaudou haitien, Paris, Payot, 1972, p. 19.

12. "La caracteristique fondamentale du Vaudou est la participation totale de l'être au cours des cérémonies. L'adepte n'est pas comme dans le Christianisme élevé spirituellement. Toute sa personne est mise en mouvement ....toutes les parties du corps vibrent sous l'empire des rhythmes du tambour." - Dr. Pierre Mabille, "Preface" in Louis Maximilien, op. cit., p. xx.

13. Vaudou worshippers use a Créole term "Gran-Met-Là", (French, "le Grand Maître) for God.

14. Apart from loas, the vaudou spirits are called anges (angels) and mystères (mysteries). Loa itself is a derivative of a commonly used Bantu verb which means 'to bewitch'. In his monumental work, Sir Harry H. Johnston, A Comparative Study of the Bantu and Semi-Bantu Languages, mentions several areas of Africa where the word from which loa is undoubtedly derived, was used. E.g. Loga in languages from Eastern and Central Africa, Loha in the Makonde language of Mozambique. In a later work, G. Malcolm Guthrie, ed. Lingala Grammar and Dictionary, Conseil Protestant Du Congo, 1935, lists loka as meaning 'to bewitch'. It was used by the Bangala tribe of the Congo River which spoke Lingala. Loka is the word in the Kikongo language of Zaire and Angola. In Swahili, the word is loga.

15. "Ce sont les dieux qui rendent fertile or stérile la terre, qui sont dispensateurs de pluie ou qui provoquent la sécheresse, qui font croître les semences ou qui les détruisent, qui garantissent les récoltes ou les ruinent. Ils protègent aussi contre les mauvais esprits invisibles, mais présents constamment, et ils gardent les hommes des mauvais sorts jetés par les magiciens." - Louis Maximilien, op. cit., p. 69.

16. Mawu is one of the more popular names for the supreme deity in Dahomey. Yet his name does not figure in the current vaudou pantheon.

17. John S. Mbiti, Introduction to African Religion, Great
    Britain, Heinemann, 1977, pp. 65-76. Of course, Mbiti
    here is not speaking specifically about vaudou spirits.

18. This point is made by George Eaton Simpson, "The Vodun
    Cult in Haiti".

19. Roger Bastide, The African Religions of Brazil, trans.
    Helen Sebba, Baltimore and London, The John Hopkins Uni-
    versity Press, 1978, p. 297.

20. J.C. Dorsainvil, Vodou et Nevrose, Etude Médico-socio-
    logique, Port-au-Prince, Haiti, Imprimerie "La Presse",
    1931, p. 158.

21. Hartley Burr Alexander, The Mythology of All Races, Vol.
    XI, 'Latin America', Boston, Marshall Jones Co., 1920,
    pp. 200, 201.

22. Ibid, p. 100.

23. Ibid, p. 72

24. "St. Patrick (died about 461). Feast day, March 17. This
    well-loved patron saint of Ireland was not of Irish
    descent nor was he born in Ireland. He was born in
    Scotland and was a Briton and a Roman by ancestry. As a
    young man he was taken into Ireland as a slave. Later,
    when he had regained his freedom and was in his own land,
    he was called by God to go to Ireland and convert the
    country to Christianity. Many legends are told about
    St. Patrick, and his feast day is universally celebrated
    among people of Irish descent." - Jessie Corrigan Pegis,
    A Practical Catholic Dictionary, New York, All Saints
    Press, 1965, pp. 232, 233.

25. Legba among the Fon (Dahomey) correspons to El-é-gbara
    or 'the powerful one' (Yoruba), A-gbara (Igbo) and
    ultimately Gabr-iy'el (Gabriel). A-gbara is the Yoruba
    word for power, corresponding to the Hebrew $g^e bu^u r$-ah.

26. J.C. Dorsainvil, op. cit., p.158.

27. Roger Bastide, op. cit., p. 265. About Saint Anthony
    the Hermit, we refer again to Jessie Corrigan Pegis,
    op. cit., pp; 235, 236: "St. Anthony of Padua (1195-
    1231). Feast day, June 13. St. Anthony, who is often
    called the wonder-worker because of the many miracles
    attributed to him, was born in Lisbon in 1195. He
    was already a Canon Regular when, inspired by the spirit
    of St. Francis, he decided to become a Franciscan and go
    to preach in Africa . Illness kept him form going to
    Africa, and for a time he lived in a cave at Sao Paulo,
    praying and doing the humblest tasks. By chance his

ability to preach was discovered by his religious
brothers, and he became a famous preacher. He died in
Padua in 1231 when he was only thirty-six years old......"

28. J.M. Salgado, Le Culte Africain Du Vodou et Les Baptisés
en Haiti - Essai De Pastorale, Rome, Université Pontificale
"De Propaganda Fide", Editiones Urbanianae, 1963, p. 31.

29. Alfred Métraux, Le Vaudou Haitien, Paris, Gallimard,
1958, p. 64.

30. Roger Bastide, op. cit., p. 265.

31. J.M. Salgado, op. cit., p. 31.

32. Louis Maximilien disagrees. He regards the death loas
as being of African origin. cf. Louis Maximilien,
op. cit., pp. 119,120.

33. Ibid., p. 66.

34. Plantains are similar to bananas. Larger in texture,
they are eaten, not as fruits but as vegetables. They
may be boiled, roasted or fried.

35. The Créole statement is often heard: "Rada loa yo doo.
Petro loa yo cho." (Rada loas are gentle. Petro loas
are hostile.)

36. Maya Deren, Divine Horsemen - The Living Gods of Haiti,
London and New York, Thames and Hudson, 1953, p. 62.

37. Houngan comes out of the Bantu languages. It could be,
as Herskovits suggests, a combination of houn (synony-
mous with vodun in Dahomey) and -gan (an ending meaning
chief)), therefore 'chief of the spirits,' but it is more
likely to be a compound of hounounga and -ganga. The latter
brings out the healing function of the individual, and
this is more in keeping with the role of the Haitian
vaudou priest.
Hounounga, among the Tenda people of Guinea, means 'the
Unknown' and refers to God. cf. John S. Mbiti,
Concepts of God in Africa, London, S.P.C.K., 1970, p. 335.
N-ganga, in the vocabulary of Lingala, means 'witch-doctor'.
cf. G. Malcolm Guthrie, op. cit.
Sir Harry H. Johnston, op. cit., shows that ganga or nanga
may mean 'doctor', 'medicine man', 'magic', 'witch' or
'witch-craft'. He again points out:
ganga = doctor, medicine man, in the Ugandan language of
   Luganda; Swahili in East Africa and languages spoken
   in Kenyan and Tanzanian villages.
ganga = witch, in languages of East Africa, as for example
   spoken among the Gogo people of Tanzania.

ganga = witchcraft, in one of the languages spoken in the
Usambara village of Tanzania.
ganga = magic, usually good magic, in the Luganda language
of Uganda; in Tanzanian languages, including Swahili.
nanga = doctor, medicine man, in the Zambian language of
Bemba; in languages spoken in Tanzania and Mozambique;
in languages of Zimbabwe, as spoken, for example, among
the Karanga people.

In my own research among African students in the Selly Oak
Colleges, Birmingham, I have discovered striking
similarities among the various words for doctor -
Mganga (Swahili of Tanzania); Muganga (Luganda of Uganda,
Kirundi of Burundi, Makonde of Mozambique); Nanga (Ronga
of Mozambique); Ngaka (Kikongo of Angola, Shona of
Zimbabwe); Nhanga (Changane of Mozambique); Onganga
(Umbundu of Angola, Oshindonga, Oshkwanyama and Oshimbadja
of Namibia).

38. In Chapter 5, we will be looking more fully into spiritual
     healing.

39. Mambo is definitely of Bantu derivation, though it is
     uncertain from which particular language. It means
     'chief', 'divine king' or 'lord' in Shona of Zimbabwe.
     Sir Harry H. Johnston, op. cit., mentions this meaning as
     obtainable also among the Karanga people of Zimbabwe, and
     in languages spoken in Kenya and Mozambique.

     It is interesting how this word mambo with its masculine
     connotations in some African countries is applied to
     a woman in vaudou. But of greater significance is
     the fact that the mambo, as priestess, is entrusted with
     spiritual authority, whereas within Roman Catholicism the
     priesthood still remains closed to women. Indeed
     the concept of mambo holds forth a challenge to many
     Christian churches, to rethink the nature of priesthood
     and ministry in so far as women are concerned. In vaudou,
     women are afforded equal status, but within Christian
     circles, where churches do ordain women, it is not
     uncommon to find that they are placed in inferior positions.
     This issue will be examined in depth in Chapter 5.

40. Maximilien suggests that hounsi is the equivalent of an
     African word vodounsi meaning 'a servant of the spirit'.
     (Maximilien, op. cit., p. 20.) He also uses the term
     hounsis-canzo, by which he describes female assistants of
     priests. (Ibid, p. 26) Apart from 'servant' or
     'devotee', the ending -si also designates the 'wife',
     hence hounsi could be correctly described as the 'wife
     of the spirit'.

41. Louis Maximilien, op. cit., p. 71.

116

42. "Aie bobo" is a ritual interjection of satisfaction
following anything done during a vaudou ceremony.
cf. Maximilien, p. 108.

43. Maya Deren, op. cit., p. 156.

44. Roger Bastide, op. cit., P. 297.

45. For detailed descriptions of ceremonies, see Louis
Maximilien, op. cit., pp. 129-145.

46. Jean Price-Mars, Ainsi Parla l'Oncle, Ottawa, LEMEAC,
1973, pp. 209ff., Alfred Metraux, op. cit., pp. 200, 201.

47. Although a houmfort is constructed for the service of
a community, a householder may set aside a special
chamber in his own abode for family worship.

48. The terms pilier-central and poteau-Legba are used by
Maximilien, op. cit., p. 34.
We may notice the strong religious symbolism of "centre".
Mircea Eliade reminds us that whether represented by a
tree or pillar, the centre usually symbolizes "access
to the sacred, to immortality, to absolute reality."
(Mircea Eliade, Patterns in Comparative Religion, London
and New York, Sheed and Ward, 1958, p. 381.) This
focal point, because of its importance, is usually
guarded very closely and access to it is very difficult.
Dr. Eliade also recalls that the central pillar had been
characteristic of the dwellings of people in ancient
Arctic, North America and Africa, and in more developed
cultures of Egypt, India, China, Greece and Mesopotamia.
(Mircea Eliade, "The Three Cosmic Zones and the World
Pillar' in Eliade, Shamanism, London, Routledge and Kegan
Paul, 1970, pp. 259-266.) There, too, "centre"
symbolized the road leading to the celestial Supreme
Being, hence sacrifices and prayers were commonly offered
at the foot of these pillars. It may therefore be said
that vaudou, in its understanding of the poteau-mitan, is
in keeping with universal symbolism. An interesting study
could emerge if a comparison were made between the
symbolism in vaudou and that as obtains in an African
country. Victor Turner, for example, has done extensive
reserach among the Ndembu of Zambia. cf. Victor Turner,
The Forest of Symbols.

49. "C'était un bâton massif que les anciens marchands mexi-
cains recouvraient de papier peint lorsqu'ils partaient
en voyage pour leur trafic. Quand le bâton était recouvert
on l'adorait comme un dieu...... Les haitiens voudouisants
ne partant pas, ont immobilisé le bâton qui est devenue le
pilier central." - Louis Maximilien, op. cit., p. 23.

50. These are known as <u>croiciner</u>. - Louis Maximilien, op. cit., p. 93.

51. This is the influence of Catholicism wherein it is customary to dedicate whatever features in the celebration of the mass.

52. A lengthy discussion of dancing and drumming appears in Maya Deren, "Drums and Dance", Chapter VI, op. cit., pp. 225-246.

53. Most writers attribute the <u>asson</u> to African influence. However, it may well have been influenced by the sacred rattle of the <u>peaiman</u> or priest of the Amerinidan Orinoco tribe. cf. Hartley Burr Alexander, op. cit., p. 296.

54. Maya Deren, op. cit., Appendix B, p. 278.

55. In <u>macumba</u> in Brazil, spirits are also invoked by "designs drawn on the ground in special chalk; these are known as <u>pontos riscados</u>." - Roger Bastide, op. cit., p. 298.

56. For extensive research on the vever, see Karen McCarthy Brown, <u>The Vévé of Haitian Vodou: A Structural Analysis of Visual Imagery</u>.

57. Il faut donc, en résumé, retenir que les vêvers proviennent des traditions religieuses indiennes, qu'ils ont été influencés par la magie européenne du moyen-âge et adoptés par le vodou dans un esprit religieux qui rejoint celui de leurs origines et que ces vêvers, observés en profondeur, loin de pouvoir servir de base à une argumentation qui tendrait à établir le caractère de magie des manifestations vodouesques, situe d'une façon nette l'esprit de religion du vodou." - Louis Maximilien, op.cit., p. 49.

58. Marassa, "twins", is of Bantu derivation. cf. Sir Harry Johnston, op. cit., e.g. <u>Maasa</u> in languages of East Africa ; <u>Masa</u> in languages of Mozambique; <u>Mapasa</u> in languages of Tanzania and other parts of East Africa; <u>Mabasa</u> in several East African languages. From my own research among students of the Selly Oak Colleges, Birmingham: <u>Mapachasa</u> in Swahili; <u>Mapatya</u> in Shona of Zimbabwe; <u>Mahahla</u> in Ronga of Mozambique; <u>Mafatlha</u> in Setswana of Botswana and Sesotho of Lesotho; <u>Omapasha</u> and <u>Epasha</u> in Namibian languages. Bastide suggests that <u>Marassa</u> in vaudou corresponds to Saints Cosmas and Damian. cf. Roger Bastide, op. cit., p. 267. Deren regards <u>Marassa</u> as corresponding to Indian twin-

heroes, the first creation of God.   cf. Maya Deren,
Appendix B, op. cit., p. 279.

59. Maya Deren, op. cit., p. 39.
Although in vaudou, twins are regarded as a blessing,
it must be borne in mind that there are old African
traditions which considered twins to be a curse. As
such, one of the twins had to be put to death to rectify
what had undoubtedly gone wrong. cf. John S. Mbiti,
Concepts of God in Africa, London, S.P.C.K., p. 82.

60. In macumba of Brazil, sacrifices may also take place
during a public ceremony, e.g. when "a cock is killed
and its blood is allowed to trickle over a woman's
body." - Roger Bastide, op. cit., p. 298.

61. Exodus 22: 29, 30.

62. Jean Price-Mars, op. cit. , pp. 207, 208.

63. Karen McCarthy Brown, op. cit., pp. 218-226.

64. Just as we do not take literally the English promise,
"If this happens, I'll eat my hat", we should not interpret the Haitian expression "Li konn mange moun" (He/
she eats people) as referring to cannibalism. The term
rather refers to a person who supposedly sends evil
spirits or spells to harm others. Only if the consequences prove fatal can it be claimed that a person has
succeeded in eating someone else.

65. This is an African concept at which we will be looking
in greater detail in our next chapter.

66. "Le rite du Dessounin n'est appliqué qu'aux initiés.
Il symbolise une nouvelle naissance, la naissance à
la vie éternelle." - Louis Maximilien, op. cit., p. 175.

67. Apostles' Creed.

68. Louis Maximilien, op. cit., P; 163.

69. cf. Peter Brown, The Cult of the Saints.

70. The idea of inflicting terrible illnesses upon people is
more in keeping with the demons in rabbinic literature
than with the evil spirits in the apocalyptic writings.
This will be looked at in the next chapter.

71. Maya Deren, op. cit., p. 26.

72. "When Paul is being consciously precise, he contrasts,
like the Gnostics, this individual, transcendent,

essentially divine spirit with both sould and body. A
positive advantage of this is that 'spirit' is sharply
distinguished from the human 'mind'($\nu o\grave{\upsilon}\varsigma$, I Cor. xiv.
14); and the negative side of it comes out in Paul's
avoidance of the word 'spirit' when he wants to describe
the profoundest 'I' of pre-Christian man." - Eduard
Schweizer et. al, "Bible Key Words from Gerhard Kittel's
Theological Dictionary of the New Testament - Spirit of
God", London, Adam & Charles Black, 1960, p. 86.

73.　According to Maximilien, bocor is the Haitian equivalent
　　　of an African term bokonon, the one who assists the
　　　officiant at a ceremony. cf. Louis Maximilien, op. cit.,
　　　p. 70.

74.　Laënnec Hurbon, Dieu dans le Vaudou haitien, Paris, Payot,
　　　1972, p. 161.

75.　In July 1975, after conducting a funeral, I noticed two
　　　young women keeping watch over a grave in the Port-au-
　　　Prince cemetery. In conversation with them, I learned
　　　that a cousin of theirs had been buried there since
　　　February, but because of the suddenness of her death,
　　　relatives kept constant watch, in shifts, to protect
　　　the body from being stolen and eventually zombified.

76.　This startling information was featured in documentary
　　　films appearing in "Newsnight" programmes of October
　　　1981 and February 1984 On BBC2 television. In reporting
　　　it here, I have stuck very closely to the text used
　　　during the programmes.

77.　These two zombies were featured on the BBC television
　　　documentary. Their stories tally with that which I
　　　had heard from colleagues in Haiti during a visit there
　　　in July 1980. Both Francine and Clervius had been
　　　interviewed by a group of leading church members
　　　attending the annual Methodist Synod in January 1980.
　　　They had been brought to the synod in an attempt to
　　　conscientize Christians about the reality of zombies -
　　　which some had been inclined to dismiss as sheer
　　　fantasy - and the implications of this modern form of
　　　slavery for the Church's stand on Christian citizenship.

78.　Max Beauvoir is a qualified bio-chemist who was educated
　　　at universities in France and the United States of
　　　America. Twenty years ago he had been chosen by his
　　　own community as a vaudou priest because the people
　　　believed that he had inherited all the necessary
　　　qualities from his grandfather.

79.　Ephesians 6: 5; Colossians 3: 22 - the most quoted
　　　passages in this regard. Yet those who argue for slavery,

using Pauline texts, avoid an exegesis of Galatians 5: 13.

80. John 7: 53 - ch. 8: 11, the story of the woman caught in the act of adultery, gives a splendid example of the value which Jesus placed upon human personality. In this incident, Jesus' actions are to be interpreted for his respect of the woman as a child of God, not for his disregard for the Mosaic Law.

81. I am indebted to F. Seal-Coon, author of An Historical Account of Jamaican Freemasonry, for pointing out this distinction to me.

82. C.C. Zain, Ancient Masonry, Los Angeles, California, copyright Elbert Benjmaine, The Church of Light, 1938, p. 414.

83. Ibid., p. 200.

84. Ibid., p. 70.

85. Ibid, p. 80.

86. Melville J. Herskovits, Life in A Haitian Valley, New York, Doubleday & Co. Inc., 1971, p. 37. Herskovits' source for this information is Pierre De Vassière, Saint Domingue 1629-1789, la société et la vie créoles sous l'ancien régime. Paris, 1909.

87. "La Maçonnerie a contribué à donner au Vaudou sa forme actuelle. Nous savons que les Loges étaient florissantes à la fin du XVIIIe Siècle à Saint-Domingue, elles contenaient des affranchis; les cérémonies qui s'y déroulaient excitaient la curiosité. Dans les desseins de certains 'vêvers' dans la hiérarchie de l'initiation, dans quelques passages du rituel, l'influence de la franc-maçonnerie est évidente." - Pierre Mabille, "Preface" in Louis Maximilien, op. cit., p. xix.

88. Maya Deren, op. cit., pp. 134, 135.

89. "...dans le vaudou nous avons affaire à une expérience religieuse authentique, un langage culturel valable comme n'importe quel autre langage, et qui satisfait le vaudouisant haitien dans sa quête de compréhension des choses de ce monde et du sens à donner à l'existence humaine." - Laënnec Hurbon, op. cit., p. 89.

90. "A la vérité, l'emploi du concept de syncrétisme cache une négation du Vaudou comme culture originale et religion vivante." - Ibid, p. 101.

91. There are numerous attributes given to God by African peoples. Hence, titles given to Him across the continent mean Architect, Almighty, Creator, Caretaker of Children, Distributor, Eternal One, Excavator, Father, Father of the ancestors, Great Spirit, Great Spider, Great One, Grandfather of all, He has not let me drop yet, Hewer, Lord of life, Master, Omnipresent, Owner of all things, Protector of the Poor, Supreme One, Wise One. cf. John S. Mbiti, op. cit., pp. 327-336. (Concepts of God in Africa).

92. Karl Barth, Church Dogmatics, Vol. 1, Part 1.

93. Karl Barth, Church Dogmatics, Vol. 1, Part 2, eds. G.W. Bromley and T.F. Torrance, translated G.T. Thomson, Harold Knight, Edinburgh, T. & T. Clark, 1970, pp. 457-472.

94. Paul Tillich, Systematic Theology, Combined Volume, Digswell Place, James Nisbet & Co. Ltd, 1968, p. 123.

95. Hugo Assmann, "The Power of Christ in History: Conflicting Christologies and Discernment", in R. Gibellini, ed., Frontiers of Theology in Latin America, London, SCM Press Ltd, 1980, pp. 134, 135.

96. H. Richard Niebuhr, Christ and Culture, New York, Harper and Row, 1975, p. 13. Niebuhr's book gives full treatment of the complex nature of the problem about deciding where God's word is pure (universal) and where it is influenced by the cultural and historical context (particular). His treatment is extensive and he refers to Scripture as well as to early theologians and philosophers.

97. Laënnec Hurbon, op. cit., pp. 217-252.

98. Amos 5: 24; Hosea 2: 19; Micah 6: 8.

99. Amos 6: 14.

100. Jeremiah 5: 15-19.

101. Isaiah 49: 6.

102. Matthew 10: 6.

103. Matthew 21: 43.

104. Matthew 8: 11, 12; Luke 13: 28 ff.

105. "Dans le Christianisme, Dieu a été le Dieu de l'homme Blanc. Sa puissance signifie oppression économique,

122

aliénation culturelle et politique pour les indigènes."
- Laënnec Hurbon, op. cit., p. 248.

106. S.J. Driver, The Books of Joel and Amos, Cambridge at
the University Press, 1901, p. 65.

107. Joel 2: 28.

108. Genesis 6: 19.

109. Isaiah 40: 5; Isaiah 49: 26.

110. Acts 2: 5 ff.

111. Acts 10: 34, 35.

112. Acts 10: 45.

113. John Hick, God Has Many Names, London, Macmillan Press
Ltd, 1980, p. 72.

114. Ibid, p. 56.

115. Romans 2: 11-16.

116. Anders Nygren, Commentary on Romans, Philadelphia,
Fortress Press, 1974, p. 122.

117. Psalm 139: 1-3.

118. A full treatment of this will appear in the next
chapter.

119. Isaiah 1: 11.

120. Amos 5: 21, 22; Micah 6: 8.

121. God, as Providence, will be dealt with in Chapter 4.

122. James G. Leyburn, The Haitian People, New Haven,
Yale University Press, 1941, p. 145.

123. In Chapter 6, we will say more about the God who,
within the broader Caribbean context, sides with
the oppressed.

124. Roger Bastide, op. cit., p. 278.

125. Louis Maximilien, op. cit., p. 80.

126. Jean Marie Salgado, op. cit., p. 34.

127. Roger Bastide, op. cit., p. 34.

128. "Pourtant, le Dieu qu'invoquent les vaudouisants
n'est pas un emprunt pûr et simple du Dieu chrétien."
- Laënnec Hurbon, op. cit., p. 123.

129. Jean Marie Salgado, op. cit., pp. 31-36.

130. "Il suffit en Haiti de se dire protestant pour prouver
qu'on ne vit dans aucun compromis avec le Vaudou. Mais
quelle est la signification du christianisme pour un
vaudouisant qui se convertit au protestantisme?
"Il semble que c'est la prise de conscience de la
faillite des esprits, c'est-à-dire de leur impuissance
à délivrer d'un malheur (maladie, mort, appauvrissement
excessif, persécutions par des sorciers, etc...), qui
amène le vaudouisant à choisir une secte protestante
comme dernière instance. Cette conversion représenterait
pour le vaudouisant un passage total hors du monde des
Loa, vers une nouvelle sphère d'existence où il ne serait
plus dépendant des humeurs de ces Loa.
"Pour le nouveau converti, il n'y a pas un anéantissement
ni une destructuration de l'univers vaudouesque, mais
un renversement de cet univers. La secte protestante
en question représente cet univers vaudouesque renversé,
c'est-à-dire l'opposé du Vaudou, dans son intransigeance
radicale vis-à-vis du Vaudou." - Laënnec Hurbon, op. cit.
p. 118.

CHAPTER 3

SPIRIT OR SPIRITS

During the discussion, in our last chapter, on the action of
the Holy Spirit as instrument of divine revelation, we noted
that spiritual gifts are the rightful inheritance of all
human flesh. In other words, spiritual revelation may be
claimed, not only by Jews and Christians, but within all of the
earth's cultures and religions God discloses Himself. This
includes Haitian culture and its vaudou religion. In this
chapter we will make a survey of spirit, as understood in
African and Biblical contexts, following which we must decide
whether an understanding of loas enhances our understanding
of the Holy Spirit. We will also have to determine whether
these spirits of folk religions constitute an authentic
Spiritual revelation, in the light of criteria which we will
establish.

Spirits in Africa

It is difficult to generalize about religious beliefs and
practices in so vast a continent as Africa. When we generalize we do so at the expense of leaving hidden the numerous
other riches of religious experience which are present.
However it is accepted that

> "in the world of spirits Africans distinguish four
> main categories of spiritual beings: the Supreme
> God, a multitude of lesser divinities and spirits,
> the ancestral spirits, and evil spirits."[1]

The focus of our attention will be the ancestral spirits since they give, by far, the best insights into an understanding of loas in vaudou.

For the African, death is not the end but rather, human life continues after death. This belief in life after death is not readily accepted in the western world. Compare, for example, the television interview in which a man facing death had been asked, "Do you believe in life after death?" His reply was, "No, I believe in the worms at the bottom of the grave."[2] In African thinking, the spirit of a person is imperishable, so that the dead person continues to exist as a member of the spiritual realm of the universe. Among ancestral spirits, there seem to be two distinct categories. John S. Mbiti[3] differentiates between the spirits of those who died long ago, and the spirits of people who died recently. Those in the former category have been forgotten and much uncertainty is connected to their present existence. There is, for example, speculation that these human spirits have become nature spirits. In order to preserve their memory, they and what they did during their lifetime have been included in folk tales, legends and historic accounts. We find some of the great leaders, heroes, warriors, in fact, the outstanding men and women of their times, fitting into this group, and very often, as folklore calls them to memory, what emerges are exaggerated human forms. Further speculation about the category of those who died long ago has given rise to a belief that these have been elevated to the

status of divinities. They are now close to God and are in a
position to intercede on behalf of mortal beings. Mbiti further
states that in some cases, since these human spirits are,
chronologically speaking, so far removed from daily memory,
many are afraid of them and think of them as ghosts, evil
spirits or other beings responsible for sickness and disease.
As to the second category of those who died recently, Mbiti
says that they are looked upon as the "living dead."[4] They
are close to the family and are still part of it. They are
interested very much in the families, and the families in turn
are interested in them.

The "living dead" can also be vengeful. If burial rites have
not been satisfactorily carried out, they can punish the family
for their shortcomings. This is true among the Ibo people, who
have two burials for the dear departed. The first burial would
be the interment of the physical body

> "soon after death, with preliminary ceremonies. Then
> after a year or less, sometimes more, the second burial
> would take place with a lot more elaborate ceremonies
> than the first. It was believed that this second
> burial was the one that helped the spirit of such
> departed elderly persons to rest comfortably with
> the ancestors in the land of the ancestral bliss,
> from where they plead effectively with the gods for
> the well-being of their children on earth. If this
> second burial was not performed, the proper inheri-
> tance of the late father's property could not be
> finally settled. What was worse, the extended
> family would be harrassed by the hovering spirit of
> the dead person who had not properly settled down
> with the other ancestral spirits."[5]

The second burial was something of a send-off party for one
undertaking his final journey into the spiritual realm. The

time lapse between first and second burials would differ
vastly from culture to culture.

Another version of second burial operative among the Shona
people is that in which the surviving relatives, upon removing
house, would collect some of the grave soil and transport it
with them to the region of their new abode, then place it in
a spot of ground. This would symbolize the continued protection of the ancestor over the family. Such beliefs hightlight
the African concept of family, namely that it is an entity
which is not limited to the nuclear family but rather includes
a wide range of social relationships. Sociologists see this
as contributing towards group cohesion.

For the African, both the physical world and the spiritual
world interact with each other. There is, on the part of the
African, a much greater understanding of phrases quoted by
western Christians about "church militant on earth, triumphant in heaven" or the "communion of saints." The matter
concerning the communion of saints will be dealt with towards
the end of this chapter. There is a deeper level of appreciation for the words of Jesus, "I go to prepare a place for
you."[6] This is why at funeral services in both Haiti and
Africa, the comforting words "we shall all meet again" constitute a real promise. In fact, it must be further pointed
out that when a new child is born into the family he or she
is carefully scrutinised, since it is believed that ancestral

spirits are often reborn in a new child. Dr. Idowu speaks of

> "the belief of the Yoruba that the deceased persons
> do 'reincarnate' in their grandhcildren and great-
> grandchildren,"[7]

and that

> "the ancestor's ori does transmigrate into the body
> of a new creation."[8]

Ancestors are regarded as much nearer to the daily affairs of human beings than God Himself. The beloved draw near at nightfall, hence no sweeping of a house is permitted after dark. It is the responsibility of ancestral spirits to supervise social and political arrangements, indeed, to take charge of all the day to day features of life in the family, clan or tribe. Small wonder it is that upon all important domestic occasions, such as birth and marriage, or in times of festivity, the ancestral spirits are included. When the Ashanti till the soil, they seek permission of the ancestors who, in effect, own the land, and who have throughout preceding generations cultivated it repeatedly.[9] So that the offering of a fowl or goat sacrificed, or the pouring of the blood on the ground, serve to emphasize the participation and approval of the ancestral spirits in what is currently taking place. Western cynics often regard such practices as "primitive" without appreciating that such gestures are designed to communicate love, admiration and respect through the use of the only ways known to human beings. When a westerner once questioned someone from a culture in which this was done, saying: "When is it that your ancestral spirits come and partake of that which you have offered them?" the reply he received was: "At the same time when your ancestral spirits come out to smell the flowers which you place on their graves."

Not only do the Ashanti offer food and drink when they are desirous of a fruitful cultivation of their land. Libations are poured out and sacrifices offered to ancestors because they do determine whether the family will experience good health and prosperity. Ancestral spirits are believed to have punished with sickness, economic loss and misfortune, those who neglected them. It is therefore important that they are kept satisfied. Within the Caribbean the practice of pouring libations to the spirits still survives in some parts, particularly at the start of some new venture such as the groubdbreaking ceremony for a new house. People quite naturally pour rum into the earth in remembrance of the spiritual presence around. Perhaps a point to note here is that in the early development of religion in Africa, the practice of offering sacrifices and libations was always reserved for the head of the family. This was his privilege by virtue of the fact that he was the senior living representative of the ancestors. In a sense, his spirit would be more in tune with theirs, seeing that he had interacted with them before they had begun their term of spiritual existence. Hence, when he performed the rite, it was done with a greater depth of meaning.

Ancestral spirits function as intercessors between human beings and God. God is often regarded as being far removed from every-

day reality, that it helps if human beings can approach Him
through someone closer to Him. The ancestral spirits, because
of their first-hand experience of the human world, are more
sympathetic to the problems experienced by men and women, hence
can communicate this more effectively to God. They are not
thought to be usurping a right which is Christ's who alone
makes intercession to God on our behalf. The prime aspect of
Christ's intercession is that which is done on behalf of
sinners for the sins which they have committed. This,
according to popular African belief, is outside the sphere of
the ancestors.

We have so far dealt with attempts by Africans to communicate
respect to their ancestors. We must now examine the manner
in which these spirits enter into communication with their
living relatives. They do this, in some cases openly, but
more often than not, through dreams and visions. Dreams and
visions constitute a phenomenon which baffles many western
minds. Are they an authentic vehicle of spiritual communication?

In the Bible, many messages from God were conveyed to His
people through dreams and visions. The prophet Joel sees all
this as a sign of the presence of God's spirit:

> "And it shall come to pass afterward,
> that I will pour out my spirit on all flesh;
> your sons and your daughters shall prophesy,
> your old men shall dream dreams,
> and your young men shall see visions."[10]

In a Biblical context, it is accepted that God employs dreams and visions to communicate with human beings and to make His will known to them.

> "In the main it must be admitted that probably a great many of the Biblical revelations must have come in sleep. Meditation on the spiritual, ethical, moral, and political problems of the day coloured the prophets' prayers; and the verses which poured forth from their lips may well have shaped themselves in the night season when they took no rest. In what ways and by what means the prophets gained the conviction that they spoke with the authority of God we do not always know; but there can be no doubt that the importance ascribed to dreams in the Old Testament record of revelation cannot be overstated."[11]

In the BBC Long Search film Zulu Zion[12] Ronald Eyre, British researcher, hears how Douglas D. Makhathini, rector of a Lutheran Theological Seminary in South Africa, had been ill and on the point of death. This was in 1948. In a dream, he was entering the pearly gates when suddenly he was confronted by his late grandmother who had been dead since 1932. She called him by name: "Duma, what are you here for?" She then proceeded to scold him with words such as "you are not ready," "you've got a lot of work still to do." In her rage, she dealt him a severe lash on his leg. "Don't come up here again," she said. When he awoke from his dream, there was, surely, a dark, black mark at the same spot on his body where he had been struck. Within a few weeks there were scales on it.

We may speculate upon this incident, wondering whether he had struck his leg against the bedpost. Suffice it to say, this was, for the rector, a genuine religious experience which, apart from signalling his restoration to health, provided him with a unique opportunity for spiritual growth. One cannot help but be impressed by these real experiences of peoples of the African continent. They say very clearly that to ask questions such as "Do spirits exist?" or "Is there any link between the physical and spiritual worlds?" is totally irrelevant. Rather, the question which needs to be posed is "What do the spiritual experiences which other people have teach me about God and about myself?"

Earlier on, we noted that in a Biblical context, God employs dreams as a means of communicating with people. But are we to take all dreams as spiritual intervention, or as the media through which some spiritual message is conveyed? I think not. Personally, there are times when I have such wild dreams purely because I have gone to bed on a rather full stomach. But there are other times when my dreams _do_ convey a message, as for example the time when I dreamt that I had smashed the right headlamp of my car. Throughout the day following that dream, I had been extra careful wherever I drove. It was not until late evening, when it became dark, that I realized what my dream really meant. I was about to drive the car to the coach station to fetch a friend when I noticed that my right headlamp was not functioning. The bulb needed to be changed. So that some dreams _do_ impart meassages. Of course, the problem which arises is how to make the distinction between

those which <u>do</u> and those which <u>do not</u>. What criteria will
determine which dreams constitute a spiritual intervention?

I agree with Professor Walter Hollenweger who, during a conversation which we had on this topic, suggested that what is
important is <u>the</u> <u>content</u>, <u>not</u> <u>so</u> <u>much</u> <u>the</u> <u>form</u>. It matters not
whether the medium is a dream, a book or a sermon. Three tests
may be applied if it is suspected that a spiritual intervention
is at hand. The first test will refer to the function which
is served. If it is πρὸς τὸ συμφέρον "for the common good"[13]
then one may, with justification, assume that it is a genuine
spiritual message. There can be no selfish end in view. What
matters is the edification of the whole body of Christ. The
second test will refer to the nature of its testimony. If it
testifies that Ἰησοῦς Κύριος "Jesus is Lord"[14] and is "not
contrary to what has come about in the incarnate Word of God,
in Jesus (1 Cor. 12.3)"[15] then it may be regarded as a genuine
gift of the Holy Spirit. The third test refers to its effect
upon <u>the others</u>[16] particularly the one who is in the position
τοῦ ἰδιώτου "of the outsider/idiot"[17]. The idiot must
be able to fall on his face and utter the "amen" of enlightenment. Paul refers, for example, to prophecy and speaking in
tongues. These are spiritual gifts in so far as others judge
them to be acceptable as vehicles of spiritual communication.
It is quite likely that in certain contexts the outsiders may
be those who are outside the normal scope of the Christian
faith, and would include other religions or other cultures

which are not usually counted as overtly Christian.

A word needs to be said about terminology used by westerners
when referring to the existing relationship between Africans
and the spirits of their family members. "Ancestor worship"
is the expression commonly used. In a sense, this term has
negative connotations, for it could suggest that worship, which
belongs to God alone, is given to ancestors.

> "The phrase 'ancestor worship' is emotionally
> charged, conjuring up primitive and heathen ideas
> of idolatry; but the phrase 'ancestor veneration'
> is neutral, and does not present us with
> incompatible alternatives, which the phrase
> 'ancestor worship' seems to do."[18]

Dr. Idowu, in discussing communion with ancestors among the
Yoruba, concludes:

> "This shows that 'Ancestor Worship' is a wrong nomen-
> clature for that which in fact is no 'worship'
> but a manifestation of an unbroken family re-
> lationship between the parent who had departed
> from this world and the offspring who are still
> here."[19]

To put it another way. What situation the term pretends to
describe is one in which people demonstrate respect for their
forefathers in a manner similar to how the English respect St.
George, the Scots revere St. Andrew, the Irish cherish St.
Patrick and the Welsh adore St. David. It is unfortunate
that non-Africans have classified all "ancestor veneration"
as a breaking of the commandment, "you shall have no other
gods before me." Even though the negative aspect of the
terminology used may, in some instances, be justified,
this is not to deny the fact that there is a positive side as

well. Where the negative side is emphasized, one must bear in
mind that Christianity itself is not free from guilt with
regards to the dead. Geoffrey Parrinder has a fitting post-
script:

> "In all these varieties of ancestral observance the
> question arises whether it is worship. This has been
> much debated, and it is of considerable importance
> in the spread of Christianity and Islam. If the
> dead are worshipped like gods, then this worship
> is incompatible with the adoration of one God.
> On the other hand if the dead are like saints, then
> certain forms of Christianity and Islam have found
> room for veneration of saints in their systems.
> In any case, both believe in a life after death,
> in the continued existence of the departed,
> and in their interest in men on earth as a
> 'cloud of witnesses.'

> "Some writers roundly declare that Africans no more
> worship the dead than they do elders and chiefs here
> on earth. They prostrate to chiefs, or kneel before
> elders and seniors, and bring to them gifts and
> requests. On the other hand, it must be said that
> the prayers and attitudes men adopt to the ancestors
> differ very little from those taken up towards the
> gods. Both are senior and potent forces, and need
> every reverence. Some would say that the gods were
> all once ancestors who have been deified, or they may
> be natural forces personified like men. Some gods,
> like Shango, clearly combine both human and natural
> attributes, the storm and the king. In the ancestral
> cults the elders of the family are priests, whereas
> in the temple of the gods there are specially
> separated priests, but this makes little practical
> difference to the types of worship offered to each
> spritual power. It can hardly be denied that prayers
> are made to the ancestors, and the only possible way
> in which such cults could be reconciled to a mono-
> theistic faith would be by permitting prayers to be
> made for the dead to the supreme God."[20]

So far, we have looked at the spirits in Africa with a view
to understanding better the nature of spirits in Haitian Folk
Religion. It is equally essential that we take a look at spirits in the Bible with the intention of making a theological

evaluation of Vaudou.

Spirit and the Bible

The Hebrew word רוּחַ "ruach" means wind or physical breath.
It refers to the life-supporting or life-animating force given
by God to the individual at creation.[21] This word always
points to God rather than to human beings. Yahweh's "ruach"
it is which accords the individual the right to live. This
idea of the ruach infused by God alone is clearly spelt out
in the famous passage in Ezekiel[22] dealing with the valley of
dry bones. When the ruach departs from a person, life is no
longer possible.[23] Yahweh alone it is who possesses the right
to recall the ruach at any given moment.[24] As Hans Walter
Wolff puts it:

> "Yahweh's breath is the creative power of life. As
> life-giving power, Yahweh's ruach also determines
> man's span."[25]

To convey the idea of the power of "ruach" various images
are conjured up throughout the Old Testament. On the one hand,
there are two words - "Word" and "Wisdom" - which are employed
to describe this creative and powerful activity of God. Yet
it must be noted that both words overlap with the idea of the
ruach being referred to. But by far the greatest wealth of
description comes across because of the various Hebrew verbs
which are used in reference to ruach. The Hebrew verb labash
(לָבַשׁ), which conveys the idea of clothing someone is used
in reference to the Spirit's possession of Gideon[26] as well as

to the empowering of persons enlisted in David's army.[27] Here
the use of the verb is figurative. So we may say, for example,
that Yahweh's spirit "clothed itself with Gideon", i.e. took
possession of him. We may even say that the spirit became
incarnate in those who were so possessed.[28] We examine another
descriptive word. The verb <u>tsalach</u> (ח ל צ) which describes
an action of <u>coming forth mightily</u> or <u>falling upon mightily</u> is
used in reference to Samson,[29] to Saul's empowering by the
Spirit of Yahweh,[30] and to David's[31] as well. The verb <u>naphal</u>
(ל פ נ) expressing the idea of <u>falling upon a person</u> is employed in accounts of the Spirit's empowering of the prophet
Ezekiel.[32] Whatever the image conjured up, the point of
emphasis is always that Yahweh's Spirit empowers individuals
to perform extraordinarily difficult tasks, so that they may
participate in the divine power. It is not irrelevant to mention in passing the parallel between the seizure of individuals
by the ruach of the Old Testament and the seizure of individuals by the loa in vaudou worship. In both cases, the idea of
superhuman power is fairly evident. Through the ruach, Samson
is enabled to tear a lion to pieces[33] and Balaam is enabled to
prophesy.[34] Through loa possession, vaudou worshippers may
roll in fire and emerge unhurt, or utter pronouncements, or be-
have in a manner which suggests that their individual personalities have been displaced by the superhuman.

Ruach, as life-giving power, seems to be a prominent idea in
the Old Testament. In fact, translating the Hebrew <u>ruach</u> into

English terminology is not without its problems. There is lacking any common agreement as to the best rendering of the Hebrew. Look, for example, at what two scholars have to say. Hans Walter Wolff says:

> "With Yahweh's ruach we must be constantly aware of the aspect of power: so when this ruach rests on the shoot of Jesse in Isaiah 11:2 we should think of his authorization. It is only through this awareness that the multifarious fine distinctions become understandable in which not only the ruach of wisdom, understanding, counsel and knowledge can be talked of, but also the ruach of might and fear of Yahweh; so that one does better to translate ruach in all cases by 'power' or 'authority' rather than by spirit."[35]

Edmond Jacob holds a different view:

> "Power and mystery, such are the two characteristics of wind, and it is because the God of the Old Testament is both power and mystery that the wind is able to express so adequately the whole nature of the divine."[36]

So that Wolff considers 'spirit' to be inadequate for translating 'ruach' and he proposes 'power' or 'authority'. Jacob, on the other hand, concludes that even 'power' and 'authority' are not satisfactory translations. My own inclination is to stick to the traditional rendering 'spirit' for no other reason than the recognition that however much we try to give a clear interpretation of 'ruach' it will still remain somewhat of a mystery, and because it describes a reality which may be foreign to Europeans, but certainly not to the Africans.

The Old Testament illustrates just the point I am making about the impossibility of ever translating 'ruach' perfectly. There are instances where it refers to the human will, the feelings

or the disposition of a person. The book of Ezra considers it
to be the will, for example the will to rebuild the house of the
Lord.[37] The prophecy of Jeremiah uses it in the context of a
will to destroy and to wreak vengeance.[38] In the Book of Job,
ruach may mean the feelings of ill-humour[39] or of mental
distress.[40] In early Hebrew tradition, there was the figurative use of the word to mean the disposition of a person.
When the person's mind and capabilities were being revealed,
then this was the action of the ruach. The interesting thing
to note about early Israelite culture is that the spirit may
move naturally from one person in a particular generation to
someone else in another generation. This was the case of
Elisha who received the spirit of Elijah after the latter
had ascended.[41] Of course, understanding how this actually
happened is quite a task, hence many prefer to speak of
Elisha as simply inheriting some of Elijah's charisma.
Suffice it to say, the idea of transference of spirit as
expressed in early Hebrew tradition is paralleled today,
as has already been alluded to, in certain parts of Africa
where a new born child is carefully scrutinised to discern any
resemblance to family ancestors.

In a more advanced stage of Hebrew tradition, ruach meant "a
sort of fluid imbued with power."[42] In Isaiah, God says "I
will pour out my Spirit upon your descendants,"[43] in Joel, "I
will pour out my Spirit on all flesh"[44] and in Ezekiel, "I
will not hide my face any more from them, when I pour out my

Spirit upon the house of Israel."[45] The idea of a fluid to
be poured out links in well with the practice of anointing a
king as symbolic of his receipt of the gift of the Spirit.
The other noticeable thing about the advanced period was what
certain scholars call "the personification or hypostatization
of the spirit"[46] where, for example, the Spirit is regarded
as giving to the Israelites rest in the wilderness,[47] or where
the Spirit is capable of leading people.[48]

One interesting aspect of ruach as we see it in the Old Testament is the general dependence upon Yahweh. In the early
tradition, the ruach "is the concrete representation of his
power and activity."[49] There is no existence apart from God.
Genesis 1:2 states that "the Spirit of God was moving over the
face of the waters." Now we must realize that this is God
Himself acting in a specific situation. Even though the
ruach may seem to act independently of him, at such times it
is still subordinate to Him.[50] The spirit still has its
origins in God, whose breath it is. Perhaps the most difficult
passage to come to terms with in this regard is one already
mentioned earlier on[51] where it would seem that Yahweh had no
part in the transfer of Elijah's spirit to Elisha. The flow
of the narrative gives the impression that this is an extreme
case of the spirit acting independently of Yahweh, one in which
there might even be the suggestion that the spirit is not
subordinate to Yahweh. However, it must be remembered that

   "by the spirit of Elijah these prophets understand

the Divine energy as the source of thaumaturgic power."[52]

Throughout the Old Testament, the ruach is Yahweh's instrument of creativity and revelation. Edmond Jacob lends support to this view:

> "It can therefore be said that the spirit is God himself in creative and saving activity; the spirit of God lies at the origin of creation (cf. Gen. 1:2), it is ceaselessly present in the form of wind, but because of the uniqueness of Israelite religion it is chiefly history which is the place of his manifestation. The action of the spirit in history has not been experienced with equal intensity in the course of the ages, but it can be said without risk of hasty generalization that throughout history it is the spirit who directs events. In the early ages the spirit acts intermittently; he falls unexpectedly upon certain persons and makes them capable of extraordinary acts ... The introduction of Yahweh's spirit at these different stages gives prominence to one of the directions of divine action in the Old Testament."[53]

The creativity and the revelation produced by the Spirit was apparent in the lives of the Old Testament prophets. In the case of the early prophets, ecstasy was the distinguishing feature of the Spirit's presence. This was so because of the close association of ecstasy and spirituality.

> "In ancient Israel the indwelling of the Spirit of Yahweh was the purpose of ecstasy."[54]

With regards to the post-exilic prophets, however, there is no suggestion that their work is to be justified or authenticated by ecstatic utterances. But the importance of the Spirit's inspiration is just as truly theirs.[55] They are equally agents of divine revelation, who call attention, not

to themselves, but to the Spirit of God who animates them. In
reference to Isaiah 63:10-11, Edmond Jacob writes:

> "One post-exilic prophet represents the holy
> spirit as the means 'par excellence' by which God
> asserts his presence in the midst of his people,
> a presence as personal as that of the angel or
> the face against whom one can revolt and who can
> be grieved."[56]

The inter-testamental period did not see the end of the Spirit's
activity in Israel.

> "In the apocrypha and pseudepigrapha, although it
> is recognized that the great period of prophetic
> revelation has passed, it is unhesitatingly re-
> garded as a possibility that even now the Spirit
> may still be granted to men."[57]

When we turn to the New Testament, we realize that the Spirit
is alive and active, and is indeed operative in the life and
work of Jesus of Nazareth.

> "In Matt. i.18, 20, as in Luke i.35, $\pi\nu\epsilon\hat{\upsilon}\mu\alpha$
> is the divine creative power, creating the life
> of this unique child..."[58]

At baptism, Jesus received the Spirit, for it descended on
Him like a dove.[59] The third gospel writer, Luke, adds that
the Spirit descended "in bodily form" (ch. 3:22). It is clear
that Luke

> "attaches importance to the objective character of
> the descent of the Spirit."[60]

A further point to be noted about Luke is that he is interested
in the Spirit as the Spirit of prophecy.

> "That Luke regards prophesying, $\pi\rho o\phi\eta\tau\epsilon\acute{\upsilon}\epsilon\iota\nu$,
> as the central and decisive activity of the Spirit, is
> shown by his insertion of this word into the long and
> otherwise almost unaltered quotation from Joel about
> the eschatological outpouring of the Spirit.(Acts 2:18)"[61]

But the fourth gospel writer

> "abandons completely the concept of inspiration,
> since it only serves to express a basic separation
> between God and Jesus which must ever be overcome
> by a third entity, namely the Spirit."[62]

In the early Church, the Spirit was a present reality.
Baptized persons received the gift of the Spirit[63] though there
is the recorded incident where the pouring out of the Spirit
preceded baptism.[64] The Spirit's presence, and how it can be
detected, are the focus of Paul's attention in his writings.
For Paul, life in the $\pi\nu\epsilon\hat{\upsilon}\mu\alpha$ is life in the new created order,
in contrast to life in $\sigma\grave{\alpha}\rho\xi$ in the flesh, which is life in
the old order. In Romans 1:3-4, the Spirit is, in accordance
with the Hellenistic thought, a celestial sphere or the
celestial substance.[65] This idea of the powerful Spirit of
God as contrasted with the weak and sinful flesh is an Old
Testament idea. For example, in Isaiah 31, those who trust in
horses and chariots are warned that their trust should be in
the Holy One of Israel. Verse 3 says:

> "The Egyptians are men, and not God; and their
> horses are flesh, and not spirit."

For a person to live in the Spirit, says Paul, he or she must
renounce the flesh, for what is flesh but dependence upon
human strength, or reliance upon the power of self. For
example, in Philippians, he speaks of worshipping God in
spirit as being opposed to putting confidence in the flesh.[66]
As he suggests to them, flesh is

> "the totality of characteristics and deeds which a

man could boast of as his own, that is, 'his own
righteousness from the law' (iii.9). 'Spirit',
by contrast, is God's power, and therefore Christ's
power."[67]

Of course, it must be said that pointing out the difference

between πνεῦμα and σάρξ is not, for Paul, an exercise in

spotting the distinction between the physical and the spiritual.

He is adamant that life in the πνεῦμα must be expressed in

material terms. In Galatians 4:6, for example, he

"can attribute to the Spirit not just the recognition of Sonship but concrete living as a Son
of God."[68]

He even spells out the material implications for πνεῦμα

in chapter 5:22, 23, the famous "fruit of the Spirit"

pronouncement.

Paul wrote to the Corinthians about the spiritual body.[69] It

is plain that his understanding of it differed from theirs

which was the Gnostic interpretation.

"They understood it as something which is already
given to the believer and simply survives death;
but he sees it as something given once and for
all by God in the resurrection."[70]

It is not that men and women deserve or merit the Spirit. It

is God who, through His goodness, gives it

"as a sign of that which is still to come."[71]

In spite of the futuristic implications of the Spirit's

appearance, Paul also concerns himself with some of the present

objective signs. In Chapter 12 of the first letter to Corinth,

he lists some of them - the utterance of wisdom, the utterance

of knowledge, faith, gifts of healing, the working of miracles,

prophecy, the ability to distinguish between spirits, speaking
in tongues, the interpretation of tongues.[72]

> "The formal sincerity between these manifestations
> and the ecstatic phenomena of the heathen world is
> so far-reaching that Paul gives the Corinthians a
> criterion by which they can distinguish the
> activities of the Spirit of God from those which
> have a different source: the criterion is the
> confession of Jesus as Lord."[73]

As mentioned earlier on, there are two other criteria which
go with the confession of the Lordship of Jesus. One is that
the "common good" must be served. The other is that the "other"
or "idiot" must thereby be edified.

One other important observation needs to be mentioned. In
contrast to Luke's concept of the Spirit's presence being validated by spectacular signs, Paul suggests that spiritually
motivated activity does not necessarily have to be out of
the ordinary. Hence in Chapter 12 of Romans, he records in
verses 7 and 8 that the gifts may include such mundane things
as serving, teaching, encouraging others, sharing, giving aid,
or being merciful. These are just as genuinely imparted by
the Spirit as any other spectacular gift, e.g. prophecy,
healing or working miracles. In fact, Paul even appears to be
uncomfortable with some of the extraordinary signs of the
Spirit. Speaking in tongues, for example, is not more important than other gifts, hence he devotes the whole of 1
Corinthians 13 to put things in their proper perspective.

Having dealt with the concept of spirit in the Old and New

Testaments, we now pay some attention to the idea of <u>spirits</u>,
again as appearing in the Bible.

Spirits in the Bible

Throughout the Old Testament period, there appear all manner
of spiritual beings as distinct from the spirit of God. There
are the angels. A little higher than human beings, they are
messengers in the court of Yahweh who execute His commands.
They are not divine, but they carry out divine instructions.
Some appear as servants, others as warriors. In this connection, we recall Jacob the patriarch and his experience with a
man who wrestled with him but whose intention had not been
to seriously hurt him.[74] On the contrary, Jacob received a
blessing. This was the religious experience which had brought
Jacob into contact with one who, though appearing as a manifestation of Yahweh and being at one with Yahweh, was still
different from Yahweh. It is difficult to define the nature
of this experience. It is quite likely that this was not an
actual physical event, but merely a dream or vision. Indeed
this is a fine example of a story dating from pre-Israelitic
or pre-Canaanean times which has gone through several stages
of oral transmission. For some, Jacob was, in the incident,
wrestling with a god, or even a river demon. The demonic claim,
though, has been stoutly refuted.[75]

In spite of the impossibility of stating with any measure of
absolute certainty what the exact details were, the Old

Testament writers did not exclude this story. Excommunication was not their policy. They incorporated it in the body of their theological narratives. In the light of the observation which we made at the end of chapter 2, these Old Testament writers would make excellent Catholic theologians. Protestants, as we mentioned, have a habit of expelling, rejecting or denying the existence of anything which cannot be easily explained. They treat such things as "superstition". The Catholic approach would be to set up a shrine, just as, in the narrative a "peniel" is created.

The other point to be noticed is that these Old Testament writers, like good theologians, do not make an issue of the fact that there is no certain name for the one who wrestled with Jacob. What they do, of a positive nature, is to elevate oral theology to a level of respectability. They valued the incident because through it there had been established a definite line of communication between God and Jacob. The latter surely learned a lesson about his own helplessness as well as a promise that if he were humble enough to submit in spiritual things, he would be allowed to prevail.

In the Old Testament era, angels have human form. Sometimes they are equated with good, particularly when they act as guardians or protectors.

> "The angel of the Lord encamps around those who
> fear him, and delivers them."[76]

"For he will give his angels charge of you, to
guard you in all your ways."[77]

It was customary for nations to have guardian angels. Israel

has Michael.[78] But sometimes angels are associated with evil

and destruction:

"And when the angel stretched forth his hand
toward Jerusalem to destroy it, the Lord re-
pented of the evil, and said to the angel who
was working destruction among the people, 'It
is enough; now stay your hand.'"[79]

The fact that angels can also be evil points to a current

belief among Israelites of the pre-exilic period that God is

the author of everything, both good and evil. For example,

it is recorded in Judges 9:23 that

"God sent an evil spirit between Abimelech and
the men of Shechem, and the men of Shechem dealt
treacherously with Abimelech."

In the first book of Samuel, we constantly encounter the phrase

"an evil spirit from the Lord"[80]

which torments Saul. At this point it is worth mentioning that

the Hebrew word רַ֫עַשׁ which is rendered _evil_ does not refer

exclusively to incidents of moral corruption, it does mean

disaster as well.[81] Whereas angels and archangels have human

form, there are other of the angelic host which have animal

form, but human faces. These are the Cherubim (כְּרוּבִים)

and Seraphim (שְׂרָפִים). The Cherubim are winged angels.

References to them appear in Genesis 3:24, Ezekiel 28:14, 16,

Psalm 80:1, Psalm 99:1 and Isaiah 37:16. A rather detailed

description of them appears in Ezekiel 1:4-28 and chapter

10:3-22. The Seraphim are mentioned in Isaiah 6:2-6. They

are six-winged angels which stand beside the throne of Yahweh
in heaven. The Seraphim are often associated with the demonic.
Although Isaiah 6 is the only passage making specific mention
of them, there are other passages, such as Numbers 21:6,8, Deuteronomy 8:15, Isaiah 14:29 and Isaiah 30:6, which are believed
to refer to them. They are thought of as fiery serpents or
scorpions. There seems to be a contradiction of ideas here,
because if the Seraphim, according to Isaiah, have hands, feet
and wings, the outward resemblance to scorpions is questionable.

Because of the insufficiency of Old Testament evidence, very
little can be known about the exact physical features of the
Cherubim and Seraphim. Archaeological research, though,
suggests that both concepts were familiar in near Eastern
lore.

> "Archaeological discoveries have shown that in
> Syria and Palestine the winged sphinx is domi-
> nant in art and religious symbolism."[82]

> "Representations of such beings, dating mostly
> from the ninth century B.C. have been found,
> e.g. at Carchemish, Nimrud, on ivories from
> Samaria, at Aleppo, and at Tell Halaf."[83]

In the post-exilic period, Yahweh is thought of as exclusively
good, and evil is regarded as originating from elsewhere,
perhaps an intermediary. It was thought, for example, that the
fall within God's creation[84] led to a race of demons, or giants.
Giants were thought of as being the offsprings of a sexual union
between a divine father and a human mother, though it must be
stressed that there is no evidence that the Hebrews believed

all giants were of divine-human origin. Not much can be said
about these giant demons who, as descendants of the fallen
angels, inhabited the earth. No support for a race of giants
is given by archaeology and paleontology. However, in post-
exilic times, they were regarded as the possible explanation
for evil. This was the sort of climate which gave rise to
the concept of Satan, the author of all evil. We see Satan
in the Book of Job assuming the role of public prosecutor.
Throughout the book, he appears to be a powerful adversary.

The function of demons is to injure the lives of people, to
spread disease and destruction. There is a subtle difference
between demons and evil spirits:

> "In the apocalyptic writings, the primary function
> of the evil spirits is to tempt men into sin. The
> criteria are therefore ethical. In the Testaments
> of the Twelve Patriarchs, specific sins are even
> personified as evil or lying spirits. (Test. Reub.
> 2:1; 3:3 ff.) This fact is clearly associated
> with the general tendency of the Testaments to term
> psychological traits and attitudes "spirits". In
> other words, in accord with normal Hebrew usage,
> the approximate meaning of "spirit" here is
> 'disposition'; the vivid language of the Testaments
> personifies this concept. Only occasionally do
> we find in the pseudepigrapha instances of demons
> that bring misfortune or are associate with magic,
> etc. (Eth. Enoch 15:11; 69:12; CD 14:5).
>
> "In rabbinic literature, on the other hand, the demons'
> function is to cause injury to life and limb; they
> are the bearers of disease, for example. Spirits
> as tempters are rarely mentioned. The rabbinic
> conception is closest to the ancient belief in
> demons, and is also found occasionally in the
> Apocrypha, Asmodeus, in the Book of Tobit (3:8, 17;
> 6:7, 14 ff.), is such a destructive demon ..."[85]

Another characteristic of demons is the association given in
the Old Testament with wild beasts,[86] particularly desert
animals.[87] Since the desert is the region of death, it would
seem appropriate that demons and demonic forces should be
linked to such a place. The Se'ir was a creature who haunted
waste places and by all appearances had his own priests (2
Chronicles 11:15). In pre-exilic times, the Se'irim were
offered many sacrifices (Leviticus 17:7). But they were also
a present reality in post-exilic times (Isa. 34:14). Azazel,
of whom we read in Leviticus 16, was probably a goat, but
certainly a powerful demon. Lilith was a demoness who could
cause disease, pestilence and death, and was very active at
night. She is reputed to have haunted the lives of various
Jewish generations. Aluquah, also beastlike, had demonic
associations.[88]

Throughout the Old Testament, communication is possible between
spiritual beings and human beings. There is continuous interaction between both their worlds. Earlier on, we mentioned dreams and visions as being a regular channel of
communication between the spirits and human beings. In the
early Old Testamental period, there had been increasing interest in the practice of occultism, whereby men and women sought
to discern the future by referring to the spirits of those who
had already departed this earthly existence. There was something rather unethical about such occult journeys because it
became more and more obvious that the people of God were placing

less and less confidence in Him and seeking the guidance of
lesser spiritual beings. It would seem that it became necessary to impose sanctions upon those who resorted to occult
practices.[89] Even Saul, the King, who had been instrumental
in waging a campaign against occultism, cannot resist it when
he is subsequently faced with a series of problems. In
desperation, he consults a medium at Endor and orders her to
conjure up a vision which he immediately recognizes as the
form of Samuel. As an ancestral spirit, Samuel leaves Sheol,
the abode of the sleeping spirits, and enters into direct
communication with the living.[90]

The New Testament world is one of people, demons and spiritual
powers. It appears more like a battleground where forces of
light are waging continuous warfare with the forces of darkness.
That the warfare is spiritual and necessitates the use of
spiritual weapons comes across clearly in the letter to the
Ephesians wherein mention is made of the principalities and
powers in the heavenly places.[91] In his letter to the Colossians, Paul speaks about the elemental spirits of the universe,[92] and in this we discern a reference to the astronomical
or astrological systems with which we are familiar in modern
society. Paul was very much concerned about the presence of
evil spirits because Jesus, during His earthly ministry, had
always been securing defeats against them. Indeed, if one
looks carefully at the New Testament, one is bound to remark
how many instances there are where Jesus conquers Satan and

his messengers. Exorcism forms part and parcel of his ministry.[93] His disciples are given the power to overcome the demons by subduing them and their chief Satan.[94]

In Luke's gospel, it is clear that the coming of the Kingdom of God symbolizes the overthrow of all evil forces.[95] This is why Paul, conscious of the world's evil, could assure his readers that Christ Jesus has definitely conquered the demons, therefore the love of God will always maintain supremacy over everything.[96]

Our survey of spirits in both Africa and the Bible has shown us some similarities between the world view of the Israelites and that of the Africans. Both groups believe in the reality of the spirit-world. It is equally true to say that since the culture of Haiti is an offshoot of African culture, that the vaudou worshippers are close in their thought patterns to the people of Ancient Israel. The God who revealed Himself in ancient Israel, through the means of spirits, dreams and visions, must be seen as operative in Haiti and employing similar methods of revelation.

Laënnec Hurbon has quite rightly refuted the claim about the religious expression of Vaudou being a mere copying from other religions. It is a mistake to suppose that God has had no unique revelation for the people of Haiti. Although western culture remains sceptical about the existence of spirits, folk

cultures across the world abound in all manner of spiritual
beings. The fact that within such cultures spirits exist
would suggest that they exercise a function, for whatever has
no function ceases to exist. We now turn to look more closely
at their function.

The term spirit is functional in so far as it provides, within
the Bible, Africa and Haiti, a meaningful description of a
certain type of phenomenon, namely the cause and the effect of
abnormal behaviour patterns observed in individuals. Outside
these contexts, spirit terminology has been supplanted by the
language of social science. From the perspective of science,
therefore, spirit merely provides a nomenclature for social and
psychological phenomena. The question yet to be resolved is
whether the social scientists are right, or whether spirits do
in fact denote an unique feature which lies outside the range
of scientific understanding. Let us pursue our enquiry,
firstly by looking at the phenomenon of loa possession in
vaudou, using spirit language, then by looking at the claims
of social science.

Loa Possession

The phenomenon of loa possession continues to baffle the majority of people. How are vaudou worshippers able to see and
converse with the spirits who exist within the universe?
During a ceremony, a scream may be heard, a fidèle may be
observed to have bulging eyes, fast breathing and after under-

going convulsions and mouthing incomprehensible utterances,
he or she enters into a trance-like state. The individual
spins, loses balance, due to muscular fatigue, and may
collapse in the arms of others of fall to the ground, either
prostrate or writhing in violent contortions. The "possessed"
individual is protected from his or her own frenzy by the rest
of the company, who provide both the physical and moral
security necessary for giving oneself entirely to possession.
When possession takes place, the person becomes the recipient
and instrument of the loa. It is as though the loa becomes
a rider who "mounts" the body and "rides" it like a horse. The
loa, now incarnate in the serviteur, has complete control of
the situation. Often at this point in the ceremony, the drums
stop beating to herald the displacement of the human personality by the superhuman. This may in a sense be regarded as
the climax of the ceremony, for the absence of spirits is taken
as a sign of their indifference or their hostility. Possession may be a matter of minutes, hours or sometimes days.
Where it is a matter of days, the individual can still go about
daily routine without any difficulty.[97] But within the context of a public ceremony, the houngan may bargain with the
loa or intercede on behalf of the serviteur especially if the
loa is seen to be punishing his "horse", such as tearing off
the expensive clothes being worn by the serviteur. Normally
when possession is unduly long, the houngan makes the individual retire to another room, and by conventional gestures,
he helps that person to return to a state of normalcy.

Possession occurs when vaudouisants exercise the discipline of complete submission to the loa. They must, upon attending vaudou ceremonies, be willing to be "mounted", to surrender their ego. In fact, there are some loas who force themselves upon unwilling individuals.[98]

Under possession, the face of the serviteur changes, the voice alters considerably and all statements uttered are pronouncements of the loa. Such utterances may be prophetic, monitory, or may involve threats to sinners. It is amazing how an otherwise ignorant individual is so able to utter profound thoughts in an eloquent manner. One writer[99] compares this to the phenomenon of speaking in tongues referred to in 1 Corinthians 14. The person is merely the vehicle through which the superhuman expresses itself. The serviteur is allowed to consume the loa's favourite food and drink and is given the loa's favourite colours to wear. All the loa's characteristics, be they masculine or feminine, good or evil, youthful or old, crafty or honest, are now embodied in the serviteur. This is probably what Maya Deren meant when she wrote:

> "In a sense, each loa is but an aspect of one central cosmic principle differentiated by the emphases which that central principle manifests according to the varying contexts in which it operates."[100]

The spirits have certain attributes which, like principles, are fixed. These attributes come to the fore when a person is possessed by them. If a person is possessed by Legba, then she/he will have the distinct expression of age in the countenance. If possessed by Damballah, s/he may crawl around the ground of the peristyle like a snake, then slither up the poteau-mitan. Under possession individuals do things which, under normal circumstances, they are unable to do.[101] Some dance with their bare feet on burning coal. Some may trample upon broken glass. Others may roll into fire, or pass the tongue over a hot iron. Yet no injury is received. In the course of the bruler-zin[102] ceremony, for example, the houngan may dip his hand in boiling dough, withdraw some of the contents, then systematically clasp the hand of each initiate. The presence of spirits helps persons to endure pain without flinching. After possession, the individual remembers nothing of his or her behaviour as a loa, and would express surprise when informed that s/he had been possessed.

Rada rites tend to produce benevolent spirits, whereas Petro rites are known to induce magical and malevolent spirits.[103] As we said earlier on, Petro loas are associated with magic and the casting of ouangas[104] or evil spells. Some writers point out that the magic altar is quite separate from the religious altar.[105] It must equally be borne in mind that vaudouisants distinguish between loa possession and possession by evil spirits. The former is desirable, the latter not.

Let us now look at the explanations for spirit which have been put forward by the social scientists.

Social Explanations

One of the noticeable things about the world of spirits and the phenomenon of spirit-possession is their reality for people who belong to the lower socio-economic classes. In other words, spirits may be described as classifying people into social groups, and those who fit neatly into the working-class bracket tend to be more spiritually minded. By contrast, the higher up the socio-economic ladder you go, the farther away you draw from the spirit world. The explanation for this could be that the more wealthy the individual becomes, the greater is his or her sense of security or independence. The less one is educated, the greater is the desire to manipulate one's environment through the spirits who wield authority in the universe. Hence in Trinidad and Tobago, there is the spirit-religion of Shango, a derivative of Yoruba traditional religion. This religion developed, in its initial stages, among African descendants of Yoruba stock, who were economically deprived. For them, Shango offered hope and assurance of better days to come. At a time when medical facilities were outside his reach, the Shango leader, with his bush medicine and magic bath, provided the working class individual with new life. At a time when social and recreational facilities were a luxury which could not be afforded, the poor man found, in his spirits, a means of meeting this need. However, as the lot of the working-class improved and as the country developed socially, economically and otherwise, spiritual expressions assumed more sophisticated forms. People now looked towards the churches

having their origins in Europe and North America to provide
them with spiritual food. Shango still exists to serve the
needs of the economically deprived, just as Roman Catholicism
and Anglicanism meet the needs of the rich professional classes.

In Haitian vaudou the masses of believers are drawn from the
working class. It was the Haitian Dr. J. C. Dorsainvil[106]
who suggested that loa possession is a phenomenon common only
among the less cultured, and that intellectual progress tends
to wipe out such cases. We have already suggested that the
second part of the statement of Dr. Dorsainvil is not altogether
true, when in the Introduction to this study, we cited the case
of two educated teenagers who were apparently spirit-possessed.
But Dr. Dorsainvil's first idea of loa possession being common
among the less cultured, which we will shortly discuss, seems
to be the echo of Malinowski's theory[107] that a belief in
spirits, sorcery and the like is rooted in psychological
reactions to those who suffer illness, misfortune, inability
to control their destiny.

Another interesting feature emerges when one looks at how
spirits are common to certain ethnic groups. In the case of
shango in Trinidad, not only are the adherents poor, but black.
With Candomblé and Macumba in Brazil, the majority of adherents
are either black or dark Mulattoes.[108] The same obtains in
Haiti. Laënnec Hurbon considers this to be not just a feature
of poor people who may incidentally be black, but as something

which is akin to peoples of African descent. He suggests
that whereas, in some types of society possession by spirits
can inspire repulsive feelings or shame, in the case of black
culture, we are confronted with a normal phenomenon, one which
helps to maintain social equilibrium.[109]

The theories of Malinowski and others may convey the impression
that spirits are operative only in the poor, Third World
countries, and there solely among the very poor. Such theories
need just one example to the contrary to be rendered void.
France is not a Third World country, yet evil spirits are
present in French society. Quite interesting in this regard
is the work of Jeanne Favret-Saada, French ethnologist[110]
who vividly describes witchcraft in the lives of peasants in
the west of France. Of course, the great thing about this
ethnologist is that she approached her research as an active
participant and became so dangerously involved that she was
almost mistaken for a sorcerer. Her findings leave the reader
with questions which anyone considering the matter of spirits
and spiritual power must ask. Whose view of the universe is
correct? Whose interpretations of a sequence of events concerning spirits is authentic? Is there a world of possi-
bilities outside the realm of science yet to be explored,
which has so far been revealed only to those who, according
to western cultural standards, are ignorant, stupid and
'victims of superstition'?

What we have just noted about France is equally true of other
developed nations across the world. The mere fact that "in
America, sixty-five per cent now believe in a personal devil"[111]
dispels any fears that only the poorer nations of the world
believe in the existence of evil spirits.

Even within the poorer countries of the world where there is
a belief in spirits, and where spirit possession is common,
the rich, educated people are just as involved as the poor.
In Brazil, although the poor are attracted to the spirit
religions,

> "we may note that present-day candomblé members
> include more and more lawyers, rich businessmen,
> and prosperous artisans, and that its priests and
> priestesses are capable of highly intelligent
> discussions with visiting ethnologists and
> respond to their arguments with sensitive
> understanding."[112]

Anthropologists have looked at oppressive societies and have
noted, and quite rightly too, that therein exists a belief in
spirits. They have assumed that oppression is a causal factor
and have sought out statistics in support of their arguments.
But what they have failed to realize is that their findings
are based purely upon statistical grounds, with little or
no relation to actual root causes. The fact that countries
have been cited where there seems to be an absence of
oppression, but where spirit belief is common, can only
suggest that oppression itself is merely a contributing factor,
not a causal one. We turn now to the psychologists and

psychoanalysts for their explanations of <u>spirit</u>.

Psychological Explanations

In seeking to explain loa possession, psychologists and psychoanalysts have dismissed the possibility of supernatural intervention. Of course it must also be said that there are
theologians who deny the reality of loas.[113] The yardstick
which is used to measure possession seems to be the same as
that used to assess the unfortunate client who had been convinced that he was a grain of corn. The psychiatrist had
spent many months convincing this patient that he was not.
The day eventually came when they held their final session
and this patient walked out of the clinic, a 'cured' man. But
five minutes had not elapsed when he burst into the office
screaming:

> "Doctor, doctor, hide me. There's a rooster outside
> and he will eat me."

> "But," said the psychiatrist, trying to reassure
> him, "have you forgotten what you've learned these
> past months? You are not a grain of corn!"

> "Yes," retorted the man, "<u>I</u> know that I am not a
> grain of corn. <u>You</u> know that I am not a grain of
> corn. But does <u>the</u> <u>rooster</u> know that I am not
> a grain of corn?"

As early as 1931, Dr. J. C. Dorsainvil suggested[114] that loa
possession was a phenomenon common only among the less cultured,
and that intellectual progress tended to wipe out such cases.
He also maintained that loa possession was <u>a</u> <u>form</u> <u>of</u> <u>religious</u>
<u>psycho-neurosis</u>, <u>characterised</u> <u>by</u> <u>a</u> <u>doubling</u> <u>of</u> <u>the</u> <u>personality</u>.

The psychologist, Emerson Douyon, has suggested that

> "spirit possession in the Haitian context represents
> an infantile reaction and requires in addition to
> specific conditioning experiences, a disturbed,
> anxious and depressed personality to be induced.
> It is also a positive mechanism for a society
> where misery, fear, anxiety, suspicion is the
> unfortunate fate."[115]

Despair is regarded as the key to the vaudou trance. Some psychoanalysts point to noise as being instrumental in inducing a certain level of consciousness, which in itself resembles the psychological state of hysteria. The drums are thought of as creating certain air waves which, apart from buffeting the bodies of the dancing worshippers, hypnotize them by means of the regular or complex rhythm patterns. The ability for unnatural physical tolerances has been described as self-hypnotism.

Louis Maximilien also sees loa possession as corresponding to a state of mental hysteria created artificially by suggestion or hypnotism.[116] He speaks of a form of self-hypnotism created by the individual who, from an early age, internalized a series of reactions relative to the religion and to behaviour associated with the loas. He knows his family loas intimately hence he can react pertinently. Maximilien, though, refutes the claim of Dr. Dorsainvil that loa possession is a doubling of the personality. Rather, it is the manifestation of an additional personality, since the true self is not completely blotted out.[117] But the idea of a state of mental hysteria is not altogether accurate, in the thinking of Jean Price-Mars.[118]

For him, hysteria is a state which can be brought on by
pathological suggestion and which can be healed by persuasion.
He thinks it unlikely that loa possession is a form of hysteria,
seeing that it is not brought on by suggestion alone. Evidence
shows that the will of the serviteur is not the determining
factor. Rather, it is the will of the loa which prevails. Nor
does a person come out of a state of possession through persuasion. Even when the houngan makes use of conventional gestures in order to help the individual return to a state of
normalcy, he is fully aware that the duration of possession
is still not his to decide. The most accurate thing to
say in this regard is that loa-possession is analogous to
hysteria, though not the same.

Another writer on the subject of loa possession, Alfred Métraux,
suggests that one cannot understand possession apart from an
understanding of the vaudou teachings concerning the souls,
viz. gros bon ange and ti bon ange.[119] At some time or other,
one of these souls, the gros bon ange, is held in abeyance.
When this happens, then it is possible for a loa to enter
and take possession of the person. This, in short, is what
possession in vaudou is all about. He objects to the description of it as a state of hysteria. He insists that the number
of persons who become possessed is too large to say that it is
a state of hysteria, unless the whole Haitian population is
seen as beset with mental problems.

But if what Douyon and Maximilien say is true, namely that
possession is a self-induced state, then we must reckon with
the fact that within the Christian tradition, this is not
unfamiliar, even concerning baptism of the Holy Spirit. Despite baptisms which may be experienced "spontaneously and
genuinely, in the setting of the psychological group pressure
of a Pentecostal meeting there are also baptisms of the Spirit
which are forced and strained."[120] And yet, this is not to
invalidate the authenticity of an experience of the Spirit, for
once a pastor, for example, has been initially baptized,

> "he learns to use levels of his soul and his body
> hitherto unknown to him, as sense organs with which
> to apprehend a psychological climate, a group
> dynamic situation."[121]

The psychological explanations for spirit behaviour are still
open to debate. It is plain that the psychologists and
psychoanalysts are not in common agreement with any one
explanation. No wonder they have not entirely convinced the
theologians, some of whom have actually encountered behaviour
patterns which could not have been altered by psychotherapy,
but by exorcism. One theologian, for example, contends that

> "Exorcism is definitely spiritual surgery, and,
> like medical surgery, it cannot be rightly com-
> prehended except by those working within the same
> healing discipline, and with an understanding
> of it."[122]

According to him, possession is not a psychological disorder,
but a state in which demons are actually at work:

> "The pastor cannot dismiss anything which is real
> to the people who turn to him for comfort and

> guidance. This is not to say that he has to
> accept without question the objective reality
> of every hallucination and fantasy which is
> described, but that he must at least start
> from a position which acknowledges that things
> may have a genuine reality for others irrespec-
> tive of his own perceptions and beliefs."[123]

One of the most interesting cases of demon possession is reported in the biography of the German pastor, Rev. John Christopher
Blumhardt (1805 - 1880). Gottliebin Dittus was a young unmarried woman who became possessed by evil spirits. The house
in which she lived was afflicted by terrible noises which
visitors to the place testified to have actually heard.
Visitors also testified to poltergeist experiences and the
teleportation of objects. They saw chairs springing up,
windows rattling, plaster falling from the ceiling, and a
general pandemonium in the house. When she had been removed
to another place of abode, the house remained haunted for a
time until her new residence began to suffer a similar fate.
Rev. Blumhardt paid regular visits to her in order to pray
with her. On such visits, he took with him medically trained
people as well as representatives of local government. Whenever Blumhardt mentioned the name of Jesus, the demon spoke
out in protest. It is noticeable that sometimes persons who
accompanied the pastor were struck by an unseen hand, but
Blumhardt himself never received a blow.

> "On one occasion after prayer, which was continued
> longer than usual, the demon suddenly broke forth
> in the following words: 'All is now lost. Our
> plans are destroyed. You have shattered our bond,
> and put everything into confusion. You with your

everlasting prayers - you scatter us entirely.
We are 1,067 in number; but there are still
multitudes of living men, and you should warn
them lest they be like us forever lost and cursed
of God.' The demons attributed their misfortune
to Blumhardt, and in the same breath cursed him
and bemoaned their own vicious lives; all the time
ejaculating; 'Oh, if only there was no God in
heaven!'

"Blumhardt held conversations with several of the
demons, one of whom proclaimed himself a perjurer,
and yelled again and again: 'Oh man think of
eternity. Waste not the time of mercy; for the
day of judgment is at hand.' These demons spoke
in all the different European languages, and in
some which Blumhardt and others present did not
recognize.

"The end came between the second and twenty-eighth
of December, 1843. After continued fasting and
prayer on the part of Blumhardt, the demons seemed
gradually to forsake Gottliebin, and instead
took possession of her sister and brother. The
first struggle took place in the person of her
sister Catherine, who at times was possessed of
such super-human strength that it took several
men to hold her. One night after hours of prayer
Blumhardt commanded the demon to come forth, when
a fearful outcry was heard by hundreds of people
penetrating to a great distance, and the demon
avowed himself an emissary of Satan. The struggle
lasted all night, and then yelling: 'Jesus is
victor' the demon departed. After this time the
three persons afflicted had no recurrence of the
'possession'. Gottliebin's health was restored.
Several physicians testify that a deformed limb
and other maladies which they had attempted in
vain to relieve her of, were suddenly cured."[124]

My own impression is that one can never be too sure whether one

is dealing with a case for the psychiatrist or the exorcist.

So that just as there are times when psychological language

is appropriate for describing certain phenomena, so too there

are those occasions when it is fully justifiable to use demon

language. In other words, both exorcism and psychiatry, in

their work, can complement each other. Masamba Ma Mpolo

touches this point:

> "Although the concepts of modern medical psychology
> appear powerful in comparison to the seeming weakness
> of those within traditional culture, it would
> probably be wise not to hold either of them as ex-
> clusive or definitive. In many ways their power
> and their weakness seem to complement each other."[125]

There are many situations in life wherein the scientist and

the theologian may discern rays of truth in each other's field.

Elsewhere we said that dreams may be interpreted as a medium

of communication employed by the spirits or they may be classi-

fied as pure psychological phenomena. An incident in the life

of Carl Jung is relevant here:

> "At that time," writes Jung, "I had to deliver a
> lecture in B. I returned to my hotel around
> midnight. I sat with some friends for a while
> after the lecture, then went to bed, but I lay
> awake for a long time. At about two o'clock -
> I must have just fallen asleep - I awoke with a
> start, and had the feeling that someone had
> come into the room; I even had the impression
> that the door had been hastily opened. I instantly
> turned on the light, but there was nothing. Someone
> might have mistaken the door, I thought, and I
> looked into the corridor. But it was still as
> death. 'Odd,' I thought, 'someone did come into the
> room!' Then I tried to recall exactly what had
> happened, and it occurred to me that I had been
> awakened by a feeling of dull pain, as though
> something had struck my forehead and then the
> back of my skull. The following day I received
> a telegram saying that my patient had committed
> suicide. He had shot himself. Later I learned
> that the bullet had come to rest in the back wall
> of the skull.
>
> "This experience was a genuine synchronistic phe-
> nomenon such as is quite often observed in connection
> with an archetypal situation - in this case, death.
> By means of relativisation of time and space in
> the unconscious it could well be that I had perceived

something which in reality was taking place elsewhere. The collective unconscious is common to
all; it is the foundation of what the ancients
called the 'sympathy of all things'. In this
case the unconscious had knowledge of my patient's
condition. All that evening, in fact, I had felt
curiously restive and nervous, very much in
contrast to my usual mood."[126]

Later on in the same book, Jung reflects upon his dream of

another person of whose death he had some foreknowledge:

"When one has such experiences ... one acquires
a certain respect for potentialities and arts
of the unconscious. Only, one must remain
critical and beware that such communications
may have a subjective meaning as well. They may
be in accord with reality, and again they may
not."[127]

Jung related his experiences using the terminology of psycho-

logy. In admitting his limitations, namely that his psycho-

logical explanations may or may not be in accord with reality,

we are reminded that whatever the terminology, we must be

humble enough to admit that no one method of enquiry can

claim a monopoly on absolute truth.

Are Other Explanations Possible?

If the phenomenon of spirit possession could be explained

simply by referring to behaviour resulting from the intri-

cacies of the human organism, then there would not be much

of a problem. What complicates the issue is the fact that

when the phenomenon occurs inanimate objects seem to lose

their normal molecular propensities. We mentioned earlier on

how burning coal, hot iron and broken glass become harmless
to the bodies of the serviteurs. Under normal circumstances,
handling such objects would have had disastrous effects for
the individual.

One explanation could be that the individuals who are supposedly possessed by spirits are not actually so, but that they are
good conjurors. They can make people believe that they are
seeing things happening which are not really happening. However, this is an over-simplification, for I have actually
witnessed such possessed individuals rolling in the fire,
dancing in it for unusually long periods with no physically
apparent disastrous effects. I am confident that from my
angle of observation I could not have been the victim of a
deception. Another possible explanation is that some chemical
substance is passed over the body of the serviteur before he
or she actually comes into contact with fiery substances.
This could be done before the start of a ceremony. One may
argue this to be the case in tourist ceremonies. I have no
evidence in support of this, but there may well be frauds in
the business. Human nature is such that the desire is always
for results, hence it is not unthinkable for some to resort
to dishonest means in order to bring about desired ends. Of
course, I am aware that even if there is watertight evidence
that points to sheer trickery in some cases, this does not
disprove the possibility of the unnatural behaviour of metals
brought on by genuine spirit-possession. The accusation of

magic is stoutly denied by houngans in charge of houmforts which
are open to the public. It is most unlikely, though, that in
vaudou ceremonies which take place in the deep countryside,
where such seeming loss of normal molecular propensities is
commonplace, that people would pander to trickery. The fidèles
do not act accordingly. They have sufficient confidence in
their loas, whom, they believe, will employ their supernatural
powers to perform remarkable feats. Furthermore, should a
serviteur suffer abrasions, this would not be frowned upon, but
rather treated as a privilege that he or she were allowed to
suffer on behalf of a loa.

We are faced with a situation in which we cannot be satisfied
with the explanations which have been put forward for the
phenomenon of spirit possession. The spirit terminology may
assuage some and anger others. The language of the social
scientist may be meaningful to some and useless to others.
The phenomenon under review is a partial enigma.

A phenomenon not unrelated to what we are discussing is that
of metal-bending. Metal-bending is the paranormal bending
of metals without actual touch by human beings. Metals may be
bent into coils, spirals, flowers, animals, abstracts and other
curious shapes. A good metal-bender may produce the deforma-
tion of cutlery or latchkeys. Professor John Hasted, modern
British researcher of Experimental Physics and Head of Department at Birkbeck College, University of London, has been

involved in research on metal benders, because of a developed interest in it following his observation of Uri Geller, the famous metal-bender. Although psychic phenomena do not rank as important on the physicists' agenda, and in spite of the real possibility of him being accused of time-wasting in this type of research, Professor Hasted persevered. He went about his investigations adopting the attitude of "Believe nothing that you hear and only half of what you see."[128]

Some of the questions asked by Professor Hasted are relevant to the behaviour of metals under spirit possession. Is the phenomenon of paranormal bending really a temporary softening of the metal? Where does the power to bend originate from? Of course, it must be stressed that Professor Hasted does not come to a belief in an outside supernatural force, or spirit, as a possible explanation for the bending of metals. For him, "the question of the reality of discarante entities is meaningless, because it is a subjective question, incapable of physical proof or logical answer, and therefore in the philosophical sense not a question at all."[129] What is relevant for our purposes is the fact that the professor accepts that our knowledge is limited, and that we do not know enough of the world to say. Our inability to explain does not mean that the phenomenon is unreal. That it exists we can be certain. Since, however, we do not know, we must encourage future research to take place so that we may gain more knowledge and further enlightenment on the subject. In his own words,

> "Of course, we do not yet know precisely what
> the reality and the detail are, but we must
> work within our limitations."[130]

Working within our limitations is of fundamental importance.

Our knowledge of the world is very limited. It is quite

likely that our view of the world is still primitive and not

as modern as we so often make it out to be.[131] Hence Alvin

Toffler writes:

> "As a novel civilization erupts into our everyday lives
> we are left wondering whether we, too, are obsolete.
> With so many of our habits, values, routines, and res-
> ponses called into question, it is hardly surprising
> if we sometimes feel like people of the past, relics
> of Second Wave civilization. But if some of us are
> indeed anachronisms, are there also people of the
> future among us - anticipatory citizens, as it were
> of the Third Wave civilization to come? Once we
> look past the decay and disintegration around us,
> can we see the emerging outlines of the personality
> of the future - the coming, so to speak, of a 'new
> man'?"[132]

Because of the limited nature of our present world view, we

are compelled to accept that certain things will remain a

mystery and that the most we can do is to offer tentative

explanations. In fact, one obvious approach to the problem

of spirit possession is to adopt the line of reasoning pro-

posed by Price-Mars, and accept it as a mystical state.[133]

Although mysticism is not an explanation in itself, at least

it is a reminder to us that the type of behaviour pattern

commonly described as spirit possession has a history deeply

embedded in religious traditions. There had been mystics

within the various Christian sects which were born out of the

Reformation. So too the dervishes or Sufis, who were the
early ascetics within the Islamic tradition, display symptoms
of mystical delirium.[134]

Rather than discard all terminology sociological, psychological, spiritual, or other - as meaningless, it seems advisable
to stick to the one which offers us a satisfactory explanation,
tentative though it may be. Since therefore, for the vaudouisants of Haiti, spirit possession constitutes a genuine
religious phenomenon, we ought to give them the benefit of the
doubt that spirits are indeed operative. The next step would
be for us to try and discover what we can thereby learn about
God and about the manner in which He reveals Himself to people
in the world of today.

Theological Evaluation

The preceding discussion has brought us to a point at which
we say that as to the question whether these spirits in
Haitian Folk Religion are a creation of the human mind or an
objective reality, it must be admitted that in intellectual
honesty, the only conclusion to be reached is that we just
cannot know for certain. They exist as a phenomenon. They
do constitute a reality for Haitians, hence they are not to
be discarded. Perhaps they also ought to be placed within
the scope of things for which we can only know in part. And
yet, one thing we _do_ know, is that whatever their exact
nature, these spirits are totally subjected to God, for they

are a part of His creation.

The question now before us is whether the spirits we encounter
in religions are able to enhance our understanding of the work
of the Holy Spirit.

In observing the phenomenon of loa-possession, we notice that
within vaudou, spiritual empowering is important. The individual who can receive power from a completely spiritual
source is to be admired. This is why tremendous admiration is
had for those who, in the context of a worship ceremony, are
chosen as serviteurs. They are regarded as specially favoured
by the loas, which in effect means that through them, the
entire worshipping community is specially favoured. But
whereas spiritual empowering in vaudou tends to be the privilege of the few, the Christian understanding of the Holy
Spirit is that the empowering is directed to the entire worshipping community. The fact is, the Holy Spirit empowers, not
only so that persons may perform spectacular feats, as in the
case of vaudou. His empowering results in simple, ordinary
activities as well. In our discussion earlier on about spirit
in the Bible, we made the point that Luke's understanding was
that the Spirit's presence could be validated by spectacular
signs, whereas Paul's concept was that spiritually motivated
activity did not necessarily have to be something out of the
ordinary. Although the spectacular may help credibility, it
must not be taken as a sign of authenticity. It is vital to

an understanding of the Holy Spirit that this must be emphasized. Otherwise the situation may arise wherin people's sole interest in the Holy Spirit is that He is a force to be manipulated for personal ends. Yet one of the criteria established by Paul is that gifts imparted by the Spirit must be $\pi\rho\grave{o}s$ $\tau\grave{o}$ $\sigma\nu\mu\phi\acute{e}\rho o\nu$ "for the common good."[135]

Sometimes in reading through the gospels, we are overcome by the distorted view of the Holy Spirit. We cannot help but notice the exceptional feats performed by those who receive the Holy Spirit. In looking at Jesus, for example, we tend to see someone who received the Spirit as a power at His birth and baptism, but seldom do we recognize that His whole life was a life in the Spirit. In reading the Pentecost Day experience we seem to notice there[136] the idea of the רוח as an external, impersonal power which enabled people to perform deeds beyond their own strength. When we view the Holy Spirit in this light, we seem incapable of remembering that His gifts ($\chi\alpha\rho\acute{\iota}\sigma\mu\alpha\tau\alpha$) are imparted, not so that individual ambitions and selfish motives may be fulfilled, but rather with a broader, more specific end in view, namely for the edification of the Church's mission in the world. John V. Taylor reminds us of this empowering with a corporate end in view:

> "What we must not do is to think and speak of the Holy Spirit as a magical power which God gives us to make us 'successful' Christians. This was the error of Simon Magus, and it continues to be the error of some revivalist and pentecostal preaching.

We must hold on to the fact that the Spirit works
by putting us in touch, making us see. It is
surely significant that, when Paul lists the
gifts and the forms of ministry with which the
Holy Spirit endowed the Church of his day, he
lumps together speaking in tongues and administration, exorcism and teaching, in complete
indifference to the distinction we now draw between natural and supernatural. The powers of
the new age which Jesus demonstrated were powers
that should be natural to any man as God intended
him to be. To say that the pentecostal movement
represents a rediscovery of the supernatural
dimension is true only if we mean a rediscovery of
the truth that every particle and process of material
existence is alive with the activity of God.

"All the Spirit's gifts are wonderful; all are
marked by a certain spontaneity; but none is meant
to be weird. They are incalculable, not incomprehensible. And, what is more important, they are
corporate."[137]

In trying to establish if there is a connection between

possession by the loas and possession by the Holy Spirit,

we must eventually come to the conclusion that there exists

a marked difference between the two. Added to what was said

above, we note the following. When a spirit possesses a

worshipper in vaudou, the latter experiences a complete change

of personality,. so much so that the individual is no longer

himself or herself but rather is completely displaced by the

loa. In contrast to this, when an individual is possessed by

the Holy Spirit, that person remains his or her original self.

According to Alan Richardson, the Spirit possesses a power which

is

"compulsive but not coercive; the Spirit guides,
leads and directs, but does not override the
personality of those who are thus directed."[138]

Karl Barth puts it another way:

> "He remains the purely other, the superior. We can
> only note what his yea is to the Word of God, this
> yea of his we can only repeat after him. As our
> teacher and leader he is in us, not as a power of
> which we might become lords. He remains himself
> the Lord."[139]

So far, we have tried to answer the question as to whether
vaudou spirits enhance our understanding of the work of the
Spirit. We have said that they merely alert us to some of
the ways in which we must _not_ think of the Holy Spirit, viz.
as an individually-oriented force which generates in people
certain superhuman powers to enhance their personal ego. The
question to which we now turn is whether these spirits must be
understood as part of the unique revelation given by God to
the Haitian people. The immediate answer one can give is that
although they do not fit neatly into the traditional category
of Christian revelation, we ought not to dismiss the possibility that God might be employing them to alert His Church to
further truths about Himself.

With reference to Paul's first letter to Corinth, we noted
that Chapter 12 suggests that one of the criteria of Christian
revelation is that it leads people to a confession of faith in
Jesus as Lord. Some of the loas, particularly those of Petro
origin, are so violently malevolent, that one can hardly hope
to credit them with a 'Jesus is Lord' motto. They would not
fit in with the categories of John who equated being _in the_

spirit with being in Christ. For John, true worship if "not
in Christ is no worship at all, no matter how spiritual."[140]
Those who adopt a Johannine approach would also reject the
possibility of benevolent loas being of God, because although
the pronouncements which they may make through the mouths of
a serviteur may serve the common good, and be in keeping with
the tenor of Christ's teaching, these spirits are implicitly
Christian and not explicitly so.

The other obvious barrier towards accepting spirits as understood within folk cultures to be vehicles of divine revelation
is the Church, whose emphasis has been on the Trinity as the
epitome of God's self-disclosure. This we dealt with in our
last chapter. And yet it must be admitted that such traditional methods of revelation are not satisfactory for every-
bdoy. G. W. H. Lampe, for example, has said:

> "I believe that the Trinitarian model is in the
> end less satisfactory for the articulation of
> our basic Christian experience than the unifying
> concept of God as Spirit."[141]

We must not remain closed to the possibility that spirits
might quite likely be tools which are being employed by God
today to make His will known to people. As hinted already,
this is a problem for Protestant theology which has for long
adopted the attitude of expelling from its system whatever
appears difficult to understand. The honest approach which
we propose is for the Church to admit its lack of experience.
As we said when introducing the section on revelation in our

last chapter, people's experiences differ and lead them
to adopt certain beliefs. If some people have an experience
which for them is a reality, how dare we claim as objective
the view that their subjective reality is merely subjective,
and that our claim to objectivity is not merely subjective!
Such a positive approach to the question of spirits, which we
now recommend, will be to the advantage, not only of the Church
in Haiti and other folk cultures across the world, but of the
Church in the west as well.

To round off the discussion in this chapter, let us take a
look at some of the benefits which may accrue when a Church
takes more seriously the terminology and the experience of
spirits.

The first thing to be said is that western Christianity will
be reminded that a conscious effort should be made to understand that there is the real possibility of interaction between the physical and spiritual worlds. This is the view of
Professor John S. Mbiti, who writes with particular reference
to the folk culture of the African continent:

> "African sensitivity to the spirit-world is some-
> thing that could enrich the rather impoverished
> type of Christianity which has come to us through
> Western thought and practice, in which the spirit-
> world is either dismissed altogether or put in the
> extreme background - except for spiritist cults
> which function outside the Church. The New Testa-
> ment is extremely aware of the spirit-world and
> its nearness to the human world. Again and again
> Jesus encounters the spirits, and one of the
> eschatological signs of His presence and ministry

is the exorcising of the spirits. The Cross is
a cosmic struggle which involves not only the human
rulers but the spiritual rulers and principalities.
Our Christian warfare is not 'against flesh and
blood, but against the principalities, against the
powers, against the world rulers of this present
darkness, against the spiritual hosts of wickedness
in the heavenly places.' Africa knows only too well
that spirits exist and form an essential part of man's
spiritual environment. The Gospel in Africa must
address itself to the spirit-world as well and not
to the human world alone."[142]

The impact of spirits in folk cultures can be such as to help

the Church spell out more clearly its doctrine pertaining to

the Communion of Saints. The statement of faith which is found

in the Apostles' Creed, "I believe in ... the Communion

of Saints" is understood to be referring to the continuing

fellowship between the Church extending throughout the ages

and linking with "angels, archangels and all the company of

heaven who," in the context of the celebration of the Lord's

Supper, "join in the unending hymn of praise 'Holy, holy, holy

Lord, God of power and might, Heaven and earth are full of

your glory, Hosanna in the highest." What better context for

translating this doctrine into terms comprehensible to human-

kind than folk culture!

Ancestor veneration ensures that the family maintains its link

with those who have departed this earthly life and are now

enjoying a spiritual existence. The doctrine of the Communion

of Saints could be all the more real if the Church seeks

always to foster and maintain a family character about itself.

The faithful departed of the Church triumphant in heaven would then be better appreciated as being intimately concerned about the affairs of the Church militant on earth. Furthermore, since Christ is Lord of both the Living and the Dead, then the links of both these groups, through Christ, should be all the more evident.

The idea of some ancestors being disposed to be vengeful, whereas Christian saints must be all-loving ought not to be a problem since in actual fact the Church has never been a perfect entity. The one weakness about the analogy is that some of the ancestors have not heard the name of Christ, and cannot be regarded as 'faithful'. But this is counteracted by the fact that Christ's death is regarded as an offering, not only to Christians, but to all people. This is the point which Paul makes in his letter to the Romans. We have already mentioned in chapter 2, that as far as the apostle understood, God shows no partiality (Romans 2:11). Although Jews may claim for themselves a special place in the plan of God, they must accept that Gentiles are equally important in His sight. Now in Chapter 3:21-26 of Romans, Paul puts forward the argument that God's saving activity is accomplished through faith in Jesus Christ, "whom God put forward as an expiation by his blood." (v. 25a) It is a benefit offered to all people, Jews and Gentiles alike, since "all have sinned and fall short of the glory of God." (v. 23) To this notion must be linked the idea which is expressed in the

second part of verse 25, that past sins are also accounted for
by Christ's death.

> "The question is why God manifested his
> righteousness in an act of redemption in
> Christ crucified. The answer is: In the
> past he had overlooked men's sins, and de-
> cisive action was necessary if his righteous-
> ness was to be vindicated."[143]

For this reason, Christ's atoning power is to be considered not
only as a present reality, but having retrospective as well
as futuristic effects. God, it would seem, had acted in
anticipation of Christ's death.

For this reason, too, Christians have prayed:

> "Almighty God, our heavenly Father, who of Thy
> tender mercy didst give thine only Son Jesus
> Christ to suffer death upon the Cross for our re-
> demption; who made there (by His one oblation
> of Himself once offered) a full, perfect, and
> sufficient sacrifice for the sins of the whole
> world ..."[144]

In saying this prayer, they have also echoed Pauline beliefs
that the death of Jesus was $\dot{\epsilon}\phi\dot{\alpha}\pi\alpha\xi$ - once for all:

> "For we know that Christ being raised from the
> dead will never die again; death no longer has
> dominion over him. The death he died he died
> to sin, once for all, but the life he lives he
> lives to God."(ch. 6:9, 10)

All those who in the past did not know His name are able to
benefit from His death.

The further question raised by all this is, then why evangelize? If in the final analysis it does not matter, because
those who did not live by faith, through ignorance of Christ,

and those who now do not live by faith, through Christ's
absence from their culture, both are assured of the benefits
of Christ's death, then Christians should not trouble themselves to proclaim Christ. Paul himself answers this
question:

> "Are we to sin, because we are not under law
> but under grace? By no means!"(Romans 6:15)

For Paul, it is not the future outcome which should be our
concern, but the quality of life in the Spirit which we now
enjoy in Christ. Since he attaches tremendous importance to
this present good quality of life, which is attained through
union with Christ, then evangelism - sharing this good news
about Christ - is incumbent upon those who have received and
accepted the Christian revelation.

Edward W. Fasholé-Luke has made some interesting observations on the relationship between ancestor veneration and the
communion of saints. His claim is that reciprocal prayer is
a logical outcome of the link with the ancestors:

> "For if it does not derogate from the sufficien-
> cy of Jesus' intercession to ask a living friend
> to pray for us, it cannot be wrong for us to request
> the prayers of a departed member of Christ, who
> is with him. Indeed, the intercession of the de-
> parted who are with Christ is a legitimate conse-
> quence of the fellowship in prayer which unites
> the whole body of Christ. The invocation of the
> departed is a practice based upon this truth; it
> is perhaps at this point that the dangers of
> syncretism are most clearly seen in the African
> situation, but it is also at the flashpoint
> between syncretism and Christian truth that a
> genuine Christian theology can be produced."[145]

The reasoning behind this cannot easily be disputed. It is
a fact that if we take the idea of family links seriously,
then mutual prayers ought to be in order. But I am well aware
that this will not be supported by the doctrinal stance of
many denominations. Methodists in Haiti are always warned
that praying for the dead is not commendable as good protestant practice. Emphasis is rather given to the idea that the
dead have already completed their time on earth, hence prayers
cannot change judgment. And yet, we are not saved on the
strength of our works, but rather upon the basis of grace,
through faith. Could not the expression of faith by the
living be to some effect in the plan of God?

Folk cultures can also challenge churches to rethink the doctrines pertaining to the existence of evil spirits and demons
in today's world, and the place of a ministry of exorcism in
the scheme of things. A closer look needs to be given to
Jesus' concern, throughout His earthly ministry, for people
who had been brought to Him possessed by demons. It is quite
likely that some were probably mentally ill patients, whose
vision of reality had been distorted until Jesus came along
and helped them see things in their true perspective. In
this regard, W. C. Willoughby has a relevant comment:

> "Much of the talk about cases of 'possession'
> among backward races must be set down to fondness
> for the exotic and the unexamined, and much to
> our failure to see that the doctrine of the
> Incarnation implies that the Lord's knowledge was
> limited by the scientific and historical horizons

of the age and nation in which he dwelt."[146]
Whether the people brought to Jesus would probably have been
cured by psychiatric treatment or not, the New Testament
described them all as having evil spirits and demons. Jesus
Himself, by His method of dealing with them, demonstrated that
demons did exist, but of greater importance was the fact that
He had power to overcome them.

On the question of demon possession, the approach of Dr. James
Cone is worthy of note. Speaking about how Jesus saw the down-
fall of Satan (Luke 10:18) he writes:

> "The reference to Satan and demons is not simply
> an outmoded first-century world-view. The issue
> is much more complex than that. Bultmann and
> his program of demythologization notwithstanding,
> the offense of the gospel is and ought to be
> located precisely at the point where our con-
> fidence in modern knowledge encounters the New
> Testament message, namely, in Jesus' liberating
> exorcisms. Unlike the fundamentalists I am not
> contending that the biblical cosmology ought
> to replace contemporary science in college class-
> rooms. Rather, I intend to make the theological
> point that the "scandal" (skandalon, stumbling
> block) is no different for us today than for the
> people who encountered Jesus in the first century.
> It is that the exorcisms disclose that God in Jesus
> has brought liberation to the poor and the wretched
> of the land, and that liberation is none other
> than the overthrow of everything that is against
> the fulfillment of their humanity. The scandal is
> that the gospel means liberation, that this liberation
> comes to the poor, and that it gives them the
> strength and the courage to break the conditions
> of servitude. This is what the Incarnation means.
> God in Christ comes to the weak and the helpless,
> and becomes one with them, taking their condition
> of oppression as his own and thus transforming their
> slave-existence into a liberated existence."[147]

When we arrive at a sympathetic understanding of the belief in spirits, then can we approach the time when the insights of the folk religions can enhance our understanding of the Christian faith. Professor Walter J. Hollenweger has a pertinent comment in this respect. Poor religion, he contends,

> "points to realities and methods in dealing with realities which some of our forefathers knew but which we have been made to forget. And that could become fatal for the future of Western Theology because it hinders a truly ecumenical and universal approach to theology. Furthermore, that process of repression and 'forgetting' could become extremely harmful when the 'demons of the past' break into our cultures (as can be seen already in the emergence of uncontrolled and sensational occultism) and find us completely unable to deal with them in a responsible and differentiated way. For this coming confrontation the religion of the poor could prove to be very much more than a poor religion."[148]

Churches in the west have begun to pay more attention to the possibility of demon possession as being something real. In fact, some churches have already begun to produce statements which offer guidelines to clergymen giving pastoral help to those who believe themselves to be possessed or whom the Minister believes to be possessed. One Church in Britain has produced the following:

(i)   These cases must remain within the context of the life and worship of the Church. Even when exorcism is practised it must be regarded as only one aspect of the pastoral ministry required.

(ii) No minister or layman should act independently in these circumstances. The Superintendent and other Ministers of the Church must always be consulted as they would be in other difficult pastoral situations. The Chairman of the District should also be asked to suggest appropriate sources of help.

(iii)   There should be a thorough pastoral investigation of the case, including, save in totally exceptional circumstances, close and continuing collaboration with those qualified in medicine, psychology and the social services, including the appropriate referral of the person seeking help.

(iv)   Since pastoral guidance is first and foremost concerned to assure people of the presence and love of Christ, it is important to follow this practice in these cases also.

(v)   The ministry of Bible, prayer and sacraments should be extended to those seeking help.

(vi)   The form of any service of healing for those believed or believing themselves to be possessed should be considered in consultation with the ministerial staff of circuit (or in one-minister circuits with those whom the Chairman of the District suggests). Such a service should not be carried out when a person is in a highly excited state. It should not be unnecessarily prolonged. Publicity must be kept to a minimum.

(vii)   Continuing pastoral care of the person concerned should involve as essential ingredients the teaching of the faith and incorporation into the worshipping community of the Church."[149]

Could it be that the Church is now coming to grips with the mistake it had been making, namely that it has never really paid attention to the possibility of demons being as real in this day and age as they had been during the time of the earthly ministry of Jesus! There is, though, a note of caution, which ought to be heeded in this matter. Professor Walter J. Hollenweger writes:

"It is not possible for me to give a conclusive judgment on this subject, even though I am certain that most phenomena of possession can be explained within the framework of modern psychiatric knowledge, even if they cannot be healed. But I agree with Albert Moll in believing that there is possibly an 'inexplicable remnant'. This

'inexplicable remnant' does not point to the
existence of demons, but to the inaccuracy
(perhaps only temporary) of our explanation
of reality. But it prevents us from making statements which it is impossible for us to test.
Anyone who uses the devil as a stop-gap to
explain the 'inexplicable' makes him a meaningless
figure."[150]

The discussion as contained in the preceding pages of this

chapter has led us to suggest that there are ways, other than

those traditionally known, whereby the Holy Spirit of God

acts as agent of divine revelation. Later on, in chapter

6, we will be looking at some of these alternative expressions

of the Spirit's activity within the broader Caribbean society.

Our immediate concern is to consolidate our understanding of

Haitian folk religion, by looking deeper into the responses

of people to God and to their spirits. Do they respond in

faith, or do they consider themselves to be victims of fate?

It is to such questions that we turn in our next chapter.

CHAPTER 3 - NOTES

1. Stephen N. Ezeanya, "God, Spirits and the Spirit World" in Kwesi Dickson and Paul Ellingworth, eds, <u>Biblical Revelation and African Beliefs</u>, London, Lutterworth Press, 1969, p. 35.

2. Extract from a film by Chris Mason, film editor, <u>The Last Taboo</u>, BBC, 1981.

3. John S. Mbiti, <u>Introduction to African Religion</u>, London Heinemann, 1977, pp. 70-73.

4. Here the term 'living dead' differs from its usage in the last chapter. There we were referring, not to spiritual beings, but to zombies - people who have been pronounced clinically dead, but are now existing as slaves.

5. Edmond Ilogu, <u>Christianity and Ibo Culture</u>, Leiden, E. J. Brill, 1974, p. 67.

6. John 14:2.

7. E. Bolaji Idowu, <u>Olodumare - God in Yoruba Belief</u>, London, Longmans, 1962, p. 194.

8. Ibid., p. 195.

9. This idea of the land belonging to ancestors is central in vaudou. Vaudouisants, who attest to the sacredness of the land, are among the most patriotic in Haiti. cf. Louis Maximilien, <u>Le Vodou Haitien</u>, Port-au-Prince, Imprimerie de l'Etat, 1945, p. 144.

10. Joel 2:28.

11. Alfred Guillaume, <u>Prophecy and Divination</u> Among The Hebrews And Other Semites: The Brampton Lectures 1938, London, Hodder and Stoughton Limited, 1938, pp. 213, 214.

12. For an account of this film, see Ronald Eyre, "Zulu Zion" in <u>Ronald Eyre on the Long Search</u>, Great Britain, Collins Fount Paperbacks, 1979, pp. 196-220.

13. 1 Corinthians 12:7.

14. 1 Corinthians 12:1-3.

15. Walter J. Hollenweger, <u>The Pentecostals</u>, London, SCM Press Ltd., 1976, p. 372.

16. 1 Corinthians 14:19.

17. 1 Corinthians 14:16.

18. E. W. Fasholé-Luke, "Ancestor Veneration and the Communion of Saints" in M. E. Glasswell & E. W. Fasholé-Luke, eds, New Testament Christianity for Africa and the World, Essays in Honour of Harry Sawyerr, London, SPCK, 1974, p. 212.

19. E. Bolaji Idowu, op. cit., p. 192.

20. G. Parrinder, West African Religion, London, Epworth Press, 1969, pp. 125, 126.

21. Genesis 2:7.

22. Ezekiel 37:6, 8-10, 14.

23. Psalm 146:4.

24. Genesis 6:3.

25. Hans Walter Wolff, Anthropology of the Old Testament, London, SCM Press Ltd., 1974, p. 34.

26. Judges 6:34. וְרוּחַ יְהוָה לָבְשָׁה אֶת-גִּדְעוֹן

27. 1 Chronicles 12:18. וְרוּחַ לָבְשָׁה אֶת-עֲמָשַׂי רֹאשׁ הַשָּׁלִוּשִׁים

28. Francis Brown, S. R. Driver, C. A. Briggs, Hebrew and English Lexicon of the Old Testament, Oxford, Clarendon Press, 1906, p. 528.

29. Judges 14:6. וַתִּצְלַח עָלָיו רוּחַ יְהוָה

30. 1 Samuel 10:6, 10; ch. 11:6. וְצָלְחָה עָלֶיךָ רוּחַ יְהוָה
וַתִּצְלַח עָלָיו רוּחַ אֱלֹהִים וַתִּצְלַח רוּחַ-אֱלֹהִים עַל-שָׁאוּל

31. 1 Samuel 16:13. וַתִּצְלַח רוּחַ-יְהוָה אֶל-דָּוִד

32. Ezekiel 11:5. וַתִּפֹּל עָלַי רוּחַ יְהוָה

33. Judges 14:6.

34. Numbers 24:2f.

35. Hans Walter Wolff, Anthropology of the Old Testament, London, SCM Press Ltd., 1974, p. 35.

36. Edmond Jacob, Theology of the Old Testament, London, Hodder and Stoughton, 1958, p. 122.

37. Ezra 1:5;

38. Jeremiah 51:11.

39. Job 15:13.

40. Job 7:11.

41. 2 Kings 2:9-15.

42. Helmer Ringgren, Israelite Religion, London, SPCK, 1966, p. 93.

43. Isaiah 44:3.

44. Joel 2:28.

45. Ezekiel 39:29.

46. Hekmer Ringgren, op. cit., p. 93.

47. Isaiah 63:14.

48. Psalm 143:10.

49. Helmer Ringgren, op. cit., p. 93.

50. 2 Kings 19:7; 1 Kings 22:21-23.

51. 2 Kings 2:9-15.

52. John Skinner, ed., The Century Bible - Kings, Edinburgh, T. C. & E. C. Jack, 1910, p. 280.

53. Edmond Jacob, op. cit., p. 124.

54. Alfred Guillaume, op. cit., pp. 290-333 make for an interesting chapter on ecstasy.

55. Ezekiel 2:2; ch. 3:24; ch. 11:5.

56. Edmond Jacob, op. cit., p. 127.

57. Eduard Schweizer, op. cit., p. 13. cf. Wisd. 9:17; ch. 7:7; Ecclus. 39:6.

58. Ibid, p. 33.

59. Matthew 3:16; Mark 1:10.

60. Eduard Schweizer, op. cit., p. 40.

61. Ibid, p. 43.

62. Ibid, p. 89.

63. Acts 2:38.

64. Acts 10:44-48.

65. Eduard Schweizer, op. cit., p. 57.

66. Philippians 3:3.

67. Eduard Schweizer, op. cit., p. 73.

68. Ibid, pp. 70, 71.

69. 1 Corinthians 15:35-50.

70. Eduard Schweizer, op. cit., p. 61.

71. Ibid, p. 64.

72. 1 Corinthians 12:8-10.

73. Eduard Schweizer, op. cit., p. 65.

74. Genesis 32:24-32.

75. Cf. Th. C. Vriezen, An Outline of Old Testament Theology, Oxford, Basil Blackwell, 1966, p. 155.

76. Psalm 34:7.

77. Psalm 91:11.

78. Daniel 10:13, 21; ch. 12:1. Michael is associated with the post-exilic period.

79. 2 Samuel 24:16.

80. 1 Samuel 16:14. וְרוּחַ רָעָה מֵאֵת וְהִוָה
    Also Ch. 18:10; ch. 19:9.

81. הָעָר adv. f. from רָעַע vb. denom. be evil, bad. This will be physical or ethical evil. רַע adj. bad, evil, unpleasant, giving pain, unhappiness, misery, harmful - "of the divine spirit as producing an ecstatic state of frenzy and violence. 1 Samuel 16:14, 15, 16, 23. 1 Samuel 18:10; 19:9 (Francis Brown, S. R. Driver, C. A. Briggs, op. cit., p. 948). The form רָעָה is also that of a noun. n.f. evil, misery, distress, injury (ibid, p. 949).

82. John D. Davis, The Westminster Dictionary of the Bible, revised and rewritten by Henry Snyder Gehman, London and New York, Collins' Clear-Type Press, 1944, p. 99.

83. The Interpreter's Dictionary of the Bible, Vol. 1, Nashville, Abingdon Press, 1962, p. 131.

84. Genesis 6:1-4.

85. Helmer Ringgren, op. cit., pp. 315, 316.

86. Psalm 22:16-21, Isaiah 13:21, 22.

87. Zephaniah 2:13-15.

88. A scholarly treatment of demons is given by John M. Hull, in _Hellenistic Magic and Synoptic Tradition_, London, SCM Press Ltd., 1974. For example, he writes: "The sub-terranean and light-hating demons were the most dangerous to men because, unable to bear light, they tried to possess men or animals, to hide in their bodies, and thus caused illness and disease. Indeed this idea is probably the root of the conception of demons as causing disease." - p. 40.

89. Leviticus 20:6-8, Deuteronomy 18:9-14.

90. 1 Samuel 28:3-25.

91. Ephesians 6:11-13.

92. Colossians 2:8.

93. Cf. John M. Hull, op. cit.

94. Matthew 10:1; Luke 10: 17-19.

95. Luke 11:14-23.

96. Romans 8:38, 39.

97. Possession is not confined to religious ceremonies. Sometimes it may occur even as a person is performing regular duties. If someone is faced with disaster, very trying circumstances or disagreeable situations, loa possession might be sought after.

98. Maya Deren was fully aware of this, as she grappled with the loa, Erzulie, who wanted to possess her. Eventually the loa prevailed. Cf. Maya Deren, op. cit., Chapter VII, pp. 247-262. It is very difficult, merely by looking at the serviteur, to discover whether possession is voluntary or not.

99. Jean Price-Mars, _Ainsi Parla L'Oncle_, Ottawa, LEMEAC, 1973, p. 193.

100. Maya Deren, op. cit., p. 95.

101. At a ceremony in the south of Haiti, during a ritual which I witnessed, the spirit being honoured was Agouet, referred to as the 'diver' or 'sea' loa. Two girls who became possessed jumped into the nearby sea and swam about like professionals, although under normal circumstances they were non-swimmers.

102. The ceremony of bruler-zin is designed to animate the spirits, for according to popular belief, these spirits have to be warmed from time to time. Hence, fire is used. We have a parallel idea in the jinns of Islam, some fiery spirits who need warmth.

103. "La crise est bien plus violente pour les loas pétro, dieux de force, dieux de la guerre." - Louis Maximilien, op. cit., p. 57.

104. Ouanga is of Bantu derivation. We noted, in a previous chapter, that ganga means witchcraft.

105. Louis Maximilien, op. cit., p. 149.

106. J. C. Dorsainvil, Vodou et Nevrose.

107. Malinowski, The Dynamics of Culture Change.

108. For a full treatment of these spirit religions, see Roger Bastide, The African Religions of Brazil.

109. "Si, pour d'autres types de sociétés, la possession pourrait inspirer de la répulsion ou de la honte, dans les cas de civilisation nègre, nous sommes en présence d'une conduite normale, ou, si l'on veut, d'une conduite qui assure l'équilibre social." - Laënnec Hurbon, Dieu dans le Vaudou haitien, Paris, Payot, 1972, p. 140.

110. Jeanne Favret-Saada, Les Mots, La Mort, Les Sorts.

111. John Richards, But Deliver Us From Evil, London, Darton, Longman & Todd, 1978, p. 32.

112. Roger Bastide, op. cit., p. 170.

113. Cf. Jean-Marie Salgado, Le Culte Africain Du Vaudou et Les Baptisés en Haiti - Essai de Pastorale, Rome, Université Pontificale " De Propaganda Fide" Editiones Urbanianae, 1963. Salgado claims that loas are nothing but the creation of popular imagination to express God's intervention in daily affairs. This is traceable, he says, to the error of perspective originating from the father of lies. (John 8:44) - p. 74. He considers vaudou to be "superstititious" and vaudou worshippers to be "poor sinners". - p. 54.

114. J. C. Dorsainvil, op. cit., p. 58.

115. Emerson Douyon, "Research Model on Trance and Possession States in the Haitian Vodoo" in Richard P. Shaedel, ed., Research and Resources of Haiti, New York, Research Institute for the Study of Man, 1969, p. 420.

116. Louis Maximilien, op. cit., p. 61.

117. Ibid, p. 55.

118. Jean Price-Mars, op. cit., pp. 183-202.

119. Alfred Métraux, Le Vaudou Haitien, Paris, Gallimard, 1958, pp. 106-125.

120. Walter J. Hollenweger, The Pentecostals, London, SCM Press Ltd., 1972, p. 332.

121. Ibid, p. 332.

122. John Richards, op. cit., p. 17.

123. Ibid, p. 192.

124. J. L. Nevius, Demon Possession and Allied Themes, Chicago, Fleming H. Revell Company, 1896, pp. 115, 116.

125. Masamba Ma Mpolo, La Libération Des Envoûtés, Yaoundé, Edition CLE, 1976, p. 141 (translated quote).

126. Carl G. Jung, Memories, Dreams, Reflections, London and New York, Collins - The Fontana Library - Theology & Philosophy, May 1974, pp. 159, 160.

127. Ibid, p. 335.

128. John Hasted, The Metal Benders, London, Routledge and Kegan Paul, 1981, p. 4.

129. John Hasted, op. cit., p. 253.

130. Ibid, p. 255.

131. In this, I am echoing the thoughts of Professor W. J. Hollenweger, with whom I agree on this point, during a discussion we had on the subject.

132. Alvin Toffler, The Third Wave, London, Pan Books Ltd. in association with Collins, 1981, p. 390.

133. Jean Price-Mars, op. cit., p. 193.

134. "Many travellers have described the dances and extrava-
gances of the dervishes. Perhaps the best account is that
given by Lane in his 'Modern Egyptians': he describes a
great ring of devotees jumping and leaping into the air
to the beat of tambourines, dancing wildly with no ordered movement until they are utterly exhausted. Lane
saw one of them rush from the dance and put pieces of
red-hot charcoal one after another into his mouth,
chewing them and finally swallowing them; while another
put a live coal into his mouth and inhaled until it was
almost white-hot ... Lane says that though he watched
them carefully he could not see any indication of pain
on their faces." - Alfred Guillaume, Islam, Great Britain,
Penguin Books, 1971, pp. 152, 153.

135. 1 Corinthians 12:7.

136. Acts 2:1-13.

137. John V. Taylor, The Go Between God, London, SCM Press
Ltd., 1974, p. 202.

138. Alan Richardson, An Introduction to the Theology of the
New Testament, London, SCM, 1966, p. 111.

139. Karl Barth, Church Dogmatics, Vol. 1, Edinburgh: T & T.
Clark, 1969, Chapter on 'God the Holy Spirit', pp.
513-560.

140. Eduard Schweizer, op. cit., p. 91.

141. G. W. H. Lampe, God as Spirit, The Bampton Lectures 1976,
Oxford, Clarendon Press, 1977, p. 228.

142. John S. Mbiti, "Eschatology" in Kwesi Dickson and Paul
Ellingworth, eds, Biblical Revelation and African Beliefs,
London, Lutterworth Press, 1969, p. 183.

143. C. K. Barrett, A Commentary on the Epistle to the Romans,
London, Adam & Charles Black, 1967, pp. 79, 80.

144. From Methodist Order of Service for Holy Communion.

145. E. W. Fasholé-Luke, "Ancestor Veneration and the Communion of Saints" in Mark E. Glasswell and Edward W.
Fasholé-Luke, eds, op. cit., pp. 219, 220.

146. W. C. Willoughby, The Soul of the Bantu, London, SCM,
1928, p. 112. An interesting critique of Willoughby's
contribution to African Christian Healing is treated by
John Rutherford, Willoughby, Missionary Practitioner and
Scholar.

147. James H. Cone, <u>God of the Oppressed</u>, London, SPCK, 1977, p. 77.

148. W. J. Hollenweger, "The Religion of the Poor is not a Poor Religion," <u>Expository Times</u>, 87/8, May 1976, pp. 228-232.

149. Methodist Church, Division of Social Responsibility, <u>A Methodist Statement on Exorcism</u>, approved by the Methodist Conference 1976.

150. Walter J. Hollenweger, <u>The Pentecostals</u>, London, SCM Press Ltd. 1976, pp. 380, 381.

CHAPTER 4

FAITH OR FATE

In order to establish whether the influence of folk religion
has been to make people faithful or fatalistic in their response
to life, let us at the very outset define our terms.

Faith

"Faith is an attitude of trust in the reality or truth of something that cannot be demonstrated or proved."[1] This is a
philosophical definition. Used within the context of religion,
faith is an implicit trust or confidence in someone greater than
ourselves, namely the Supreme Being whom we all call God.
Christianity defines faith in relationship to Christology.
Apart from the Christ event, it is meaningless to talk about
religious faith.[2] This truth comes across clearly when we
read the account given in Chapters 11 and 12 of the Epistle to
the Hebrews. There it is stated that

> "faith is the assurance of things hoped for, the conviction
> of things not seen." (ch.11: 1)

Then follows the explanation. Several men and women who lived
in the Old Testament times were people of faith. They had
been motivated by faith, venturing as they did into the unknown,
never seeking comfort and security, but ever willing to face
danger and certain death, having as their chief source of
comfort the assurance that they would eventually be reunited
with God. According to F.F. Bruce:

> "Their lives were regulated by the firm conviction that
> God would fulfil the promises He had given them, and in
> death they continued to look forward to the fulfilment
> of these promises .... but the full realization of
> the promises had to await the day of Christ."[3]

To many people today, their approach might appear somewhat

naive, yet the nature of their faith is upheld as virtuous:

> "So real was that fulfilment to them that it gave them
> power to press upstream, against the current of their
> environment, and to live on earth as citizens of that
> commonwealth whose foundations are firmly laid in the
> unseen and eternal order."[4]

The unseen basis of faith, though, is Jesus Christ, whom the

writer to the Hebrews describes as "the pioneer and perfecter

of our faith" (ch. 12: 2). As pioneer, it was Jesus Himself

who had guided the men and women of pre-Incarnation times along

the path of faith. As perfecter, this Jesus showed what faith

is all about by His complete submission to the will of God.

He endured all suffering, even to the point of death on the

cross. He now enjoys communion with God, which in itself may

be described as the ultimate goal of faith.

The letter of James suggests that "faith by itself, if it has

no works, is dead" (James 2: 17). Because of this, some

Christian writers have laid an undue amount of emphasis on the

practical aspect of faith. Although works are important as a

demonstration of the power of faith, we have always to remem-

ber that there are many works which are performed by unfaithful

people. Rudolf Bultmann has described faith mainly in terms of

action.[5] In his interpretation of Paul, Bultmann says:

"For Paul the acceptance of the message in faith takes
the form of an act of obedience because of the fact that
the message which demands acknowledgement of the
crucified Jesus as Lord demands of man the surrender of
his previous understanding of himself, the reversal of
the direction his will has previously had."[6]

He goes on to say that faith is

"the free deed of obedience in which the new self constitutes itself in place of the old."[7]

Then again,

"It is evident that 'faith' has the character of obedience
and is an act of decision."[8]

But to say that faith is an _act_ is incorrect terminology since
faith is basically the description of an attitude. I agree
with Robert Campbell Roberts' opinion expressed as follows:

"Unlike Bultmann, the New Testament never calls faith an
act, or speaks of '_the act_ of faith'. It does, however,
describe many acts which we could reasonably call acts
of faith."[9]

Of course, Bultmann is not the only theologian to use the term
act in describing faith. Karl Barth also does it, though in
his usage of the term we detect

"a mere infelicity of speech, an awkward expression
inherited from German philosophy."[10]

Whereas the general pattern of Bultmann's thoughts on faith
would suggest that calling faith an act is no accident, in the
case of Karl Barth, we have the suggestion that, as far as he
is concerned, faith is an _experience_ which is grounded in the
God who revealed Himself in Jesus Christ. Barth writes:

"Let us hold on to the fact that faith is experience, a
concretely fixable temporal act of this man's or that,
the act, in short, of acknowledgement. But it does not
go without saying that experience is real experience,
experience of the Word of God. Of no experience as such,
however perfect a form it may have, could this be said.
Therefore, it is not as experience that faith is faith,

i.e. real experience, although it is certainly experience.
Or, the act or acknowledgement is not as such acknowledgement of the Word of God. Nor is it so in virtue of any
degree of perfection with which it may be achieved. But
it is the Word, it is Christ, to whom faith is related,
because He gives Himself as object to it, who makes faith
into faith, into real experience. Of course, because He
gives Himself to it as object! For faith is not already
faith because it has or is a relation - it might in fact
be an objectless relation with an imagined object - but
because the Word of God is given to it as the object of
this connection, as the object of acknowledgement and
therewith as the ground of real faith."[11]

In any attempt at determining whether or not folk religion has
caused Haitians to be faithful, we must admit that the specific
revelation of God in Christ is not automatically implied. Faith
in Christianity may not be defined apart from Christology, but
as we have established in the two previous chapters, divine
revelation is such that the only meaningful way to talk about
belief, trust or confidence is in reference to the spirits.
Hence, as we examine attitudes and responses to life within
Haitian culture, our mention of faith will be in relation to
the loas, or in relation to God who is Lord of the spirits.

Fate

Fate is the term used to describe a power which determines the
appointed lot or ultimate condition of the individual. The
person held in the grips of fate does not necessarily deny that
good things may be in store for the future, but he or she lives
with a trembling fear that evil will eventually triumph. Such
an individual exists as a virtual prisoner, trapped, completely
impotent, entirely at the mercy of forces outside personal

control. Fatalism is the expression of an attitude of respect for this predetermining power greater than ourselves. It is the

> "belief that events are irrevocably fixed so that human effort cannot alter them, though sometimes things appear otherwise. 'What is to be, will be'."[12]

Within the Christian tradition, fatalism is often associated with Calvinism, whose message of absolute predestination proclaimed that God has foreordained all that is to come to pass and that the whole of humankind has already been allocated. Some will reap damnation, others will have salvation and eternal life. This doctrine seems to describe a God who is not the father of Jesus Christ.[13] However, the letter to the Ephesians states:

> "For by grace you have been saved through faith; and this is not your own doing, it is the gift of God."(ch. 2:8)

This stresses that the individual may respond, in faith, to God's gift of His Son Jesus Christ. Here there is no question of damnation for some, salvation for others. All may, through faith, receive salvation.

Predestination demotes humankind in order to promote divinity.

> "This fantastic exaggeration of the divine initiative into a fatalism is repugnant not merely because it dehumanizes man but also because it presents us with a God who is not worthy to be worshipped........"[14]

John Macquarrie, with whom I agree on this point, suggests that as we peruse the New Testament, we cannot extract the sayings and fit them neatly into either a universalistic scheme or a predestinarian scheme.

> "A true fatalism therefore exludes free will, and thus
> human responsibility."[15]

Part of Methodist tradition, for example, seeks to justify a

doctrine of free-will. John Wesley preached thus in one of

his sermons:

> "'And God' the three-one God, 'said, Let us make man in
> our image, after our likeness. So God created man in
> His own image, in the image of God created He him' (Gen.
> i. 26, 27): - not barely in his natural image, a picture
> of His own immortality; a spiritual being, endued with
> understanding, freedom of will, and various affections;
> nor merely in his political image, the governor of this
> lower world, having 'dominion over the fishes of the
> sea, and over all the earth': but chiefly in his moral
> image; which, according to the Apostle, is 'righteousness
> and true holiness' (Eph. iv. 24). In this image of God
> was man made........... But although man was made in the
> image of God, yet he was not made immutable. This would
> have been inconsistent with that state of trial in which
> God was pleased to place him. He was therefore created
> able to stand, and yet liable to fall. And this God
> Himself apprised him of, and gave him a solemn warning
> against it. Nevertheless, man did not abide in honour:
> he fell from his high estate. He 'ate of the tree
> whereof the Lord had commanded him, Thou shalt not eat
> thereof'. By this wilful act of disobedience to his
> Creator, this flat rebellion against his Sovereign, he
> openly declared that he would no longer have God to
> rule over him; that he would be governed by his own will,
> and not the will of Him that created him........"[16]

The God who is the Father of Jesus Christ does not treat us

like puppets, but has given us the freedom either to seek

salvation or to court damnation.

It is interesting to notice how Barth interprets the free will

which, as human beings under God, we are supposed to have. He

maintains that God, out of his freedom, has opted for

predestination, and that in so doing God is answerable to no

one but Himself:

"Must we know an inner reason for this choice, a justification for God on account of the freedom which He takes
to Himself and possesses, when He speaks to man, now of
adopting him, now of rejecting him, of illumining one
with His light and blinding another with the same light,
of dealing with one as Peter and with another as Judas?
A sufficient justification for this view, as for the
dogma of predestination generally which at this point
comes within range, is that the decision made in the Word
is God's and therefore it is a righteous and a good
decision."[17]

In discussing predestination, Barth speaks of a freedom which

is God's prerogative. Even when freedom of choice is imparted

to us as a gift from God, it still has to be remembered that

God is author of that freedom:

"Faith and unbelief, obedience and disobedience are only
possible in that as our action in the judgment of God
they are the answer, one way or the other, to His Word
addressed to us. In faith and in obedience my own
resolution and choice are genuinely good before God,
I exist, whatever else may be said of me, according to
the Word of God, I have adopted and received His grace.
In unbelief and disobedience my own resolution and choice,
whatever else may be said of them, are genuinely bad
before God, I exist in contradiction to the Word of God,
I have not adopted His grace. In one way or the other it
is I - so that it is my, my extremely responsible
decision. But it does not depend upon my decision for
this character which it has, for my choosing now the
good, now the bad. But what this decision of mine means,
which I achieve with free will, is that in one case its
meaning is a step to the right, in another a step to the
left, that my choice one way is faith and obedience, while
my choice another way is denial of both - this characteristic of my decision is the truth, inherent in it, of
the divine decision about me. By addressing me, God
has regarded me as the man I am to myself as I am. The
new quality which I acquire through the Word of God is my
peculiar and essential quality. It is this peculiar and
essential quality of mine that I cannot give myself.
Only God can judge me. Thus I am altogether the man
I am by virtue of God's decision. In virtue of God's
decision I am by my own decision a believer or an
unbeliever."[18]

When one looks critically at fate, one observes that there exists a dualism. It is the dualism between man's condition and God's will. The human condition may be described as a hopeless one - sickness, poverty, ignorance, pain, suffering and a general state of misery. God's will appears to be fixed. Things are exactly as He wants them to be. The fatalist accepts the dualism with an air of resignation, suggesting that nothing can be done to change it, for his understanding of God is that He is the One who never changes. As far as this line of reasoning goes, the physical and moral state of humanity will remain constant throughout a lifetime. What happens in the hereafter has already been determined by God, and this cannot be altered. In contrast to the fatalist, the individual guided by faith seeks to change the dualism. For him, it is possible to bring about an end to sickness, poverty, ignorance and the rest. This general state of misery can be changed through an act of faith, a faith in the God who is lord of both parts of the dualism. The fact is that the faithful individual has a totally different concept of eschatology. Whereas the fatalist understands eschatology as a future wrapped up solely in God, the Unchangeable, the latter sees eschatology as a God-given future in which human beings are allowed to take the initiative and become actively involved.[19]

Fate, as we have just noted, is the opposite of faith. We said earlier on that in searching for evidence of faith in vaudou, we will be searching for a God who is Lord of the spirits. We may here add that as far as fate is concerned, our responsibility will be to detect spirits which appear to be independent and outside the control of God.

Let us, in the first instance, look for evidence of faith within vaudou.

Faith Within Vaudou

It is fair to say that in the historical context, people have always had an implicit trust in the power of God or of His spirits to effect changes within the human condition. Put rather bluntly, theirs was a faith that the spirits would act as agents of political revolution. In the days of slavery in the West Indies, the Africans prayed to their spirits, requesting that these reward them with freedom from bondage. In Saint Domingue, the spirits seemed to have been against the idea of the country remaining ever a colony of France, so much so that they incited individuals to rebel against the status quo. In our treatment of the historical background of folk culture in Haiti[20] we referred to François Makandal, a Muslim from Guinea who, with his companions, had terrorised the plantations in a bid for freedom. When Makandal was eventually arrested and thrown into a fiery furnace, he became possessed by a spirit and so managed to escape. Although recaptured and killed, people were terribly impressed by what had happened to him and were convinced that the spirits favoured their cause for liberation.

As we peruse further the annals of Haitian history, we notice
that it was the famous Boukman, another spirit-filled individual who, on the night of August 14, 1791 conducted a vaudou
ceremony at which all participants pledged their allegiance
to the cause of the slave revolt. This initiated a chain of
events leading to political freedom from France in 1804. In
fact, not only Makandal and Boukman, but others of the early
leaders in the struggle for political independence - Hallou,
Hyacinthe, Lafortune and Toussaint - had believed in a power
within self which could alter what in the eighteenth century
seemed to have been a fate imposed on their country. They knew
that if they acted positively, the spirits would support them
and twist things to their advantage.[21]

The early Haitians have been expounding, in their own way, a
theology of hope long before it was popularized as a new
phenomenon in Latin America, Germany, the rest of Europe and
North America. They may not have testified to the presence
of Christ, or have expressed awareness of the hope born out of
the cross, but certainly the knowledge of their spirits' presence
helped the early Haitians to become aware of a new life and
hope which was theirs, namely, a hope in God "as the ground of
liberation, and not as the enemy of freedom".[22] Or to use
other terminology of political theology, vaudou in its early
stages represents the theology of liberation carried out to
its logical conclusion.[23]

These early Haitians rejected fatalism in preference for the positive outworkings of faith. They did not regard as irrevocably fixed the existing political state of affairs in their country. For them, change was possible if they took the matter into their own hands. In so doing, they reflect what Christian theologians of liberation today affirm about the gospel which

> "declares that the reality of the present is to be found in its potentialities for the future, but in the very process of pointing to this reality the gospel lays bare self-deception, rejects fatalism - even when it is blasphemously called the will of God - and requires us to become agents of change............................. The Jesus who is proclaimed is not an example of patience and submission to fate."[24]

By successfully championing the cause for Haitian liberation, vaudou has emphasized a sober truth which all who fight in the interest of freedom must note. It is this, that oppressed peoples will only be freed when they themselves act out the role of liberators. As Paulo Freire says:

> "In order for the oppressed to be able to wage the struggle for liberation, they must perceive the reality of oppression, not as a closed world from which there is no exit, but as a limiting situation which they can transform. This perception is necessary, but not a sufficient condition by itself for liberation; it must become the motivating force for liberating action. Neither does the discovery by the oppressed that they exist in dialectical relationship as antithesis to the oppressor who could not exist without them in itself constitute liberation. The oppressed can overcome the contradiction in which they are caught only when this perception enlists them in the struggle to free themselves."[25]

It is being over-optimistic for one to expect the oppressor to become the liberator. Like the Pharaoh whom Moses encountered

the typical oppressor hardens his heart since any form of
liberation in favour of those whom he is oppressing will pose
a serious threat to his power, prestige and safety. The
early Haitian revolutionaries knew that if they did not act
decisively to change their country's political climate their
people would have continued to bear the French yoke for a
long time to come.

> "For self-sacrifice and heroism," writes C.L.R. James,
> "the men, women and children who drove out the French
> stand second to no fighters for independence in any place
> or time. And the reason was simple. They had seen at
> last that without independence they could not maintain
> their liberty, and liberty was far more concrete for
> former slaves than the elusive forms of political
> democracy in France."[26]

Christians usually engage in heated discussions as to whether
violence can be justified as a vehicle of revolutionary change.
There are those who suggest that since Christ is the Prince of
Peace as foretold by the prophet Isaiah (ch. 9: 6), then the
Christian must always be committed to adopting peaceful methods
in any bid for political change. There are others who hold to
the view that although the Christian must strive towards the
creation of peace, there are times when the achieving of such
ends can come about only through the use of violence. Moltmann,
for example, argues that

> "violence, construed as the love which desires to put an
> end to evil, cannot be approved but it can be answered
> for."[27]

There are still others whose exegesis of Christ's words that
he came not to bring peace but a sword (Matt. 10: 34) causes
them to argue in favour of an unconditional use of violence

being compatible with Christianity. Interestingly enough,
such questions are not of prime concern to vaudouisants. As
far as they are concerned, they cannot spare themselves the
luxury of such debates, for as they see it, life is a matter
of survival at whatever cost. As mentioned in Chapter 2,
their understanding of eschatology is not one involving judgment, heaven and hell. So that the question of the rightness
or wrongness of violence, the love or the hatred which may
motivate it, will not occupy any place of priority on their
agenda. For them it is the end, not the means, towards
realizing political change.

The majority of Haiti's five and a half million inhabitants
live under conditions of poverty. They feel oppressed socially,
economically and politically, despite the fact that they threw
off the French yoke nearly two centuries ago. There are reports
that members of the country's League for Human Rights have
been victimised, and that limitations have been imposed upon
the freedom of radio stations, newspapers and political parties.
The mere fact that people have elected not to remain silent
in the face of injustices, suggests that they do not conceive
of themselves as hopelessly existing in the grips of fate.
They believe that they can now do something in a positive manner
which will be to their benefit in the future. The desire to be
freed from misery has caused some Haitians to take a leap of
faith, namely venturing out into the seas in tiny little boats
bound for the United States of America, the Bahamas, in fact

anywhere which would provide a haven for them. This we discussed in the Introduction. Many of them suffer torture, disease and even death as they make their bid for freedom. With dogged determination and with faithful fearlessness they move on, following what they understand to be the only clear path of liberation open to them.

Naturally we may want to question whether the act of fleeing their country is, for these refugees an expression of faith. It was Gustavo Gutierrez who suggested that faith teaches us that every human act which is oriented towards the construction of a more just society has value in terms of communion with God.

> "Spiritual life and experience," he says, "is something we are used to viewing as apart, far removed from such impure human realities as politics. But we must now move in a different direction. Instead of looking for an encounter with the Lord through contact with poor individuals in isolation, with 'nice' poor people, we must seek that encounter through contact with the oppressed, with all the members of a particular social class who are fighting valiantly for their most basic rights and for an altered society in which they can live as human beings."[28]

Now in general terms, fleeing one's homeland is a negative move and is questionable as a means of constructing a more just society. Moltmann's observations are valid that

> "one does not move to another country to find freedom and God. One remains where one is in order to correspond to the conditions of the coming kingdom of God through the renewal of the heart and by practical transformation of social circumstances. The front line of the exodus is not emigration, but liberation through the transformation of the present. For in the present, where we always are, the powers of the past wrestle with the powers of the future, and fear and hope struggle for domination. By changing ourselves and the circumstances around us, by

anticipating the future God, we emigrate out of the past into the future."[29]

Yet although Moltmann may be right in his description of what generally occurs, his observations are not applicable to Haiti where, given the present political situation, it would be an over-simplification to expect a practical transformation of social circumstances through a renewal of hearts. It is much more complicated than that. Hence the mass exodus of citizens ought not to be condemned as a negative move, but must be understood as a device which could induce a serious re-examination of the image which Haiti projects on the international scene and an alleviation of some of the severe social conditions under which people live.

Fate within Vaudou

In the preceding section, we have established that people have in the past and do in the present act decisively in response to the politico-socio-economic situation in Haiti. But there are significant numbers of persons who do not find themselves impelled into action, but rather accept events with a sense of resignation. Surrounded as they are by situations of depression, many have adopted an almost totally negative attitude to life. There is the feeling that absolutely nothing can be done to bring about a radical change in their hopeless situation. A sort of dependency syndrome has developed whereby everything is left to fate. According to Harold Titus, fatalism

"is in part an emotional reaction growing out of the fact that man lives in a universe which far exceeds his power to understand and control. Fatalism is most prevalent

> in areas where hopeless misery exists without any effort
> to relieve it and in areas without advanced means of
> scientific and social control."[30]

Historical records tend to support this fact that social,
political or economic oppression force persons into developing
feelings of resignation. The slaves who were brought to the
Caribbean and the Americas wanted to maintain their African
identity, they wanted their freedom, they had no desire to
give up their culture. But when several attempts at bringing
about the desired changes in their condition, namely a series
of revolts, amounted to nothing, several of them trusted less
in the power or the efficacy of human effort.

There are some people who, in their desire to seek peaceful
coexistence, leave everything to the spirits. The conviction
among many vaudouisants is that their spirits will set things
right if there is corruption or oppression. So they sit back
and passively accept what they believe to be the wishes of the
spirits. Naturally, this may be interpreted as an act of faith,
namely implicit confidence in the powerful God, who is lord
of the spirits. But it may equally suggest that instead of
inspiring faith within people, these spirits act as agents of
fate and of political control. They bear a resemblance to the
ancestral spirits in Africa who are understood as working
together with human beings for the building of community. By
their very presence and participation in social and political
arrangements, they instil a great sense of patriotism, of

national pride and are seen to give approval to the status
quo. In fact, several political leaders in Haiti have exploited this position of immunity from spiritual critique and
judgment, and have threatened that the spirits would be avenged,
should anyone dare to incite a revolution against the established authority. One of the country's most popular leaders
of the past has been accused of having exploited this to his
own advantage.[31]

I now cite two incidents of my encounter with vaudou worshippers who would fit into the category of persons who adopt a
fatalistic approach to life.

Incident No. 1

In July of 1977 I had the opportunity of talking to a farmer
in a little village to the north of Haiti. A week prior to
this encounter, he had suffered a terrible loss. Three of
his five children had died, each one within the space of twenty-
four hours of the other's death. Since all of his children
had apparently been in good health, the explanation of their
sudden deaths was the retributive action of the farmer's _loa_
protecteur.[32] According to his story, he usually held a
portion of his garden in reserve for his loa protecteur.
Nothing had ever been cultivated in that particular spot
which he regarded as sacred. One day he decided that he would
act contrary to custom and he actually began cultivating the
sacred parcel of land. His loa intervened. (Here I am not

sure whether this intervention was in the form of a dream, or
through someone possessed by his loa.) His disrespectful deed
was condemned, and his loa promised that the punishment which
he was about to receive would be greater than he could bear.
No effort on his part could restore to life the three children.
He remained convinced that the dead trio was the outcome of an
act of vengeance wreaked upon him by his angry spirit.

From this incident, we may infer that in vaudou, many people
conceive of themselves as victims of fate. Yet even as we
observe in this incident the farmer's acceptance, with certain
resignation, of the lot which had been imposed upon him by his
loa, we detect also a type of faith. It is the faith that the
loas may be trusted to do whatever they consider to be just in
any given situation, regardless of how much pain and suffering
may be inflicted as a result. This is the sort of example
which we crave after within Christianity, for so often believers
are apt to lose their faith in God whenever they encounter
suffering and hardship in life.

Incident No. 2

The second incident is that of a visit which my wife and I had
paid to a home in the north of the country. We had known this
family through their teenaged daughter who used to be a member
of the youth fellowship. She described her parents as Catholics.[33] Our visit to her home had been paid about two days
before we were due to leave Haiti to proceed to our next

appointment with the Methodist Church in Great Britain. Throughout that visit, we noticed that although the atmosphere was
cordial, the girl's mother had been a bit tense. When our visit
came to an end and we bade the family our 'au revoirs' the
mother breathed a sigh of relief and made a confession to us.
All along she had been thinking that the purpose of our visit
had been to announce to the family that we would be taking away
their daughter. Consequently, she had been tense throughout
the conversation, dreading as she did, the moment of that
fateful announcement, which in fact never arrived. She admitted
that if indeed we had decided to take her daughter along, she
would be bound to accept this as her lot. She said to us that
in her life she had learned never to fight against that which
had been predestined by God and His spirits.

This story is suggestive of a belief in fate which vaudouisants
entertain. And yet, like the first incident quoted, this one
gives further support to the idea of a tremendous faith which
Haitians have in the God who is Lord of the spirits. Other
true-to-life incidents may be cited with the same result.
Paradoxical though it may seem, the fate which pervades Haitian
culture is in itself an expression of faith. Fertility is
another area which is controlled seemingly by fate, hence
childless wives hardly ever entertain the idea of consulting
the obstetrician or gynaecologist to determine the root cause
of their infertility. For one thing, there are not that many
doctors available to the masses of people in the rural areas,

so that even if the intention was there, to actually pursue it would be well nigh impossible. On the other hand, people so afflicted have such a tremendous depth of confidence in God, that if a cure is indeed possible, there would be no need for them to rush to the medically trained practitioner, but rather their God could be trusted to intervene.

An expression common among Haitians is "Si Bon Dieu vlé."[34] This is uttered whenever reference is being made to some future undertaking on the person's part. According to this line of thinking, individual effort will always be counter-productive unless it is God who wills it. Consequently, many live in fear that the spirits might be very displeased if one should dare to oppose or to change what has already been decreed. They feel duty bound to their loas. They fear that neglect of these spirits would result in sickness, crop-failure, death or some other misfortune. But although fear is a very real element in vaudou, it must not be thought of as the basic component of the vaudouisants motivation to worship. Laënnec Hurbon maintains that fear is not the cause but merely the result of a fatalistic streak in vaudou.[35] There are some truly religious attitudes within the context of vaudou ceremonies which are a permanent fixture and which constitute a solid base upon which to build any religion. For example, the attitude of complete submission to the will of God, which is often interpreted as sheer fatalism, is something which western Christianity craves for its faithful followers.

Deductions

From the foregoing it is possible for us to deduce that folk religion has so influenced Haitian society that there now exists a dualism. Diagramatically, it may be represented as follows:

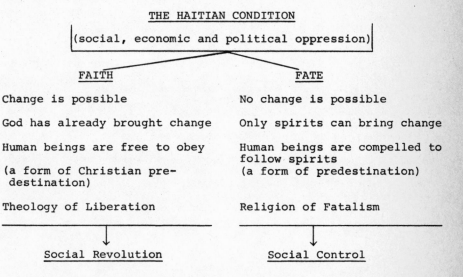

THE HAITIAN CONDITION
(social, economic and political oppression)

FAITH	FATE
Change is possible	No change is possible
God has already brought change	Only spirits can bring change
Human beings are free to obey	Human beings are compelled to follow spirits
(a form of Christian pre-destination)	(a form of predestination)
Theology of Liberation	Religion of Fatalism
↓	↓
Social Revolution	Social Control

On the one hand, there is a faithful stream which emerges. The visitor who arrives for the first time in Haiti cannot help but notice the tap-taps[36] which ply along the roads, displaying a variety of religious themes: La Sainte Vièrge, Le Regard Divin, Merci Seigneur, Dieu le Seul Espoir. The message which comes across is clear. These people recognize divinity within their midst. They are a people of faith. On the other hand, there is a fatalistic stream. This is undoubt= edly the result of too much preoccupation with the conditions of social, economic and political oppression which the population must endure. It is expressed in the fear of persons that they might be consciously or unconsciously disobeying the spiritual powers, or in the acceptance without question of undesirable conditions such as human infertility.

Faith and Fate, as the two operative principles within Haitian society, come to the forefront at different times. It may be said that sometimes the society appears to be dominated by the guidance of a positive faith which could culminate in revolution. At other times it seems that the society is being held within the grips of fate, thereby ensuring social control. Yet the element of fate which we find in folk religion must not be interpreted to mean absolute fatalism. W.C. Willoughby makes this observation about Bantu religion which contributed to the evolution of Haitian folk religion:

> "There is also something akin to fatalism in this faith.
> Accidents don't happen; congenial circumstances come from
> the favour of spirits, and unwelcome events from their
> wrath. Every occurrence is specifically ordained by
> unseen beings of some grade or other; spirits of the
> home and clan, earthbound spirits of wicked people,
> kinless spirits of more aboriginal races than one's own,
> spirits of the newly dead that have been enslaved by
> knavish neighbours, and spirits of things that may be
> called into play by anybody who knows how. Sagacity or
> fatuity, forethought or thriftlessness, idleness or
> industry, skill or clumsiness, is but as the small dust
> of the balance; the world is full of spirits, and the
> spirits send what they will to men. What they send
> depends more upon their character than upon that of the
> recipients. This is not quite the same thing as fatalism;
> for spirits can be influenced, according to their order,
> by punctilious conformity to custom, or by religious
> rites, or by redoubtable magic; but when piety is equated
> with prosperity and defined in terms of conventionality,
> fatalism draws perilously near. Fortunately, nobody
> quite conforms to this view of life; men are everywhere
> a bit bigger than their beliefs; but there is the belief."[3]

The conclusion which we must come to is that the Haitian brand of fate has engendered a positive outlook on life. I agree with the Reverend D. Alain Rocourt[38] as he expressed it in a conversation which we had on the subject of fatalism. He suggested that Haitians generally trust in Providence, or the beneficent care of God. Paradoxically though it may sound, theirs is a fate which is faith in a good God. Often Haitians may be overheard saying "Bon Dieu bon, oui!" ("Yes, God is good!") meaning that there can be only goodness emanating from this God. The goodness of God, used in this context, does not refer to a state of morality so much as it expresses the confidence that God will bring to pass whatever is to the individual's best advantage. Under extreme suffering the faithful individual does not sink into the depths of despair, but is hopeful that better days will come. Even if, from the point of view of lessening of physical pain, there are no better days, then the believer is still confident that there must be some positive or creative aspect to his or her suffering. The oft repeated phrase "Pa gin problem"[39] is a further indication of this positive outlook which Haitians have upon their seemingly hopeless situation.

All things considered, faith permeates the society. To the background of social, economic and political oppression, there is still heard the song of thankfulness and hope:

> "Thank you, good God
> For these things which nature has brought us
> Thank you, good God
> That misery's now ended for us

> Corn is sprouting
> Mushroom's growing
> Who were starving
> Will be eating
> Come, let us dance Congo
> Come, let us dance Petro
> Our Father God in heaven above
> Misery's ended for us, misery's ended for us
> Misery's ended.
> Thank you, good God, thank you, good God."[40]

Haitians are in a position to sing because they have the necessary survival equipment for their situation - faith! This faith has undoubtedly been one of the positive influences of folk religion upon the culture. In the next chapter, we will explore in greater depth the ways in which Christians and vaudouisants live out their faith in response to the needs of the Haitian community.

CHAPTER 4 - NOTES

1. Harold H. Titus, Living Issues in Philosophy, New York, Van Nostrand Reinhold Company, 1970, p. 539.

2. πίστις,-εως, ἡ 1. in active sense, faith, belief, trust, confidence, in NT always of religious faith in God or Christ or spiritual things. -G. Abbott-Smith, A Manual Greek Lexicon of the New Testament, Edinburgh, T. & T. Clark, 1964, p. 362.

3. F.F. Bruce, Commentary on the Epistle to the Hebrews, London, Marshall, Morgan & Scott, 1977, pp. 303, 304.

4. Ibid, p. 343.

5. For a full discussion on this, see Robert Campbell Roberts, Rudolf Bultmann's Theology: A Critical Interpretation, London, SPCK, 1977, pp. 285-325.

6. Rudolf Bultmann, Theology of the New Testament, I, II, trans. Kendrick Grobel, New York, Charles Scribner's Sons, 1951 & 1955, p. 315.

7. Ibid, p. 316.

8. Ibid, p. 317.

9. Robert Campbell Roberts, op. cit., p. 310.

10. Ibid, p. 318.

11. Karl Barth, Church Dogmatics, Vol. 1, Part 1, The Doctrine of the Word of God, Edinburgh, T. & T. Clark, 1969, p. 263.

12. Harold H. Titus, op. cit., p. 539.

13. In all fairness, Calvin is not to be completely blamed for the doctrine of absolute predestination. In fact, this doctrine is itself traceable to St. Augustine and Thomas Aquinas. But what Calvin was undoubtedly attempting to do was to emphasize God's initiative in the matter of salvation. Perhaps Calvin failed to communicate the idea that God's initiative does not exclude human initiative. What he succeeded in conveying was that Christ's reconciling work, through the Holy Spirit, is essential. Personal attributes on the part of the individual are of little importance.

14. John Macquarrie, Principles of Christian Theology, London, SCM, 1971, p. 303.

15. Ibid, p. 303.

16. John Wesley, Forty-Four Sermons, London, Epworth Press, 1946, p. 515.

17. Karl Barth, op. cit., p. 182.

18. Ibid, pp. 183, 184.

19. I am indebted to Rev. William Watty, President of the United Theological College of the West Indies, for discussing with me the interplay of faith and fate within folk religion. He has been of tremendous help in formulating and crystallizing these ideas about the dualism.

20. Chapter 1.

21. Of course in making this claim, we must note that there are certain critics of Haitian history who disagree with the idea of vaudou being influential in Haitian politics. cf. Harold Courlander and Rémy Bastien, Religion and Politics in Haiti. But theirs is a minority opinion. It is generally felt that part of the reason for the intolerant attitude of heads of State towards vaudou after independence was that these leaders knew of the religion's political potential.

22. Jurgen Moltmann, The Experiment Hope, London, SCM Press Ltd, 1975, p. 51.

23. In Chapter 6 we will be looking at the theology of liberation in greater detail.

24. J.G. Davies, Christians, Politics and Violent Revolution, London, SCM, 1976, p. 101.

25. Paulo Freire, Pedagogy of the Oppressed, translated by Myra Bergman Ramos, Great Britain, Penguin Books, 1977, pp. 25, 26.

26. C.L.R. James, The Black Jacobins, New York, Vintage Books, 1963, p. 357.

27. Jurgen Moltmann, op. cit., p. 143.

28. G. Gutierrez; "Liberation Praxis and Christian Faith", in R. Gibellini, ed. Frontiers of Theology in Latin America, London, SCM, 1980, p. 16.

29. Jurgen Moltmann, op. cit., p. 59.

30. Harold H. Titus, op. cit., p. 187.

31. cf. Bernard Diederich & Al Burt, Papa Doc: Haiti and
     Its Dictator, Middlesex, Penguin Books Ltd, 1972,
     pp. 345-357.

32. Loa protecteur is the term for the protective spirit
     in vaudou. Its functions are similar to that of the
     guardian angel in Catholicism.

33. It is quite normal for Haitians to use the term "Catholic"
     to mean "vaudouisant". This is because of some of the
     parallels found in both religious systems, which we
     described in Chapter 2.

34. "Si Bon Dieu Vlé" is the Créole expression for the French
     "Si le Bon Dieu veut", i.e. "If God wills".

35. Laënnec Hurbon, Dieu dans le Vaudou Haitien, Paris,
     Payot, 1972, p. 165.

36. "Tap-tap" is a Créole expression meaning "very quickly".
     It is popularly used to refer to the brightly coloured
     and locally-built lorries and buses which are a means
     of public transport throughout the republic of Haiti.

37. W.C. Willoughby, The Soul of the Bantu, London, SCM,
     1928, pp. 434, 435.

38. Rev. Rocourt is the Director of the Department of Lay-
     Leadership Training for the Methodist Church in Haiti.
     The conversation referred to took place during a visit
     to Haiti in July 1980.

39. "Pa gin problem" is the Créole expression for the
     French "il n'y a pas de problèmes', i.e. "There's
     no problem".

40. This is a translation which I have done for a Haitian
     liturgical song made popular by the well-known group
     "Les Gitans":
          Mèsi bon Dieu
          Gadé tou sa la natu poté pou nou
          Mèsi bon Dieu
          Gadé ki jan la misè fini pou nou
          Mayi pousé
          Diondion levé
          Min tout moun ki grangou
          Pralé manjé
          An nou dansé Kongo
          An nou dansé Petro

Papa bon Dieu
Ki nan siel la mizè fini pou nou
Mizè ya fini pou nou, mizè ya fini pou nou
Mizè ya fini, Mèsi Bon Dieu, mèsi Bon Dieu."

CHAPTER 5

CHURCH AND COMMUNITY

The Church is the Body of Christ. If it is to be true to that title, then it must not exist for itself. It must serve the community in which it is placed. Christ described Himself as having come "not to be served, but to serve."[1] His presence is all the more real when the Church addresses itself to the particular needs of the community - hunger, thirst, loneliness, nakedness, sickness, political injustice - "As you did it to one of the least of these, you did it to me."[2]

> "Much has been written about 'the Servant Church'. In practice many have interpreted this as the Church working for the world, that is, the Church being the humble, uncomplaining and unpaid servant of the world which presents itself as customer, client or boss. The servant ministry of Jesus was otherwise. He was servant to all but none were his bosses or his customers. He came to work with us. He is Emmanuel which means 'God is with us'."[3]

For the Church to serve most effectively, it must know the community inside out.

The Haitian Community and The Church

As we already said both in the Introduction and in chapter 1 the Haitian community is a predominantly rural one. About eighty percent of the population live in the countryside, where they remain vulnerable to an endless number of problems - overpopulation, poor housing, poor sanitation, drought, crop failure, soil infertility, hurricanes, malnutrition, disease, inadequate medical facilities, insufficient educational opportunities, poor communication systems, absence of proper social services. As a Third World country, it ranks among the poorest, receiving external aid to the tune of 110 million U.S. dollars. This represents 46 percent of the country's total budget. The average annual per capita income has been estimated at 100 U.S. dollars.

Ever since March 28, 1860 when the famous Concordat had been concluded between Pope Pius IX and President Geffrard, Haiti has remained a predominantly Roman Catholic country. The State continues to grant to Roman Catholicism privileges which are not automatically enjoyed by Protestantism. Upon his ordination, a Catholic priest is accepted as assermenté, which gives him the right, among other things, to celebrate marriages which are simultaneously religious and legal. His Protestant counterpart must sit an examination in order to be registered as a marriage officer. It is usually at a Roman Catholic Church that important government functions necessitating Christian blessing will take place. The President of the Republic, Jean-Claude Duvalier got married in 1980 at the huge Catholic Cathedral in Port-au-Prince. So prestigious is the State religion

Chart 5.1

Catholics	70.0%
Vaudou	20.2%
Protestants	9.8%

Religion in Haiti - General

that it is no surprise that it is embraced by 70 percent of the total population. (See Chart 5.1) Vaudou is estimated at 20.2 percent. Its actual strength may not be as modest as shown in these statistics.[4] There had been in the past so much persecution meted out to Vaudou, that people were wondering whether it was really beneath their dignity as human beings to practise it. For fear of being ridiculed some vaudouisants proclaim themselves Catholics.

Chart 5.2

Pentecostals	36.84%
Baptists	26.33%
Methodists	13.15%
Adventists	5.26%
Anglicans	2.63%
Others	15.79%

Religion in Haiti - Breakdown of
Protestant Groups

Protestantism continues to grow in Haiti. One estimate claims that by the mid-eighties, the figure will increase from 9.8 percent to 15 percent and that by the end of the eighties it will be 20 percent.

There are more than 250 Protestant missions operating in Haiti. The Pentecostals are the largest such group (Chart 5.2). These include the Church of God, Church of God in Christ, Church of God of the Apostolic Faith, and the Assemblies of God. The Baptist Church is strong, particularly because American Baptist Mission Societies took a special interest in the country during and after the American Occupation (1915-34). Among those present

are the Independent Baptist, Evangelical Baptist, Conservative
Baptist, Ebenezer Evangelical Baptist, and Jamaica Baptist
Missionary Society. Methodism includes the Methodist Church
of Haiti, Wesleyan, Haitian Union Methodist Episcopal, African
Methodist Episcopal and Free Methodist. The Adventist and
Anglican Churches are by comparison smaller bodies. In the
chart, 'Others' refers to religious organisations such as the
Un-evangelised Fields Mission, Holiness Faith Mission, Naza-
rene Church, Maranatha, Salvation Army, Jehovah Witnesses and
Reorganised Church of Latter Day Saints. Indeed there is an
abundance of religion in Haiti. To deal with the total
religious picture would be a monumental task.[5]

The Church - and here I use the word broadly to mean the ecumenical Church - sees its service mainly in terms of development which is the most obvious need of the Haitian community.
Poverty is a way of life for thousands. Some literally starve
to death, not having had the material resources necessary to
provide themselves with food, shelter and clothing. Church
congregations often function as social welfare agencies,
making handouts available to the less fortunate. Whenever
people are beset with serious financial crises, occasioned by
the illness of a child or by death within the family, they
wend their way to the priest or pastor seeking a way out of
their predicament. This is a situation open to abuse in that
some who are not deserving receive assistance. The Church,
however, is convinced that isolated instances of exploitation

should not deter it from providing a service which is genuinely needed.

The Church has responded remarkably well to the educational needs of the community. It ably supplements the work of government in this sphere. The school enrolment rate is 40 percent of the school-age population. The drop-out rate is 50 percent at primary level.[6] Catholic and Protestant Churches can boast of hundreds of day schools providing an education for the country's youth. The Methodist Church of Haiti, which has 115 congregations, is responsible for 52 schools serving a total of 6500 pupils. Many of these schools have had very humble beginnings such as under a tree or in somebody's backyard. With the help of charitable organisations such as Church World Service, Oxfam and World Vision Interntional, these schools provide children with a hot meal, books, clothes and medical care. Such items cannot easily be provided by the masses of impoverished parents. Education for adults is offered through adult literacy programmes (cours d'alphabetisation). One benefit which accures to the Church is that more of its worshippers are able to read the Bible and follow the hymns in the hymnals. But the functional aspect extends into community life. The farmer learns to read scales or to make proper use of the instruments he will need for levelling his land and for combatting soil erosion. The housewife learns to read a tape measure which ensures her taking proper measurements for making the family's clothes.

Hygiene, Agriculture, Farming and Domestic Economy are common
lecture topics during cours d'alphabetisation. It is in such
a way that rural folk are liberated from ignorance to become
capable of participating sensibly in the development of their
community. The manner in which teachers are trained for service in the rural community reflects the Church's deep commitment to development. At one training institution, the Centre
Pédagogique Rural Protestant located at Frères, near Pétionville, the students are exposed not only to courses that
relate directly to teaching skills, but to the practical
sciences of agriculture, farming and animal husbandry. Male
and female trainee-teachers alike invest much time, during
their three years' preparation, in tilling the soil and taking
care of poultry, pigs, goats and cows.

Health constitutes another aspect of the Church's involvement
in development. 50 percent of children die before reaching
the age of 4. 80 percent of children under six years of age
have malaria, or are vulnerable to other diseases - diarrhoea,
pneumonia, tuberculosis, typhoid and tetanus. Life expectancy,
though statistically given as 52 years, is probably 40. There
is one doctor for every 15,000 residents.

> "As a result of these conditions, the blood of sur-
> viving Haitians is among the richest in the world
> in antibodies, which accounts for a thriving trade
> in blood, organised by the Minister of the Interior,
> in collaboration with three American pharmaceutical
> laboratories - Armour Pharmaceutical, Laboratories
> Cutter and Dow Chemical.

> "There is a permanent reserve of 6,000 donors who

give blood every week for a monthly salary of
12 dollars. Voluntary donors receive 3 dollars
per litre. Each month, five tons of blood are
shipped to the USA."[7]

Some churches have built hospitals, though the majority have
opted for health centres, dispensaries and mobile clinics.
Obviously the latter are more beneficial to people who would
normally have to travel far, on foot, from their hilly communities to the nearby town hospital for medical tratment. These
smaller health units are staffed by the minimum number of
medically qualified personnel, the vast majority having been
trained on the job. This demonstrates that health is not just
something for the professional.   It is the responsibility
of the entire community. This is the reason for which health
centres often invite the people of the community to attend
hygiene lessons and nutrition classes which have been organized
for their benefit.

Development in Haiti has always been done with a view to
improving the urban areas. Governments have concentrated on
Port-au-Prince, the capital, because this is where the tourist
planes and boats stop regularly. If a poor impression is given
to foreign visitors upon their arrival, then this could mean
a recession of the country's tourist trade. As a means of
participation in the liberation of those that are oppressed, the
Church is constantly reaching out to the rural areas, impoverished as they have been through drought, deforestation and

the absence of good roads. It attempts to work, not _for_ the
rural folk, but _with_ them, digging artesian wells, building
water storage cisterns, constructing roads, planting trees,
experimenting with new techniques of farming and agriculture,
setting up workshops and co-operative societies. Although
Church action has inspired thousands to accept Jesus Christ,
the motivation is not securing converts. Empire building is
alien to the thinking of most of these Christian denominations.
The Methodist Church of Haiti, for example, has a numerical
strength of 13,000 although its programmes serve an estimated
rural population of 100,000. This same church, for example,
made it clear in a statement approved by its January 1978
Synod, that it participates in development simply because
God is calling His Church to liberate the Haitian from those
forces which prevent the full development of his or her potential as a child of God:

> "1.-L'Eglise Méthodist d'Haiti déclare sa foi en
> la volonté de Dieu de libérer l'homme Haïtien
> des entraves qui l'empêchent de réaliser toutes
> ses potentialités d'enfant de Dieu. Elle
> croit fermement aussi que la mission que Dieu
> lui a confiée, aussi bien qu'à d'autres, c'est,
> en suivant les directives de son Esprit et les pres-
> criptions du message de la Parole Vivante et
> écrite, de travailler de toutes ses forces à
> cette libération pour une promotion spirituelle,
> morale et matérielle de toute la communauté dans
> la justice et l'amour.

> "2.-L'Eglie c'est le rassemblement du peuple de Dieu
> en marche vers la plénitude du "Royaume". Cette
> marche exige une participation de tous et de
> chacun pour la libération intégrale, individuelle
> et collective car le plan initial de Dieu, qui
> avait pour but le bonheur de l'homme, a été
> contrarié par le péché.

L'incorporation de l'homme dans l'Eglise entraine
par voie de conséquence son engagement dans le
combat contre le péché sous toutes ses formes y
compris l'injustice sociale, économique et
politique, l'exploitation de l'homme par l'homme,
l'ignorance et toutes les misères qui sont causes ou
conséquences du péché.

"3.-Le développement est pour nous un ensemble de tâches
interférentes à partir des besoins réels de l'in-
dividu et de la communauté. Il concerne non seule-
ment ses besoins "élémentaires" (nourriture-travail
-habitat) mais comprend également la liberté d'expression et le droit de s'exprimer et de recevoir
des idées et des impulsions, de participer à la
formation de sa propre existence et de contribuer,
à déterminer l'avenir de la communauté haïtienne
au fur et à mesure de sa prise de conscience des
causes de tout ce qui déshumanise sa vie, de leurs
conséquences et de leur interrelation. La
participation de l'Eglise au développement se
situe pour nous non pas spécifiquement au niveau
des "techniques" mais plus fondamentalement au
niveau de la conscience de l'homme, de sa motivation
et de sa participation effective au développement.

"4.-C'est au nom de sa Foi en un Dieu Père, en Jésus-
Christ pleinement Dieu et pleinement Homme pro-
clamant la libération totale en l'Esprit, que le
Chrétien s'engage pour l'accomplissement d'une
action de libération tout en sachant que le
développement ne peut être que relatif puisque
sa Foi lui apprend que ce développement ne sera
intégral qu'avec le retour du Christ, prototype
de l'Homme Nouveau vers lequel nous devons
marcher."

This rationale is itself based on that prepared by an ecu-

menical body dedicated to development in Haiti.

It is clear that both Catholic and Protestant Churches are

heavily involved in rural development, working alongside

non-church organizations to bring about the liberation of

Haiti from a state of misery and depression. The themes

of liberation and development will be looked at in much

broader contexts when we focus our attention, in Chapter 6,
upon the ingredients of theological speculation within the
Caribbean.

Vaudou and the Haitian Community

If the Church is working for individual as well as community
development, Vaudou is working particularly towards the former.
This is so because the latter presupposes access to considerable financial reserves, which the Church secures because
of its partnership with congregations in rich, developed
nations across the world. Vaudou is unable to undertake
community development projects because it is at one with the
dispossessed majority. Even as the Church renders service,
it must always be alert to the political implications of its
involvement in development. A Haitian friend of mine, Dr.
Charles Roumain, used to warn that the role of the Church is
not political but social and religious. As far as Vaudou is
concerned,

> "in addition to being functionally effective at the
> village level, it does not challenge the sovereignty
> of the state as do Catholicism and the more estab-
> lished Protestant faiths."[8]

It concentrates on providing the individual with an emotional
framework with which to cope with his immediate environment.

> "It is a religion tailored for the Haitian, geared to
> his life and spirit. It provides a structure of
> beliefs that explain the mysteries of life and
> death; rituals of thanksgiving, consolation, healing,
> and protection; sanction for social acts, such as
> marriage; a sense of communion; a spiritual identi-
> fication. It channels pleasure rather than curbs
> it. In it there is a primitive release and

> purgative from heavy hearts rather than the
> accumulation of sin-inspired guilt. It has
> survived and grown as a working belief that
> acknowledges and deals liberally with the
> practicalities of a harsh life - food,
> shelter, sex, disease."[9]

What Vaudou has succeeded in doing for the rural Haitian is
to make him or her proud of self as a creature made in the
image of God. It has made the individual develop a love for
the folk culture which permeates life. This is something
which the majority of Protestant churches in Haiti have,
until now, proven themselves incapable of doing. Monseigneur
François Gayot, Bishop of Cap-Haitien, in a critique of
Roman Catholicism[10] has said that the Church used to see
traditional evangelism as giving to people a new culture
and stripping them of the old. The new was French, the old
Haitian. French culture had:

a system of communication	- French language
a system of family union	- Marriage
a system of religious expression	- Catholicism

Haitian culture had:

another system of communication	- Créole language
another system of family union	- Common-law
another system of religious expression	- Vaudou

During the anti-superstition campaign of 1941, there was a
very militant pastoral action aimed at repressing various aspects of Haitian culture. Eventually it became clear to the
Church that there must be a new pastoral orientation which

would foster social and cultural values. There must be the use of Créole, the language of the masses, for transmitting the religious message; acceptance of the drum in worship; awakening the laity to their responsibility.

In 1966, with the appointment of Haitian bishops, the Roman Catholic Church was becoming more indigenized. Today there are more folk masses which, in effect, constitute the people's offering of worship to God in their own culture. This is a step in the right direction. Protestantism, though, is more conservative in its approach to worship. The most popular hymnal, Chants d'Espérance, contains French hymns and a smaller collection of Créole hymns. The latter are merely translations of eighteenth century English hymns. There is a great need for hymns written by Haitians and using the bouncy rhythmic idioms of local music. The conservative nature of Protestant worship is partly due to a fear that in employing Haitian cultural idioms, converts won over from vaudou would revert to their former practices.

Worship expressions within vaudou incorporate music, dance, art, drama and other facets of the folk culture. In so doing a balance between the sacred and the secular is maintained. Whatever takes place during vaudou worship is in some way related to what people actually experience every day. Consequently, people find less difficulty in relating to vaudou than they do with Roman Catholicism and Protestantism.

One critic has given the following appraisal of vaudou:

> "If it has had more meaning to most Haitians
> than Christian doctrine, it is because Christianity
> has seemed to offer only doctrine and guidelines
> to behaviour, whereas vodoun offers doctrine,
> social controls, a pattern of family relations,
> direct communication with original forces, emotional
> release, dance, music, meaningful socializing,
> drama, theater, legend and folklore, motivation,
> alternatives to threatening dangers, individual
> initiatives through placation and invocation, treat-
> ment of ailments by means of herb lotions and
> rituals, protection of fields, fertility, and a
> continuing familiar relationship with the ancestors."[11]

This marriage between liturgy and life which we find in vaudou,
and which seems absent from the greater part of Christianity,
indicates a need for the Church to constantly re-examine its
theology as understood on Haitian soil. But it is not an
issue confined to Haiti. It is of crucial significance for
the future of Caribbean theology as a whole. We will devote
more time to this in the next chapter.

This happy relationship between liturgy and life is possible
within vaudou, because the houngans live among the people,
quite unlike the religious leaders of the main-line churches.
They tend to enjoy a lifestyle far removed from that of the
masses. The Roman Catholic priest's separation from his
people began when he had been accepted for seminary training.
Then, he had been required to sever ties with his family and
commence living as a celibate, espoused to the Church. At the
completion of theological training, he soon discovered that
seven years of institutional life had made him forget how to
live and work alongside men and women in the rural milieu.

Compare him with the houngan and there is a world of difference. The houngan has always maintained his links with the people whom he serves, hence he can understand better and relate more meaningfully to the people. All this suggests that the future of Caribbean theological education, in so far as it relates to the preparation of ministers and priests, must lie in the ability of seminaries to produce men and women who will no longer be middle-class or elitist in outlook, fit only to serve the structures created by a middle-class Church. But these seminarians will understand the needs, aspirations, the very pulse-beat of the poor who are a majority within the Caribbean. This is one aspect of the way forward which will be expanded in the final chapter of the thesis.

But let us turn now to yet another sphere in which vaudou seems to be issuing a challenge to the Christian faith.

Attitudes to Women

One of the ways in which Vaudou is more of a liberating force than Christianity is in its attitude to women. In Vaudou, women may become priests, in which case they are referred to as mambos. As

> "in West African religion, women priests are generally on the same level as men, and women devotees and mediums far outnumber the men. Christianity has not yet made sufficient use of women preachers and spiritual leaders."[12]

This accusation ought to be levelled particularly against those churches in the Caribbean whose origins are in the

European and North American continents. Indigenous Christian churches, like the Spiritual Baptists of Trinidad, have always accepted women as spiritual leaders. A male member of this denomination is content to describe himself as the spiritual son of Mother X. In vaudou, there is no prejudice against women being vested with spiritual authority because of the way vaudouisants understand divine revelation. We recall that the loas whom God sends may either be male or female. Whenever someone becomes possessed by one of these loas, he or she assumes the spirit's characteristics. It is quite normal for a man to become possessed by a female loa or for a woman to become possessed by a male loa. In vaudou, no monopoly of spiritual power is granted to either of the sexes. Has the Church anything to learn from this?

(a) To What extent is the traditional attitude to women in the churches theologically justified?[13]

One reason for the absence of women in spiritual authority within those Christian denominations which do exclude women from their ministry or priesthood comes from their exegesis of Scripture? We may think, for example, of the second account of Creation in Genesis (ch. 2:18-24) which states that woman has come out of the rib of man. The exegetes who would argue against women in the ministry will interpret this passage as a sign that women must be subservient to men, because God had ordained this from the very beginning. Men being dominant, there are certain privileges which they must

enjoy, but which their female counterparts cannot partake
of let alone enjoy. However the exegetes who are favourably
disposed to the priesthood of women will see differently,
namely that God's creation attests to the equality of men and
women. For an example of the latter type of exegesis, we are
well advised to consult the famous Behold the Rib sermon[14]
of the black preacher:

> "So God put Adam into a deep sleep
> And took out a bone, ah hah!
> And it is said that it was a rib.
> Behold the rib!
> A bone out of man's side.
> He put de man to sleep and made wo-man,
> And men and women been sleeping together ever since.
> Behold the rib!
> Brothers, if God
> Had taken dat bone out of man's head
> He would have meant for woman to rule, hah
> If he had taken a bone out of his foot,
> He would have meant for us to dominize and rule.
> He could have made her out of back-bone
> And then she would have been behind us.
> But, no, God Almighty, he took de bone out of his side
> So dat places de woman beside us;
> Hah! God knowed his own mind.
> Behold the rib!"

Of course, the inferior or subordinate status of woman is
not confined to an exegesis of the second account of creation.
Everywhere in the Hebrew Scriptures women are portrayed in
an inferior light.[15] There is the case of Lot who, in order
to protect his male guests, offers his two daughters to the
men of Sodom for them to do as they pleased (Gen. 19:8). There
is the judge Jephthah who willingly sacrifices his daughter
in order not to break a vow which he had made (Judges 11:29-40).

Elsewhere in the book of Judges, we read of women being compelled to satisfy the sexual desires of men, of women being killed and dismembered (Judges 19). In the books of the law, women do not fare any better. They are numbered among the chattel of men (Exodus 20:17; Deut. 5:21). If found guilty of fornication, the penalties meted out to them are often more severe than they would be for men (Deut. 22:13-21). In matters pertaining to divorce, they are treated as disposable commodities, hardly as persons who have rights (Deut. 24:1-4). Added to the foregoing is the fact that because of their regular menstrual periods, they are considered more unclean than men and therefore unfit to be priests (Levit. 15).

Another reason for the absence of women in spiritual authority is the argument about the maleness of God.[16] Some critics have looked at Genesis 1:27 and have drawn the conclusion that it is in man alone that the image of God may be reflected. If we look again at the verse in question, what do we see?

> "So God created man in his own image, in the
> image of God he created him; male and female he
> created them."

In the first part of the verse, man is used collectively to include both sexes. The Hebrew word אִישׁ does not just mean masculine man, but a range of meanings:"man, human being; one, anyone, each other."[17] In other words, it is a collective man. If this understanding of the collective nature of אִישׁ is not clear in the first part of the verse, then the second part of the verse spells it out, viz. male and female he created them.

Over against the argument about the maleness of God there are

passages of Scripture which reveal <u>female imagery about God</u>.

In Deuteronomy 32:18, God is a mother:

> "You were unmindful of the Rock that begot you
> and you forgot the God who gave you birth."

In Psalm 22:9-10, God is a midwife:

> "Yet thou art he who took me from the womb;
> thou didst keep me safe upon my mother's breasts.
> Upon thee was I cast from my birth,
> and since my mother bore me thou hast been my God."

In Isaiah 42:14, God is likened to a woman in travail:

> "For a long time I have held my peace,
> I have kept still and restrained myself;
> now I will cry out like a woman in travail,
> I will gasp and pant."

Of course in this particular verse, the pain of labour is not

as important as the end result, namely the actualization of

a new hope. This view is reflected in Dr. Frances Young's

comment that

> "the ensuing verses probably imply that this
> labour of God's is a labour to bring forth a new
> people, restoration, new life, new hope. It is
> interesting that elsewhere the Hebrew verb for
> a woman giving birth, and travailing in the
> process, is used of God bearing Israel and giving
> birth to his own people (Deut. 32:18)."[18]

A similar type of image of God as expressed in feminine

terms appears in Isaiah 46:3, 4, where we are presented with

a loving, caring mother:

> "Hearken to me, O house of Jacob,
> all the remnant of the house of Israel,
> who have been borne by me from your birth,
> carried from the womb;

> even to your old age I am He,
> and to grey hairs I will carry you.
> I have made, and I will bear;
> I will carry and will save."

We note that in the New Testament, Jesus also made use of female imagery. He says, for example:

> "How often would I have gathered your children together as a hen gathers her brood under her wings." (Luke 13:34; Matthew 23:37)

So there are passages which suggest that it is not only the male, but also the female who is able to reflect the divine image. In spite of this, there is no Biblical precedent for ordaining women to the priesthood. The reason for this glaring omission is cultural, rather than theological. One has got to understand the context in which the ancient Israelites presumably formulated their ideas of a male dominated priesthood. They did it as a reaction against the religion of Canaan. In the Baalist cult of the Canaanite religion, there were the sanctuary prostitutes or "consecrated women". The original intention had been that these women who involved themselves in the fertility rites of nature religions were to partner the god in his work. The rationale had therefore been a sacred one, and this was understood by the Canaanites. But the Israelites, looking on as outsiders to Canaanite culture interpreted sanctuary prostitution as an immoral institution. In fact there is a severe warning given in the law books, that

> "there shall be no cult prostitute of the daughters of Israel." (Deut. 23:17)

In Hosea too, sanctuary priests are an abomination (Hosea 4:
12-14).

It would have seemed that the responsibility of Yahweh's
people lay in avoiding any confusion between their worship,
and the worship of local Canaanite religions. Hence the Israelites were doing all in their power to distance themselves
from the Baalist cult. They reasoned that to include women as
priests would, in their cultural context, be counter productive. Today the Roman Catholic Church has continued the
practice of debarring women from the priesthood with no regard for the fact that this attitude cannot be theologically
justified.

Many persons who oppose the ordination of women state rather
glibly that Jesus did not choose women to be His disciples.
Yet their argument is not extended to include criteria other
than sex. If, for example, ethnicity was cited, then this
would undoubtedly deter the vast majority of the world's
population from ever becoming priests. I think it is important for us to see this as a cultural issue, rather than a
strictly theological one. In the world of the New Testament,
there had been cultural restrictions imposed upon women,
so that although they could perform certain roles just as
competently as men, seldom were they allowed to hold positions
of absolute authority. And yet, we must not forget that they
did play a significant role.[19] The Incarnation was made

possible through a woman, the Virgin Mary. Jesus often sought rejuvenation at the home of Mary and Martha (Luke 10:38-42). In the account of the crucifixion women are the ones who remain loyal whereas the all-male disciples forsook Him and fled. The first to receive the good news about the resurrection were the women who had gone to the tomb to anoint the Lord's body (Luke 24:1-12). Just as the apostle Paul defends his apostleship[20] with the claim that its authenticity springs from his having experienced the Risen Lord and having received the commission to preach the Gospel, so too is it true that women have also fulfilled these criteria for apostleship. Women were present in the life and witness of the Early Church.[21] This was in fulfilment of prophecy, for at Pentecost, they also received the Spirit.[22] Phoebe, of whom we read in Romans[23] probably belonged to an order of deaconesses. During his third missionary journey, Paul encountered at Caesarea four unmarried women who prophesied.[24] There appears also to have been an order of widows, judging from a passage in a letter to Timothy.[25]

As mentioned above, although women perform an active ministry in the New Testament, there is no precedent for the ordination of women to the priesthood. Paul's teaching on the subject of women's involvement in church life is not always clear. On the one hand we hear him handing out instructions that women who pray and prophesy must do so with their heads covered,[26] while on the other hand he forbids women to preach and pro-

phesy in public.[27] They are to remain silent in the churches.
When Paul spoke about "oneness in Christ"[28] he was not implying
"sameness". Rather he was trying to show that in Christ,
there ought to be no difference in the value or worth of
individuals, even though the roles which each performed were
different. As far as Paul is concerned, therefore, no
distinct words of support are found for the ordination of
women.

We have already established that the male-dominated priesthood
model emerged out of cultural contexts. It may equally be
argued that on general Biblical grounds there is no support
even for the structural model of priesthood as obtains, for
example, within the Roman Catholic tradition. According to
Dr. Mary Hall, holder of the Roman Catholic lectureship at
the Selly Oak Colleges, Birmingham,

> "The understanding of priesthood as a canonical,
> hierarchical state with exclusive access to
> sacramental ministry is not found in Scripture.
> It is a later development in the history of
> the Church. It was not established before the
> end of the first century or the beginning of the
> second century. The responsibility for
> ministry,or service, was shared by various groups
> within the community."[29]

If the Roman Catholic Church has been prepared to accept a
model of priesthood which certainly evolved later than New
Testament times, presumably under the guidance of the Holy
Spirit, then why must not this Church accept that there is
other guidance being offered today? Why is there such re-
luctance on their part to be guided by current movements for

the liberation of women and the granting of equal rights to
them? Should not one see in this the work of the Holy Spirit?
Is not this Spirit pointing to the need for more sectors of
the Christian Church to entrust women with spiritual authority?

The answer to the questions outlined above lies in the tendency, particularly of Anglo-Catholic and Roman-Catholic
churches, to narrow the scope of Spiritual revelation to the
Bible and Tradition. However, as we already argued in chapter 2, we do God an injustice when we try to limit His
revelation to confined structures and not allow Him the freedom to speak through the world's cultures. The Church must
sincerely believe that God continues to reveal Himself in the
world. It must trust the Spirit to lead it into new ways of
doing things. It must be willing to respond creatively to
the situations in which it finds itself.

(b) Does Haiti challenge the Church to re-assess its
     attitudes to women?

In Haitian society, where it is very obvious that women can
and do exercise spiritual authority, the Church must be
prepared to seriously entertain the idea of female priests.
One has merely to look at the number of women who have been
enlisted in religious orders in comparison to the number of
priests (Chart 5.3). There is always twice the number of women
to men. This was the picture in 1977 if one were to make an
inspection of all the seven geographical areas into which the

Chart 5.3

	Priests	Religious Srs.
Port-au-Prince	140	358
Cap-Haitien	86	176
Hinche	17	44
Jérémie	23	39
Cayes	76	133
Gonaives	32	66
Port-de-Paix	24	44
	398	860

Distribution of Roman Catholic Priests

and Sisters - Haiti 1977

work of the Roman Catholic Church may be divided.[30]

We notice that the trend of more women to men continues throughout the years. (Chart 5.4)

Chart 5.4

Year	Priests	Religious Sisters	Year	Priests	Religious Sisters
1970	382	804	1974	382	796
1971	391	799	1975	403	828
1972	419	792	1976	404	835
1973	392	775	1977	398	860

Roman Catholic Priests and Sisters in Haiti - 1970 to 1977

Chart 5.5

Year	Communicant Members			Adherents
	Male	Female	Total	
1975/76	1492	2338	3830	5231
1976/77	1625	2558	4183	10203
1977/78	1552	2740	4292	11125
1978/79	1650	2949	4599	12197

Membership of the Methodist Church of Haiti, 1975-1979

Within Protestantism the same is true that there is a majority of women, indicating a tremendous amount of leadership potential among them. In the figures obtainable for the Methodist Church of Haiti[31] (See Chart 5.5) the women far outnumber the menfolk. It is a pity that the figures comparing male and female are given only in the cases of those who are communicant members. The adherents, or those who are attached to the church, but do not yet receive the sacrament of the Lord's Supper,[32] are far more numerous. If the figures were available, then it is almost certain that these would reveal the general trend of female domination. However, Protestantism in Haiti allows women to enter into the ranks of spiritual authority whereby they may serve as ministers of the Gospel and as deaconesses. This is still not the case with Catholicism, which until today has closed the doors of priesthood to women.

It is rather shocking that this prejudice against women should
prevail within a Caribbean cultural context, because within
Caribbean culture women are not inferior beings, except within
the Church. In other words, they are powerful, wielding as
they do tremendous influence in the household. In fact,
sociologists cite the Caribbean as an example of where the male
figure is marginal to the life of the home or the domestic
arrangements of the family.[33] The absence of the father-
figure may be due to the fact that he spends most of his time
socialising with his male friends rather than at home with
his wife and children. In extreme cases, such as one-parent
families, it is the mother who may be present. Consequently,
when one talks about God, it seems more reasonable to speak
of the motherhood of God, for this is the true image reflecting love and concern. Naturally one accepts the father-
hood of God concept as an ideal, perhaps one to which all
earthly fathers must aspire. Yet, surrounded as the Caribbean person is, by loving mothers and grandmothers, it seems
a shame not to capitalize on the motherhood image in impar-
ting theological concepts to the society.

Of course, in arguing for greater usage of female imageries
about God, we must be aware that whatever the imagery, there
will still be weaknesses. In this connection, it is interesting to note what one feminist theologian has to say.
Mary Daly comments as follows:

"Why indeed must 'God' be a noun? Why not a verb
- the most active and dynamic of all? Hasn't the
naming of 'God' as a noun been an act of murdering
that dynamic Verb? And isn't the Verb infinitely
more personal than a mere static noun? The an-
thropomorphic symbols for God may be intended to
convey personality, but they fail to convey that
God is Be-ing. Women now who are experiencing the
shock of nonbeing and the surge of self-affirmation
against this are inclined to perceive transcendence
as the Verb in which we participate - live, move, and
have our being."[34]

What in Vaudou is accepted as commonplace, namely the priestly

role of women, is something which numerous churches through-

out the world are now struggling to come to terms with. There

have been concerted efforts by the World Council of Churches[35]

to facilitate dialogue in this direction. To this day, the

ordination of women

"constitutes one of the biggest hurdles to the
unity envisaged by the ecumenical movement."[36]

It is hoped that as the dialogue continues, God may reveal to

His entire Church, as He has certainly done within Vaudou, that

women are to take their rightful place alongside men in giving

spiritual direction to His people.

Health and Wholeness

If vaudou summons the Church to a serious reappraisal of its

attitude to women, it is equally challenging through its

approach to health and wholeness. We said earlier on that

vaudou is not involved in promoting comprehensive health

development schemes. Its effectiveness on the level of com-

munity development is seen only in so far as it provides the

individual with an emotional framework within which to cope
with his/her immediate environment.

In the following section, let us say more about how vaudou is
involved in health care, after which we will deal with its
implications for the Church.

(a) Indigenous Therapy

Vaudouisants believe that their loas have the power to inflict
and to prevent sickness, hence prayers are always offered on
behalf of those afflicted. Some types of illness necessitate
the wearing of charms. Some will require a ritual bush bath.
Quite common, too, is the belief in the cathartic effect of
the mud bath, which is specially indulged in on the feast-day
of Saint James (Fête de St. Jacques). There are certain cases
for which anointing with oil is prescribed. As we already
pointed out in an earlier chapter, exorcisms are conducted
in order to treat cases of demon possession and mental illness.
When placed alongside the various modern methods of medical
care in the west, some of the vaudou remedies may seem absurd,
or far-fetched. Yet we must remember that in times past some
similarly absurd methods had been employed with good effect.
We will refer to this later on as we survey healing in the
time of the Ante-Nicene fathers and doctors of the first few
centuries. We may mention that mud had been used by Jesus to
heal a blind man.[37] It is not unrelated to note that today
mud is finding its way onto commercial shelves in cosmetic form.

We mentioned, in chapter 2, that the training for a houngan
includes a study of leaves, plants and their medicinal properties. He must also be familiar with the use of holy water,
anointing with oil and the part which they play in the healing
process. He must equally be able to distinguish between
natural and physical ailments requiring herbal treatment, and
unnatural or spiritual ailments which warrant ritual treatment.
In other words, the houngan makes proper use of traditional
medicine.

> "Traditional - or indigenous or folk - medicine is the
> sum of knowledge and practices, based on practical
> experience and observation, which have been handed
> down from generation to generation. Traditional
> healers may use medicines made from local plants,
> minerals or animal substances. They may use
> sacrifices and purifying rituals of a religious
> nature. All these procedures reflect the beliefs
> and attitudes of their community about what causes
> illness and how to prevent it, and about what being
> healthy means."[38]

The houngan, by virtue of his training, knows all the elements of healing which are natural to the immediate environment. When we consider that the drug used by houngans and
bokors to zombify people (as discussed in chapter 2) has
awakened the curiosity of western medical scientists who are
aware of its potential for open heart and brain surgical
operations, then we realize that the approaches to health
care within vaudou may not be as absurd as they appear to
be on the surface.

In treating his patients, the houngan always takes seriously
their beliefs as to the causes of their illness. In folk

cultures, demon possession is commonly cited as the root
cause, and persons are apt to blame a particular person
for their state of ill health. Westerners very seldom take
persons from folk cultures seriously. They say:

> "Africans are neither obsessed by nor even,
> paradoxical though it may sound, possessed by
> spirits. The whole purpose of many possession
> cults is to prove that man can master the destiny
> spirits sought to impose upon him. The
> possessed do not aim so much at definitely
> throwing out the spirits by which they were
> initially seized against their will but rather
> at reaching the point where they are in full
> possession of their spirits. Though the African,
> like most men, can be overtaken by events at the
> outset, he is sufficiently resilient and resource-
> ful to eventually reassert control over the circum-
> stances which his spirits symbolize."[39]

This may be a way of explaining away illness caused by
"possession" but the houngan in Haiti knows only too well
that rationalization is no cure for what his patient is experiencing. In fact, t he houngan succeeds because he
seems to understand even better than the qualified medical
practitioner the human interplay whereby sickness might be
caused through psychological factors, breakdown in human
relationships, indeed through a series of complex factors.
Added to this is the fact that the houngan knows his limits
and is sufficiently humble and honest to refer to the pro-
fessionally trained those cases which are beyond him. Part
of this may be due to the fact that he dare not fail his
clientele, because his reputation depends upon the number of
cures he succeeds in bringing about.

> "If the medical profession is to accomplish any-
> thing in Haiti, it must begin by abandoning the

ancient prejudice against the houngan and re-
linquishing the melodramatic images of
'witch doctors'."[40]

In fact, as we shall see later on, there are some countries

which are making a conscious effort to view positively the

offerings of traditional medicine towards the health and

wholeness of communities and societies.

We turn now to look at some of the implications for the Church.

(b)   Healing in the Bible

Vaudou challenges the Church to take the world of the Old

Testament more seriously. This was a world in which abnor-

malities in life were the result of Yahweh's visitation.[41]

According to Dr. Philip Potter,

> "In the Old Testament sickness, disease and
> disabilities are regarded not merely as physical
> realities which are inevitable, but as the results
> of individual disobedience or, as in the case of
> Job, as the permitted work of the Adversary, the
> personification of the evil forces in the world.
> The Psalmist calls on the believer to bless the
> Lord 'who forgives all your iniquity, who heals
> all your diseases' (Ps. 103:3)."[42]

Sickness is also the result of corporate disobedience. The

prophets constantly remind the Israelite nation to return

to Yahweh in order that the nation may be restored to health

and wholeness. And not only is this applicable to Israel, but

to other nations as well. This may be illustrated in reference

to Isaiah[43] where

> "the earlier prophet Isaiah sees Egypt and
> Assyria, representatives of the world power,

as participating with Israel in God's healing
and blessing, thus bringing about the end of
war and oppression."[44]

Even though we may not agree with the Old Testament idea of
all illness being the result of human sinfulness, yet we
cannot lightly dismiss the idea that some types of illness
may be traceable to some spiritual causation, as we have
already discussed in Chapter 3. So too we have to recapture,
as they did in Old Testament times, and as they do within
Haitian vaudou, that sense of trust in God who is able to heal
all diseases. It is lamentable that more confidence seems to
be placed by Christians in western medical science than in
the God who is lord over all. But this point will be developed
later on.

Vaudou is also a challenge to the Church to take the ministry of healing much more seriously than it does at present.

"The gospels reveal an unquestioning tradition
that Christ's commission to the Church included
not simply the command to preach but also the
command to heal and, even more definitely, to
cast out demons."[45]

Mark's gospel states:

"And these signs will accompany those who believe:
in my name they will cast out demons; they will speak
in new tongues; they will pick up serpents, and
if they drink any deadly thing, it will not hurt them;
they will lay their hands on the sick, and they
will recover."[46]

In western cultures, where there is not a widespread belief
in demons, it may not be all that urgent for a ministry of
exorcism to be enforced. On this point, Don Cupitt and
G. W. H. Lampe have written:

"It is, we think, mistaken to suppose that loyalty
to Christ requires the Church to try to recreate,
in late twentieth-century Europe, the outlook and
practices of first-century Palestine. Such an
attempt invites ridicule, not to mention the
harm that may be done."[47]

And yet, such a ministry ought not to be completely dismissed

either. As we said in chapter 3, there is evidence that

spirit possession is real in England, so much so that some

churches have been offering to their pastors guidelines for

dealing with people believed to be demon-possessed. However,

where the Church exists within cultures that acknowledge the

existence of evil spiritual forces, it is a mistake for church

leaders to adopt the sceptical approach of the west. Rather,

the Church must follow the pattern set by vaudouisants and

wage the spiritual battle without fear.

The Church today must convince itself that it also is offered

by Christ the opportunity to share fully in the ministry of

healing. The disciples, and eventually the elders of the

Early Church, were convinced that they had been given this

authority by Jesus to heal. After all, in the case of the

disciples they had witnessed endless numbers of persons being

healed by their Lord and Master, sometimes by the imposition

of hands and at other times through the initiative of the

sick person in reaching out and touching His garment.

"The healing of the body and the forgiveness of
sins are one action and this action is based on
Jesus' will to heal and people's faith and trust
in him, their openness to him, their willingness
to be exposed to his judgment on what divides

them in themselves and from others. There is no
dualism between body and spirit. Healing means
the restoration of wholeness to the person and
restoration to the life of the community. Hence
Jesus' typical word to the healed is: 'Your faith
has saved you; go into peace' (Luke 8:48)."[48]

This he said to the woman who had had the flow of blood for

twelve years. To blind Bartimaeus, He said,

"Go your way; your faith has made you well." (Mark 10:52)

The oneness of bodily and spiritual health is mentioned by

Robert Lambourne:

"The common use of $\sigma\acute{\omega}\zeta\epsilon\iota\nu$ for salvation from
sin and from disease reaffirms the Hebraic view
of the close relation between sin and suffering
and between healing and salvation."[49]

Lambourne goes on to say:

"By the common usage of 'saved' for what faith
in Christ does for the sick man and for the
sinner the states of sin and redemption, sickness
and healing, are made to illuminate each other.
So a 'healthy' man is one who has been saved by
faith in Christ; he has been joined to him in a
life of obedience to the Father, love of all
men, self-sacrifice and suffering, joy and
crucifixion. Conversely a 'redeemed' man is
one who shares in Christ's reversal of the work
of Adam, whose flesh shares in the making of all
things new, the cosmological redemption, and
so can share physically and materially in what
Christ has done for mankind, whether through
anti-slavery legislation or antibiotic research
or the mercy of a home-help. The mutual
illumination of 'healing' and 'redemption',
'wholeness' and 'salvation' rests on historic
fact, the fact that there was in Palestine under
Christ, and there is in the world under Christ
today, a real relation between health and
redemption. But both our spiritual state and our
physical health share in the consequences that
follow from the fact that we live in the
times between Christ's having struck the decisive blow, and the final rounding up of all
the forces of evil."[50]

Whereas the faith of the individual is important for healing
or the forgiveness of sins, there are recorded incidents in
the ministry of Jesus where it was clearly the faith of others
which precipitated divine activity. At Capernaum there had
been the classic instance of the healing of a slave because
of his master's faith,[51] as well as the healing of a court
official's son.[52] So too the paralytic who had been let down
through the roof to the feet of Jesus and received healing
had been blessed on account of the faith of his friends.[53]

The therapeutic method of anointing[54] with oil in Ancient Near
Eastern times and common among pre-Christian Jews as a remedy
for fever and other illnesses, was also employed as a method
by certain sectors of the Early Church. Mark tells us that
the disciples themselves had healed many sick people in this
fashion.[55] In the Epistle of James, an admonition is given:

> "Is there anyone who is ill? He should send for
> the church elders, who will pray for him and rub
> olive oil on him in the name of the Lord."[56]

It is significant that anointing had been done 'in the name
of the Lord,' for Jesus is Himself the Messiah, the One anoin-
ted by God's Spirit, who shares His anointing with His followers.[57] Also significant is the follow-up in the following
verse:

> "and the prayer of faith will save the sick man,
> and the Lord will raise him up; and if he has
> committed sins, he will be forgiven."[58]

Apart from healing which may come about by God's grace
through the spiritual gift of faith, there is healing

brought about through a combination of forgiveness and prayer. We have already established the fact that in several parts of the Bible, sickness and sin are related. Although Jesus denied that this is a general rule[59] he did show, as in the case of the paralytic at Capernaum, that sometimes to ensure complete restoration to health, the person's sins must be forgiven. James's advice is:

> "Therefore confess your sins to one another, that you may be healed. The prayer of a righteous man has great power in its effects."[60]

In the Early Church, healing was the responsibility of the entire congregation. It was not left to the specialists. The epistle of James does not say that the 'elder' must be summoned to the sick person's bedside. It says 'elders'. The elders were acting on behalf of the entire Christian community. The problem is that down through the ages, the Church has always left the task of healing to individuals. Dr. Lambourne laments this excessive individualism, which has so gripped the Church that its healing model is an individualistic rather than a corporate one.[61] Gradually, such mistakes are being discovered:

> "Health and wholeness are now realised to be wider than the individual, and it is realised that there can be no perfect wholeness except within a perfectly whole society."[62]

Commenting on this same theme, John V. Taylor has written:

> "But although the gift of healing has been manifest in the life of the church, albeit spasmodically, throughout its history, for most of the time it has been avery different thing from the 'charisma'

which we see in the New Testament. The change,
I suggest, was due to the determined attempt to
institutionalize the Holy Spirit in the life of
the Church. Instead of being the creative Lord
and initiator of all the communal responses of
the church, he is treated as a thing - a force to
be manipulated, a fluence to be placed at the
disposal of bishops and priests and dispensed
sacramentally and in no other way."[63]

Let us spend some time now looking at how healing was ex-

perienced historically, as the Church moved out of the New

Testament era into post-Biblical times.

(c) Healing in the Post-Biblical Age

By all appearances, the Church was embarrassed by incidents

of healing which occurred after the New Testament era. They

were many and varied, a regular feature of the life of the

Church. Some of them were just as absurd as what we today

associate with healing activity in Haitian vaudou. Perhaps

it was for this reason that church historians have paid

attention to church councils, theological debates and creeds,

while deliberately stifling information about approaches to

health and wholeness. One writer who has done extensive

research on these veiled evidences of healing is Professor

Morton T. Kelsey, to whom I am indebted for most of what

follows in this section. He has shown that after the

apostolic period, the Church was active as a healing agent.[64]

In support of this, he has made use of the writings of many

of the well-known early fathers.

Quadratus, writing in second century Rome, testified to the
reality of physical healing in the lives of people. Justin
Martyr, also writing in the second century Rome, describes in
his Second Apology to The Roman Senate how exorcisms are
conducted in the Name of Jesus Christ. He rejoiced that the
charismatic gift of healing was being received and used to
good effect by Christians. Irenaeus, originally from Smyrna
but living in Gaul, gives out a plea in his Against Heresies
that Christians were healing people, not deceiving them. He
describes the healing of bodily infirmities and different
diseases, exorcisms and raising of the dead, this last one
having been made possible through the prayer and fasting of
a church. Irenaeus also remarks that no fee was charged by
Christians for these works of healing. Origen of Alexandria,
in his third century work Contra Celsus, mentions that Christians were expelling evil spirits and performing many cures.
According to him, even Greeks and barbarians who became
Christians, shared in these healing miracles wrought in the
name of Jesus. Origen also points out that demons were
expelled from the bodies of animals.

Cyprian, of third century Carthage in North Africa, speaks
in one of his letters about a serious illness which had been
cured by baptism. Tertullian, also of the third century, in
his protest to the North African proconsul against persecution, states that common people as well as men of great
rank (whose names he specified) were being forever delivered

from devils and healed of diseases. Theophilus of Antioch
refers to physical healing and the exorcism of demons. St.
Eugenia is reported to have healed, through prayer, a noble-
woman of Alexandria. Minucius Felix, who wrote about the end
of the second century, speaks of the exorcism of demons. So
too, Arnobius and Lactantius, who wrote at the beginning of
the fourth century, mention spiritual healing and acts of
exorcising demons.

Professor Kelsey makes the point that in order to bring about
cures, various methods had to be employed. These included
prayer, laying on of hands, oil, fasting, forgiveness of
sins, baptism, Communion, exorcism, sign of the cross. He
explains that healing and exorcism did not constitute functions
unique to the priesthood. Lay persons served as healers and
exorcists. Several of them banded themselves into lay orders.
The numbers had grown to such a tremendous amount in the fourth century that the order was abolished, as a result of which
the healing ministry had been narrowed down to include only
the ordained. Professor Kelsey is also careful to stress that
the manner in which the church faced persecution was in itself
a tribute to the very real healing ministry to which its
members had been committed;

> "For nearly three centuries this healing, centrally
> experienced, was an indispensable ingredient to
> Christian life. The same strengthening force was
> at work, not only in dealing with physical and
> mental disease, but in meeting persecution. The
> power, the same profound experience, was given to

> these men and women to meet agonizing death, often
> by slow degrees, without yielding to save themselves
> by repudiating Christianity. Thus the martyrs, too,
> stood as continuous evidence of a power able to
> strengthen them beyond normal expectations of human
> life, and of the Christian's relation to the source
> of that power."[65]

When, following the victory of Constantine and the Edict of

Milan in 313, the Church became accepted by the authorities,

hence no longer faced persecution, healing activities con-

tinued, but only to a minimum. The early doctors of the church

record acts of healing. Theirs was a Platonic view of the

world, in that they regarded the physical realm as being heavily

influenced by the spiritual. Spiritual healing was therefore

of importance to them. From the East there were at least five

persons concerned about healing. Athanasius (296-393) in wri-

ting about the desert monks spoke of healing as a gift given

by God through personal devotion to Christ. Basil the Great

(329-379) voiced his appreciation for spiritual healing as

well as healing through medical science. Gregory of Nyssa

(331?-396) described St. Macrina's healing of a child's eye

infection as well as the amazing deeds of Gregory Thaumatur-

gus. Gregory of Nazianzus (329?-389) was one whose healing

works were associated with dreams. John Chrysostom (345-407)

spoke of the healing of body and soul at the shrines of mar-

tyrs.

From the West there were at least six names which one could

easily cite as being interested in healing. Ambrose (340?-

397) lists the healing of a blind man, bringing a dead child back to life and the exercise of power over unclean spirits. Augustine (354-430) in his City of God records healing miracles which took place in his own diocese of Hippo Regius. When, for example, a shrine of St. Stephen had been placed in his church, several healings took place. It is recorded that Augustine himself became a healer nearing his death. Jerome (340-420) although he wrote about healing which took place in relation to other people, tended to treat it not as a real phenomenon, but as a symbolic act. Gregory the Great (b. 540) in his Book of Pastoral Rule implied that sickness is inflicted by God in order to correct individuals, or to chastise the faithful. Sulpitus Severus, writing about the same time as Gregory, gives accounts of the healing and the exorcisms effected by St. Martin of Tours. John Cassian, in his book Conferences discusses at length the question of the divine gift of healing. He considers healing to be demonstrative of the power of God. He warned that too much emphasis must not be placed upon body healing so that we forget the soul.

As the centuries progressed, and as there were changes in the world view as well as in the concept of God, people became increasingly sceptical about some of the miracles of healing which were reported. Lay persons were discouraged from engaging themselves in acts of healing. Only the priests, through sacramental acts, could do this. The therapeutic

act of anointing with oil, within the Catholic tradition,
soon lost its original significance. This was due, in no
small measure, to Jerome's translating of the word 'heal'
as 'save'. Consequently, it became extreme unction, a sacramental act of preparation for death, since now it had become
a tool of salvation, not of health. What was happening was
that the church leaders were claiming a monopoly over healing.
Even the medically trained were viewed with suspicion. There
was a widening rift between medical science and theology. The
church wanted sick people to confess, not to be treated by
physicians. The Roman Catholic Church had been so powerful
that

> "from 1566 on, to obtain a licence to practise
> medicine, doctors were required to swear that
> they would stop seeing a patient on the third
> day unless he had confessed his sins and had a
> statement signed by his confessor to show for
> it. The Roman Synod renewed this decree in
> 1725 with added penalties."[66]

Clearly the church was shifting its emphasis from healing
to forgiveness.

If Jerome contributed to the decline of the church's
interest in a healing ministry, so too did Thomas Aquinas.

> "Aquinas had no real place for religious
> healing in his systematic thought, and his
> basic ideas gradually gained acceptance
> among Protestant thinkers as well as
> Catholic theologians. It is impossible
> to understand the intellectual rejection
> of the healing ministry in modern times
> without following his reasoning closely."[67]

Yet in spite of those who sought to curb the healing activities of the Church, there still exists a long catalogue of names of persons who availed themselves of gifts of the Holy Spirit. Among them would be included Martin Luther, George Fox, John Wesley,[68] St. Francis Xavier and St. Vincent of Paul. The result of all this is that today there are conscious attempts being made by Christians to regain what seems to have been an art lost throughout the centuries, namely the art flowing from the spiritual gift of healing.[69]

(d)   Health - the People's Responsibility

The fact that in Haitian vaudou, health is seen as the responsibility of persons who are not as qualified as the western trained medical practitioners, indicates a truth which ought to be noted. It is that in any society, health care must not be left in the hands of the professionals. Rather, it is the people's responsibility. In the book, Health by the People[70] the importance of people-centred approach to health is highlighted. When health is seen as the responsibility of professionals, e.g. doctors only, then there is bound to be frustration, particularly in rural areas throughout the Third World, where the ratio of doctors is one to a thousand patients. However, when all participate - professionals, non-professionals, skilled, unskilled - when all see it as their responsibility, then there is hope for success.

Carroll Behrhorst's project in Guatemala[71] is a fine example
of a community health approach. The community itself takes
the responsibility for choosing those whom it wants to be
trained to take care of itself. So too, in the Aroles'
project in Jamkhed, India[72] it is the community which
selects its promising people for medical training. Some of
the persons selected may be illiterate, but they usually
show a willingness to learn and eventually emerge as capable
functionaries. Health care in the People's Republic of China
deserves special mention. When Mao-Tse-Tung and the Chinese
Communist Party assumed power in 1949, the ensuing Cultural
Revolution stressed, among other things, that

> "Chinese traditional medicine should be integrated
> with Western scientific medicine - that is, instead
> of competing, the practitioners of the two types of
> medical care should learn from each other.

> "Health work should be conducted with mass par-
> ticipation - that is, everyone in the society was
> to be encouraged to play an organized role in the
> protection of his own health and that of his
> neighbours."[73]

This type of approach to health was to produce those peasant
health-workers who came to be known as "barefoot doctors".
They evolved in the rural areas near Shanghai, and helped

> "to provide environmental sanitation, health
> education, preventive medicine, first aid, and
> primary medical care while continuing their
> farm work."[74]

These

> "barefoot doctors are encouraged to use a wide range
> of both traditional Chinese and Western medicines
> and some have become skilled enough to perform
> limited forms of major surgery."[75]

Vast successes are listed, for example, fewer deaths in babies
and young children.

> "Other achievements of the Chinese health care
> system include technical advances such as the
> treatment of widespread severe burns , the
> replantation of severed limbs, and - most
> recently - new uses of techniques derived from
> traditional Chinese medicine. These have
> included the employment of acupuncture to pro-
> duce hypalgesia during surgical procedures,
> thus avoiding the dangers to certain patients
> of general anaesthesia, and the study of
> a number of traditional herbal medicines in an
> attempt to isolate and identify active extracts
> and to determine their effectiveness using
> scientific criteria."[76]

One writer has given an evaluation of what has just been
outlined in the following manner:

> "The experience of China has shown that indigenous
> healers can be trained and integrated in the
> general health system. Indigenous systems of
> health care function among large populations in
> the developing world, and in some countries,
> such as India, the system is well established
> although unrecognized. Further integration
> of these indigenous practitioners - professionals,
> nonprofessionals, faith healers, magic healers
> - into the state system calls for more research
> and information."[77]

In the examples of Guatemala, India and China, and indeed in
a host of other countries - Cuba, Indonesia, Iran, Niger,
Tanzania, Venezuela - the message is the same. People
participation is crucial for the health of any community or
society. This ought to be the norm at all stages of health
care, preventive as well as curative. Dr. Philip Potter has
put forward the case for the latter as follows:

> "First we have been learning, especially through
> the Christian Medical Commission, that

the healing process involves the sick being enabled
to participate in the diagnosis of their disorder,
and in the responsibility for finding and carrying
out its cure. Only thus can they mobilize their
'life-force' for being healed. Too often have
people been left mystified and ignorant about what
is going on, and so the process of healing has been
impeded. Too often have they felt their situation
to be hopeless and have resigned themselves to their
fate in despair. By engaging people in facing up
to the real nature of their illness, they can be encouraged to have the will to be healed. This is
precisely what we have been learning in the ecumenical movement not only about persons but about
our societies."[78]

One village health care handbook has given the following six

rules[79] which are pertinent to what we have been saying:

1. Health care is not everyone's right, but
   everyone's responsibility.

2. Informed self-care should be the main goal
   of any health program or activity.

3. Ordinary people provided with clear, simple
   information can prevent and treat most
   common health problems in their own
   homes - earlier, cheaper, and often better
   than can doctors.

4. Medical knowledge should not be the guarded
   secret of a select few, but should be freely
   shared by everyone.

5. People with little formal education can be
   trusted as much as those with a lot. And
   they are just as smart.

6. Basic health care should not be delivered,
   but encouraged.

(e) Wholeness - An End to Compartmentalization

One obvious barrier to wholeness lies in the fact that

medical science and theology have for long existed in two

different compartments. And yet, they both contribute to
health. In fact, we may list fields other than medicine
and theology, which are usually placed in separate compartments, where they are not considered as having anything to
do with health. Dr. Michael Wilson has sounded a warning
about this tendency to compartmentalize.

"Health," he says, "is the wider context within
which medicine, teaching and politics are practised."[80]

He laments the narrow approach in which doctors may feel that
specialized knowledge about diseases means that they are
equipped as agents of health:

"Doctors are authoritative on the subject of illness,
but in matters of health carry the same authority
as, for example, teachers, mothers and environ-
mentalists."[81]

Commenting on the idea of general practitioners, he says:

"Because so much illness in the West is emotional,
and has family and social roots, it is questioned
whether our general practitioner should be pri-
marily a medical man trained in hospital medicine.
The need is for a man or woman with much more
social understanding who is well versed in human
behaviour; someone with a more general doctor/
nurse/social work type of training. It is possible
that the knowledge and skills required are too
great for an individual, and that the general
practitioner should be a troika of nurse, doctor
and social worker. Leadership would not necessarily
rest always with the doctor; this is a situation
derived from the clinical model of health.[82]

On the specific question of the compartmentalization of
medical science and theology, Dr. Wilson has said:

"Even a Christian mission hospital may fail to
preach a gospel relevant to the whole of life;
for unless the hospital can be seen to be part
of the life and good news of the local church-
community, unless priest and doctor on the
mission station are seen to be members of the

same 'Body', then the very work of curing the sick
may bring glory to Western technology, rather than
glory to the Lord of life."83

The existing dichotomy did not exist in the past.

"The cold estrangement between religion and science
is in fact a modern aberration for which both
religious people and scientists must be held
responsible and which has in effect created on
both sides a distorted view of man and an
inadequate understanding of both sickness
and health.84

Consequently, it is important that this breach between

medical science and theology be healed. Medical prac-

titioners and spiritual healers must be willing to collabo-

rate and in humility to acknowledge that all healing comes

from God.

"Divine healing is becoming a live issue
again in the churches after years of neglect and
we are discovering how much we depend on God
for our own health because of the way he has
made us total, integrated beings. We are
realizing that the same mystery out of which we
have been made, can break in upon our lives.
Perhaps we should see every act of healing,
whether by medical science or faith, as Divine
Healing. Perhaps if we recognize this more,
we could see even greater wonders in our daily
lives. God can, in various ways, break through
in health."85

Vaudou has helped the rural communities in Haiti to avoid

the dichotomy between the religious and the secular which

exists in secularist socieities. The houngan is one who

combines religion and science, one who, because his gifts

are so numerous, may best be described as a man of 'charisma'.

The Hebrew prophet of old used to be that sort of person.

He functioned as God's mouthpiece and at the same time he was

the guardian of the 'shalom' - health or well-being - of the
community. He was both prophet and healer. The increased
secularization of societies has resulted in increased
specialization, so that in the domain of health, different
people fulfil different aspects. The doctor, nurse, politician, policeman, teacher all address themselves to
specifically defined areas which, in the long run, contribute
to the "well-being" of the community. Just as health and
wholeness may be embodied in the houngan, so too the Church
must concentrate on the totality of the healing ministry.
A Methodist Statement on healing says:

> "The Church is called to be a community in which
> the constant, total healing work of the Holy
> Spirit is taught, sought and experienced. The
> Spirit of healing is present in the worship,
> sacraments, preaching, prayer, fellowship and
> pastoral and social ministry of the Church.
> This is its normal activity and all its members
> are called to be involved in it."86

The involvement of all members in the healing ministry of
the Church is of vital importance.

> "The Church's ministry of healing is in the
> world, and it is laymen and lay women who are
> most in touch with those who are in distress.
> They are at the frontier of the Church's work.
> Because so much medical work is secular, it is
> no answer to try to recover a ministry of
> healing centred upon the church building, or
> upon an ordained ministry, as if this could
> give us back the 'spiritual factor' that is
> missing. We must recover the sense of true
> ministry among lay people; and equip them for
> the Church's work where they already are - in
> the world."87

This consciousness of lay responsibility is growing more and more in Haiti. In rural communities, whenever people are sick, others rally round to express their concern. Prayer meetings are the norm and these take place in the homes of those afflicted, regardless of the presence of priest or ordained minister. Catholics, Protestants and Vaudouisants alike have taken this ministry of healing very seriously and this must be the dawning of a new day, a foretaste of things to come.

One word, though, still needs to be said about the clergy. The vaudou priest is able to exercise a healing ministry because of his training which has been geared towards this end. Christian priests and ministers need to receive similar preparation if indeed they and those over whom they will exercise spiritual leadership and guidance are to contribute to health and wholness within their communities. One writer has echoed the following sentiments:

> "We pray for the time when theological colleges
> will have chairs of Divine Healing. The occupant
> of that chair, instead of sharpening the intellects
> of students by hammering into them the theories
> and ideas of, say, Karl Heim, Rudolf Bultmann,
> Karl Barth, Soren Kierkegaard, Martin Heidegger,
> Oscar Cullmann, Karl Jaspers, Paul Tillich and
> all the rest of that galaxy of intellectual
> stars, familiarity with whose works may prove
> a mark of culture and theological erudition, will
> impart the Secret of the Kingdom of God which
> Jesus entrusted to His disciples. That Secret
> throws wide the "everlasting doors" of the
> personality for the entrance of that Holy Spirit
> and His power which Jesus promised."88

The principle of making theological students more aware of divine healing is a good one. I will, though, question the setting up of a "chair", because divine healing is not something which is taught. Our understanding of the Scriptures suggests that we are here dealing with a gift which is imparted by the Holy Spirit. So that the principle is laudable, but the chair concept is a fallacy.

Conclusion

The Church in Haiti, acting as the Body of Christ, is seeking to respond to the needs of a rural community beset with endless socio-economic problems. It considers itself called of God and guided by His Spirit to concentrate upon development. Its programmes in education, health and rural rehabilitation are expressions of this. It is equally true that apart from being seen in terms of improvement to the community, development is channelled towards the liberation of the individual from ignorance or other states of powerlessness which prevent the development of one's full potential as a being made in the image and likeness of God. The insights of Vaudou are not to be dismissed lightly. Its contribution to the liberation of women presents the Church with the challenge of rethinking its theology pertaining to the ordination of women. So too it offers insights into health and wholeness mainly because it successfully incorporates the sacred and secular into its system without compartmentalizing them. Finally, the fact that in Vaudou the spiritual leaders are so closely identified with the masses means that it has something to teach the Church about service. It is only when the Church, through its priests, ministers and people are closely associated with all levels of the community, can it be the incarnation of the Servant Christ, working, not _for_, but being Emmanuel, working _with_ God's people.

CHAPTER 5 - NOTES

1. Mark 10:45.

2. Matthew 25:40.

3. George Lovell, The Church and Community Development - An Introduction, London, Grail/Chester House Publications, 1972, p. 5.

4. These statistics are based on figures obtainable from the Département des Cultes, which acts on behalf of the Government Ministry having oversight of religious affairs in Haiti.

5. Considerable research into the history and practices of these denominations has been undertaken by the renowned Haitian scholar, Dr. C. Pressoir, Le protestantisme Haitien.

6. "The Hell that's Haiti" in Caribbean Contact, Vol. 9, no. 7, Barbados, November 1981, p. 4.

7. Ibid, p. 4.

8. R. P. Schaedel in Courlander and Bastien, Religion and Politics in Haiti, Washington DC, Institute for Cross Cultural Research, 1966, p. xv.

9. Bernard Diederich & Al Burt, Papa Doc - Haiti and Its Dictator, Middlesex, Penguin Books Ltd., 1972, pp. 349, 350.

10. François Gayot, Evangelisation and Development in Haiti.

11. Harold Courlander and Rémy Bastien, op. cit., p. 21.

12. G. Parrinder, West African Psychology, London, Lutterworth Press, 1951, p. 223.

13. For a brief but good introduction to the dilemma, see Phyllis Trible, "Feminist Hermeneutics and Biblical STudies" in The Christian Century, Vol. 99, no. 4, Chicago, Illinois, Feb. 3-10, 1982, pp. 116-118.

14. Langston Hughes and Arna Bontemps, eds. Book of Negro Folklore, New York, Dodd, Mead and Co., 1958, p. 234.

15. For a full account, see Phyllis Bird, "Images of Women in the Old Testament", in Rosemary Radford Ruether, ed., Religion and Sexism - Images of Woman in the Jewish

and Christian Traditions, New York, Simon and Schuster, 1974, pp. 41-88.

16. When the debate for the ordination of women to the Anglican priesthood got underway, opinions were expressed about the necessity of having presiding at the Lord's table only those who could represent the maleness of God. One critic scoffed at the idea of a pregnant woman priest ever officiating at the Eucharist, because this would be most "unsightly". Someone cynically remarked that some of the priests already have a pregnant look, yet this has never been proven to have detracted from a worshipful atmosphere.

17. Georg Fohrer, ed., Hebrew and Aramaic Dictionary of the Old Testament, London, SCM Press Ltd., 1973, p. 12.

18. Frances Young, Can these Dry Bones Live?, London, SCM Press Ltd., 1982, p. 48.

19. Cf. Constance F. Parvey, "The Theology and Leadership of Women in the New Testament" in Rosemary Radford Ruether, op. cit., pp. 117-149.

20. Galatians chapters 1 and 2.

21. Acts 1:14.

22. Acts 2:17, 18.

23. Romans 16:1.

24. Acts 21:9.

25. 1 Timothy 5:9-16.

26. 1 Corinthians 11:5.

27. 1 Corinthians 14:34, 35, and 1 Timothy 2:12.

28. Galatians 3:28.

29. Mary Hall, in a lecture on Ordination of Women delivered to Selly Oak Colleges' Students, February 1982.

30. Statistics from PRO MUNDI VITA - HAITI, 19/1980.

31. Statistics from Annual Synod Reports, Methodist Church of Haiti.

32. Many <u>adherents</u> have not yet become <u>communicant members</u> because they cannot read or write. Usually an oral examination precedes acceptance as candidates for Holy Communion and it is to be understood that hundreds of illiterates fail. Although this system has the virtue of highlighting how seriously Church membership is taken in Haiti, and how in the Haitian situation where the vaudouisant may be theologically in a muddle, the Christian is expected to be intellectually clear about the tenets of his faith, however, there are injustices within such a system. For one thing, it means that the only persons who will eventually become accepted as full members of the Church are those who by virtue of their education have entered into the framework of the middle classes. They are not the very poor. There are serious implications in this for a ministry to be carried out among the masses of God's people, who are poor. We will return to this issue in the final chapter, when we will be discussing the way forward for the Church.

33. For arguments in support of the matrifocal nature of Caribbean society, see Edith Clarke, <u>My Mother Who Fathered Me</u>, which is a study of the family in 3 selected communities in Jamaica. See also M. G. Smith, <u>West Indian Family Structure</u>, which records the findings of research done in 1953 and 1955 on homes in the islands of Carriacou, Grenada and Jamaica. In a large percentage of these homes, the fathers are absent, and even if present physically and acknowledged as titular head, they are still marginal. Hence the justification for the claim of matrifocality.
Some reject the idea of matrifocality. cf. L. Morris, <u>Women Without Men</u>, the British Journal of Sociology, vol. XXX, no. 3, September 1979, pp. 322-40. cf. also F. Henry and P. Wilson, <u>The Status of Women in Caribbean Societies - An Overview of their Social, Economic and Sexual Roles</u>, Social and Economic Studies, vol. 24, no. 2, June 1975. They claim that in the political, economic and social spheres, the man is dominant. However it still stands that the female figure is more powerful as an example of loving care.

34. Mary Daly, <u>Beyond God the Father</u>, Boston, Beacon Press, 1977, pp. 33, 34.

35. See Constance F. Parvey, ed., <u>Ordination of Women in Ecumenical Perspective</u>, Geneva, WCC, 1980. Cf. also Susannah Herzel, <u>A Voice for Women</u>, Geneva, Women in Church and Society, WCC, 1981.

36. Susannah Herzel, op. cit., p. 66.

37. John 9:1-12.

38. Jeanne Nemec, "Rediscovering an Ancient Resource - A New Look at Traditional Medicine", in Contact 58, Geneva, CMC, WCC, October 1980, p. 1.

39. "Obsession With Possession" in Pro Mundi Vita: Dossiers, July-August 1977.

40. Maya Deren, Divine Horsemen - The Living Gods of Haiti, London and New York, Thames & Hudson, 1953, p. 164.

41. For a development of this, see Morton T. Kelsey, Healing and Christianity, London, SCM Press Ltd., 1973, pp. 33-38.

42. Philip Potter, "Healing and Salvation" in The Ecumenical Review, Vol. 33, no. 4, Geneva, WCC, October 1981, p. 332.

43. Isaiah 19:22-25.

44. Philip Potter, op. cit., p. 332.

45. John V. Taylor, The Go Between God, London, SCM Press Ltd., 1972, p. 205.

46. Mark 16:17-18.

47. Don Cupitt, G. W. H. Lampe, "An Open Letter on Exorcism" in Explorations in Theology 6, London, SCM Press Ltd., 1979, p. 51.

48. Philip Potter, op. cit., p. 333.

49. R. A. Lambourne, Community, Church and Healing, London: Darton, Longman & Todd, 1963, p. 98.

50. Ibid, p. 101.

51. Matthew 8:1-13.

52. John 4:47-53.

53. Mark 2:1-12.

54. An in-depth study of anointing is currently being pursued by Mark Turner, "The Holy Spirit and the Sacraments", post-graduate research, University of Birmingham.

55. Mark 6:13.

56. James 5:14.

57. 2 Cor. 1:21; 1 John 2:20.

58. James 5:15.

59. See for example his words in reference to the man who had been born blind, in John 9:3.

60. James 5:16.

61. R. A. Lambourne, op. cit., pp. 124-143.

62. Ibid, p. 90.

63. John V. Taylor, op. cit., p. 208.

64. Morton T. Kelsey, op. cit., pp. 129-156.

65. Ibid, p. 154.

66. Ibid, p. 212.

67. Ibid, p. 213.

68. John Wesley's treatise on medicine was published in 1747, and reached its twentieth edition in 1781, and its thirty-sixth in 1840. For its contents, cf. William H. Paynter, ed., Primitive Physic. A Book of Old Fashioned Cures and Remedies, Plymouth, Parade Printing Works Ltd., 1970.

69. One interesting venture in this regard is the healing community, 'Burrswood' at Groombridge, near Tunbridge Wells in England. It is part of the Dorothy Kerin Trust. Dorothy Kerin had been miraculously healed of tuberculosis in 1912, following which she dedicated her life to healing.

70. Kenneth W. Newell, ed., Health By the People.

71. Carroll Behrhorst, "The Chimaltenango Development Project in Guatemala", in Kenneth W. Newell, op. cit., pp. 30-52.

72. Mabelle Arole and Rajanikant Arole, "A Comprehensive Rural Health Project in Jamkhed (India)", in Kenneth W. Newell, op. cit., pp. 70-90.

73. Victor W. Sidel and Ruth Sidel, "The health care delivery system of the People's Republic of China," in Kenneth W. Newell, op. cit., pp. 1-12.

74. Ibid, p. 6.

75. Ibid, p. 7.

76. Ibid, p. 10.

77. V. Djukanovic and E. P. Mach, eds. Alternative approaches to meeting basic health needs in developing countries - Geneva, A joint UNICEF/WHO study, 1975, p. 100.

78. Philip Potter, op. cit., p. 334.

79. David Werner, Introduction in Where There is No Doctor.

80. Michael Wilson, Health is For People, London: Darton, Longman & Todd Ltd., 1977, p. 86.

81. Ibid, p. 90.

82. Ibid, pp. 103, 104.

83. Michael Wilson, The Church is Healing, London: SCM Press Ltd., 1966, p. 65.

84. William Watty, "Man and Healing - A Biblical and Theological View" in Contact, no. 54, Geneva, CMC, WCC, December 1979, p. 2.

85. Ibid, p. 7.

86. A Methodist Statement on The Church and the Ministry of Healing, approved by the British Conference, 1977, p. 5.

87. Michael Wilson, The Church is Healing, London: SCM Press Ltd., 1966, p. 101.

88. J. Cameron Peddie, The Forgotten Talent - God's Ministry of Healing, Collins, Fontana Books, 1975, p. 117.

CHAPTER 6

THEOLOGY AND CARIBBEAN EXPERIENCE

One of the legacies which the Haitian people have undoubtedly retained from the era of colonial rule is its cuisine. The creativity of the French, combined with the necessity imposed upon poor people to prepare dishes which were tasty without being too costly, has made Haitian food a rather exciting affair. I would spare the reader the details of a diversified menu, and simply point to one meal which is common to most Haitian kitchens. 'Bouillon!' This is a kind of soup, well-flavoured with meats, vegetables and ground provisions of various sorts. The average housewife would prepare a 'bouillon' for her family on Saturday which gives her the opportunity to use up food left-over during the week.

Bouillon provides a helpful analogy in so far as describing Caribbean theology is concerned. We will not be able to understand theological thinking in the region, unless it is realized that Caribbean people have inherited much from their past of slavery and colonialism. Now there is a struggle to be freed from foreign impositions and external restraints, and a conscious attempt to be fashioned into the people whom it is believed God would want them to be. Theology in such a complex society is like a bouillon in the sense that much use is being made of the variety which is on offer, even the left-overs which have been thrown out by other people.

Before we delve into a description of the ingredients of this
bouillon let us say something about theology itself.

Theology is sometimes regarded as a speculative exercise.
Viewed in this fashion, it is the sum total of theories about
God which are propounded by academics and mystics who have
undergone a series of reflections on the spiritual life. True
theology is more than just a theoretical exercise which is
undertaken by academics and mystics. It does not emerge in
a vacuum but rather it is a practical discipline which seeks
to discover the reality of God within concrete historical
settings. God is forever entering into dialogue with humankind.
In Chapter 2, we described God's self-disclosure through nature,
Holy Scriptures, salvation history, the Holy Spirit, the Church
and Christian tradition. We also noted that divine revelation
is affected by social, economic and political factors. Today
God continues, through His Holy Spirit, to reveal Himself to
people. In Chapter 3 we established the criteria for genuine
spiritual revelation, when we alluded to Pauline passages in
1 Corinthians 12 and 14. Such a revelation would testify to
the Lordship of Jesus, would serve the common god, and would
result in the edification of others, even those who are
normally outside of the Church. Whatever the social or cultural
environment, God reveals Himself. In fact, it must be said
that it is on account of such concrete factors - social and

cultural - that people may experience Him one way or another.

Karl Marx rightly affirmed that

> "consciousness can never be anything else than conscious
> existence."[1]

Thought has no independence from social existence. Individuals
who have remained alert to what is taking place in the world
around them have had the experience of God speaking to them
out of their situations. To borrow the words of Lukas Vischer,

> "theological reflection should result from direct contact
> with the realities we experience today."[2]

Following on from this premise, we would have to admit that
there must be different theologies for different people. It
also calls into question the age-long practice by denominations
to legislate that all their followers, irrespective of what part
of the world they may be and under whatever social, economic
and political situations they exist, must swear allegiance to
a neatly packaged list of doctrinal stances. Indeed, indigenous
theology is a grim reminder that true theology is contextual
in nature and cannot be dished out onto so-called universal
platters.

It is outside the scope of this study to discuss the questions
which follow from this, namely, How can indigenous theologies
be part of one and the same Gospel? How can different exegeses
be part of the same exegesis? How can different forms of
revelation testify to the oneness of revelation? How can
different liturgies be part and parcel of the same liturgy?

How do all these expressions of Christianity lend support to the universality of the faith? These questions are dealt with elsewhere.[3] Our immediate task is to focus on theology within the Caribbean context.

PART I -   <u>BOUILLON: The Ingredients</u>

PART II - <u>BOUILLON: The Flavour</u>

Part I - BOUILLON: The Ingredients

Missionary Theology

Missionary Theology was one of the first types of theology known in the Caribbean region. It arrived with the Spanish towards the end of the fifteenth century. The Spaniards had begun exploring after the incentives occasioned by the papal bulls which granted them the exculsive rights to territories touched upon, provided that no Christian prince was already in possession of them. For example, the Papal Bull, 'Inter Caetera' of May 3, 1493, issued by Alexander VI, awarded them ownership of lands discovered in the Indies. Who should own what territory was arrived at by the Pope's fixing of a demarcation line drawn through the world. By the Treaty of Tordesillas, June 7, 1494, Portugal and Spain made some adjustments to this demarcation line, which had been drawn. The aim had been to produce a more satisfactory arrangement. Since Pope Julius II ratified this agreement in 1506, it meant that the way was open for Spain to conquer lands in the Caribbean region.

As the Spaniards colonized and fully exploited the lands which came under their control, they baptized men and women into the Roman Catholic faith. Christianity must have seemed to be a very cruel religion to the original Amerindian tribes which inhabited the region. The Spaniards preached the Gospel of love, but took away their possessions, including their very lives. In an account of Spanish activity in Hispaniola, Las

Casas recorded that

> "The Spaniards in about eight and thirty or forty years
> have unjustly put to death above twelve million of your
> subjects; and what an incredible damage must your Majesty
> have further sustained by these massacres, as they have
> hindered all these people from multiplying...............
> They don't much concern themselves whether the Indians
> live or die, provided they reap some advantage by their
> labour."[4]

In the island of Jamaica, Spanish rule (1502 - 1655) succeeded

in destroying the Arawak Indians, their number being estimated

at sixty thousand.[5] Following the annihilation of the

original inhabitants within the Caribbean, the Europeans

captured Africans and brought them as slaves in order to

fulfil the demands for cheap labour. Much has been written

about the slave enterprise and the horrors of it.[6] Such

atrocities committed in the name of Christianity have earned

the following comment from Dr. Phillip Potter:

> "When Christopher Columbus landed in the Caribbean he
> planted the cross as one of his first acts. But it was
> the Arawaks and Caribs, and the blacks and later white,
> Indian and Chinese indentured labourers who bore that
> Cross for centuries."[7]

Missionary theology, clothed in Roman Catholic garb, held sway

in the early days of Spanish rule. The Crown tolerated no

other religion apart from Catholicism, hence it was not

surprising that Church and State were so closely allied in the

colonies. Theologizing within such a context, because it was

done by those who represented the administration, not the

masses of oppressed people, served to preserve the 'status

quo', not to challenge it.

England and other European powers came in to the picture of
colonial activity when they openly contested Spain's claim
to exclusive rights within the New World. There soom emerged
the principle of "effective occupation", which was the tool
devised by Spain's rivals to determine the ownership of
territory. England, having built up her naval power during
the sixteenth century, was able, at the start of the seventeenth century to secure colonies in the Caribbean. In 1627,
the island of Barbados was colonized. In 1655, Jamaica was
seized from Spain. 1675 saw St. Kitts and Nevis added to her
possessions. Unlike the Roman Catholic Church which sought, in
the Spanish and French colonies, to Christianize the slaves
who had been brought from Africa, the Church of England served
only the needs of the establishment. In fact, very early in the
slave trade, the English had shown little or no regard for anything
or anybody but for the building up of the British Empire. This
point comes across quite vividly in C.L.R. James' description of the
horrors suffered by slaves who had been packed in "trunks" or "dens
of putrefaction":

> "The Africans fainted and recovered or fainted and died,
> the mortality in the trunks being over 20 per cent.
> Outside in the harbour, waiting to empty the trunks
> as they filled, was the captain of the slave-ship, with
> so clear a conscience that one of them, in the intervals
> of waiting to enrich British capitalism with the profits
> of another valuable cargo, enriched British religion by
> composing the hymn 'How sweet the Name of Jesus sounds'!"[8]

This trend of the Church serving the interests of the planter class
continued throughout the seventeenth and eighteenth centuries, hence
the overall theological picture was a reflection of the white settler
and officials' understanding of God. There were certain clergy in

Jamaica who refused to conduct worship services if there were no white people in the congregation. It mattered little to them that the masses of people were black and enslaved. Theology disregarded the social context in which the Church had been situated. It did not focus on the needs of a slave society, nor was its intention to produce Caribbean Christians, for it had been formulated beforehand in Europe. It was completely alien to the majority of people in that society. In fact the African slaves who had their traditional forms of religion found it difficult to come to terms with the culture of the Church. When they tried to inject elements of their own culture into religious life, elements such as drumming and dancing, dreams and visions, they were made to feel that their culture was not acceptable to the Christian God. Gradually, people within the Caribbean seemed to be hearing God saying to them that as a people, they were valuable only in so far as they mirrored the actions of foreigners. Once they were their own true selves, they could not be His people.

The Church of England supported a theology which catered only to the privileged minority. But what more could be expected of a church which in itself was in dire need of reform. The clergy who found their way into the Caribbean were not amongst the most devoted or well-equipped; some were gamblers and drinkers; some were unfrocked priests, and many were absentees; some soon became planters and merchants. Leslie, writing in his History of Jamaica, 1740 states:

> "The clergy here are of a character so vile that I do not
> care to mention it; for except a few, they are generally
> the most finished of our debauchers. Messrs. Galpin,
> Johnson and May are indeed men whose unblemished lives
> dignify the character they bear. They generally preach
> either in their own churches, or to a few in some private
> house every Sunday; but for others their church doors
> are seldom open."[9]

For such reasons much respect for the Church was lost.

Apart from the Roman Catholic and Anglican brands of theolo-

gizing which appeared on the Caribbean scene, there emerged

some Protestant movements whose theologies seemed to pay more

attention to the harsh realities of life. Whereas before the

Church, represented by Roman Catholicism and Anglicism,

exercised a role supportive of the Crown, now the Church,

represented by Moravians, Methodists and Baptists, seemed to

have shifted its theological stance in regards to the instit-

ution of slavery. The State on the one hand was trying to

maintain slavery whereas the Protestant Church often opposed.

Indeed, these Protestant groups, as we shall see, did not

direct their missionary activity solely towards the planter

class as the Church of England had done. They worked among

the slaves, hence they were more likely to be affected by the

inhumane and un-Christian treatment meted out to followers of

theirs. Freedom seemed to be a commonplace word among

Protestant missionaries. Initially, this freedom did not refer

to a state of being liberated from actual physical chains.

The Moravian mission's founder, Count Nikolaus von Zinzendorf,

shortly after they had begun work in the Virgin Islands during

the 1730s, is reported to have said at a meeting that conversion

to Christianity would free people from their wicked habits
and thoughts, though not giving them freedom from the control
of their slave masters. The actual words spoken during his
address to the converts in St. Thomas on February, 15th, 1739
were:

> "God punished the first negroes by making them slaves, and
> your conversion will make you free, not from the control
> of your masters, but simply from your wicked habits and
> thoughts, and all that makes you dissatisfied with your
> lot."[10]

Zinzendorf and his fellow missionaries usually stressed law and
order, not revolt against their servile condition. But the
very fact that Moravians, Methodists and Baptists had been
prepared to preach the Gospel to the slaves was a highly revolutionary affair which could lead the movement for complete
freedom one step nearer its goal.

Methodism was introduced into the region during the 1760s,
the venue being the island of Antigua. Nathaniel Gilbert,
lawyer, politician, and Speaker of the House of Assembly, was
also a slave-plantation owner and preacher. In 1758, following
a bout of illness, he took the family and household slaves to
England, where they all heard John Wesley preach. In 1760,
back again in Antigua, Gilbert gave up his career in law and
politics and announced the Good News both to slaves as well
as to whites. Methodist work continued to grow through the
evangelistic zeal of the converted slaves. An added impetus
came with the arrival in 1778 of the shipwright, John Baxter,
who was also a Methodist local preacher. It was Baxter who in

1783 completed the building of the first Methodist chapel in St. John's, Antigua. Following the visit of Dr. Thomas Coke to the Caribbean in 1786, twelve missionaries were sent out from England. By the year 1788, there were one thousand Methodists in Antigua alone.[11] The Baptist Church in Jamaica was founded in 1783 by two American blacks, George Liele (Lisle) and Moses Baker. In 1792 the Baptist Missionary Society was formed in England. It was not until 1814, following an invitation extended by the local Jamaica Baptist Church, that the first English missionaries arrived. They

> "acquired a growing following among the slaves, and by
> 1831 they had built 24 churches, enrolled 10,000 members
> and claimed another 17,000 'inquirers'."[12]

In 1794 the Church of England set up a Society for the Conversion and Religious Instruction and Education of the Negro slaves in the British West Indies. In 1795 the London Missionary Society was founded. In the year 1800 there was the founding of the Scottish Missionary Society, and in 1803 the Bristish and Foreign Bible Society.

The dawn of the nineteenth century in the Caribbean saw the Church becoming increasingly concerned about getting rid of slavery. The more the missionaries preached, the more suspicious planters became. These planters feared that slaves would get new ideas about their worth as human beings and rebel against their servile condition. They wanted to ensure that preaching showed that a man could be a good Christian and a good slave at the same time.[13] They resented the idea

of brotherhood in Christian teaching. They became openly
hostile to the missionaries and so influential were they in
political life that tough legislation was passed in the colonies.
Laws demanded that preachers be in possession of licences to
preach. Laws forbade religious services between sunset and
sunrise which obviously made it difficult for any slave to
attend. Since Sunday was declared market day for slaves, it
meant that the works of Sunday schools, Sunday Church services
and Bible Study groups were terribly undermined. Despite this
the missionaries were active, teaching slaves to read and write.
But the price the missionaries paid for all this was great.
They were often accused of sedition. They were thrown in prison
after trials which had been concocted in the aftermath of slave
rebellions. For example, Baptist, Methodist and Moravian
pastors were blamed for the 1831 rebellion in Jamaica as a
result of which their chapels were attacked and they themselves
abused or imprisoned.[14] Clearly, the Church was seeing itself
more and more in terms of a force for the liberation of its
people. This was to be understood, seeing that by the 1830s
the slaves were in the majority within the Churches. The
Methodist Church records that in 1833, there were 23,000 slaves
out of its 32,000 members in the West Indies.[15] This incidentally was the largest slave membership of any church. As the
nineteenth century progressed, with the humanitarian movement
against slavery becoming increasingly effective, the theology
of the Church was beginning to reflect more of the majority
understanding of God. This was, to say the least, dangerous

to the solidarity of white society.

Slavery was abolished in 1838 and the nature of Caribbean
society underwent a change. A Trial or apprenticeship period
had been decreed to facilitate the transition from a slave to
a free society. It is significant that after 1838 many
missionaries, particularly Baptists and Methodists, migrated
to the United States of America. These had been largely the
ones closely allied to the ruling class. It must be remembered
that clergymen had held civil and political offices, functioning
as Justices of the Peace, Councillors and, in one case cited
in the Leeward Islands, Speaker in the Assembly. There were,
within their ranks, many a powerful figure. Loss of status
came as their signal to depart. Throughout the post-emanci-
pation period, into the days of colonialism, there still remained
within the Church a very strong element which sought always to
court the favour of the establishment. This was inevitable
because although the Church incorporated freed men and women
of African origin, indentured labourers from India, China and
other parts of the world who had come to the Caribbean under
a work contract, the people who held the positions of leadership
in both Church and State were white. The Church tended, in
such a situation, to oil the machinery for colonialism and
imperialism. The Church, like the State, was foreign. It
served as an agent of the 'status quo' in so far as it did
not pave the way for resistance, confrontation and revolt.
In the face of opposition and injustices of all kinds, it

remained silent, choosing not to participate in political
decisions.

In looking at missionary theology as an ingredient in the
bouillon of Caribbean theology, we may state that this is one
of the left-overs which Caribbean theologians are now trying
to do without. Reflecting on how this brand of theology has
presented to Caribbean people a concept of God which does not
reflect their experience of Him, the late Dr. Idris Hamid
wrote:

> "God is really foreign to us. In the religious imagination
> of our people he is a benign white foreigner - 'an
> expatriate'. Even the categories of our religious
> experiences are imports which do not reflect our cultural
> and native experiences. We experience God as an outsider
> in the bad sense of that encounter. He is not the God
> in our history and of our destiny. In fact He has not
> been God for us, but against us."[16]

Naturally, while appreciating the sentiments expressed by
Dr. Hamid, we are equally aware that there are times when God
has to act against us, in order to emphasize that He is for
us. The people of Israel, for example, had this sort of
experience of Yahweh. During their days of slavery in Egypt,
it seemed that their God had forsaken them, or had been
completely opposed to them. But in the midst of their despair,
Yahweh sent Moses to be the instrument of His love and concern
for them. They were eventually delivered from their misery
in Egypt and in looking back on the incident, could celebrate
their God (Exodus 13: 14) for having acted in their favour.

Idris Hamid has also this pertinent comment about the missionary era:

> "Its theology in almost every aspect fell prey to the
> dominating colonial ethos of the era. The theology of
> salvation, that is, how a person or a community conceives
> of salvation, as well as such concepts of sin and even
> the theology of the cross, were all made to fall in line.
> Jesus on the cross was often presented as the ultimate
> example in obedience and acceptance of the cruelties of
> the ruling power, with the subtle undertone of passive
> acceptance of one's fate as a necessary religious act.
> It is more than coincidental that the theology of the
> Church so well fitted the inner immoral logic of
> colonialism and the interest of the oppressors. This
> twist therefore made the old missiology a theology of
> oppression despite the good intentions and great sacrifices
> of Church workers and representatives."[17]

In actual fact, then, missionary theology which prevailed during

the first four hundred years of the Church's history in the

Caribbean so influenced people that they did not consider as

worthwhile the native experience of God. This truth is

reflected in the manner in which theological colleges, up

until the 1970s, have been stimulating their seminarians. The

themes of the Incarnation, Trinity and Atonement have been

presented through the eyes of European thinkers, who hail not

only from the colonizing nations of England, France, Spain and

Holland, but also from Sweden, Switzerland and Germany. What

seemed to come across to theological students was that in order

for a Caribbean Christian to be counted as a theologian, he or

she must be a Gustaf Aulen, an Anders Nygren, a Karl Barth,

an Emil Brunner, a Rudolf Bultmann or some other European, but

definitely not someone born and bred in the Caribbean. Obviously

much benefit has been derived from the theological reflections

of such erudite scholars. With their insights, our understand-

ing of God has been greatly enhanced. Because of them, too,

we have come to appreciate the fact that theology is culturally
conditioned. But in the process of receiving from others, we
have neglected ourselves. We have denied our very existence
as a Caribbean people. We have chosen to let God speak to us
out of the situation in Sweden, Switzerland, Germany and the
rest of Europe, while not paying any attention to His voice
resounding clearly across the Caribbean.

> "The tragedy of colonization and the theology which inspired
> it is that for all this and because of all this Caribbean
> man, oriented to Western values, has become a caricature.
> Few peoples of the world have become so uncreative,
> unoriginal, unproductive and imitative as the peoples of
> this area, and nowhere is this barrenness of thought and
> copy-cat mentatlity so depressingly evident than among
> the Christians of the Caribbean. This is the final verdict
> on colonial theology."[18]

The challenge facing the Caribbean Christian now is for him or
her to come out of this present stupor and theologize in the
light of current realities faced by us as a people. In so
doing, our theology would embrace such relevant ingredients as
Development, Castroism, Liberation, Blackness and Rastafarianism.

Development

If the 1960s saw the Caribbean moving away from colonialism
towards independence, with August 1962 marking the shift in
political status of Jamaica and Trinidad and Tobago, the 1970s
saw the people of the Caribbean seeking desperately to come to
terms with their state of under-development. It is noteworthy
that the Church was very much in the forefront of such an
activity. Christian Action for the Development of the Caribbean
(CADEC) had been busily engaged in organizing seminars and

conferences on the theme of development. Its publication, Caribbean CONTACT, the region's monthly newspaper, had been helping its readers to become more aware of some of the root causes of under-development. Because of some of its articles, this newspaper came under fire from conservative Christians who accused it of being too "political", "revolutionary" and "Marxist-inspired", and suggested that the Church was seriously misguided in this new line of approach.

Perhaps the most significant contribution to the issues of under-development had been the Caribbean Ecumenical Consultation for Development held in Trinidad from November 15th to the 22nd, 1971. It was sponsored by the Steering Committee of the Caribbean Conference of Churches (in formation) and the Joint Commission of the World Council of Churches and the Pontifical Commission on Justice and Peace (SODEPAX). This Committee was chaired by the Roman Catholic Archbishop of Kingston, Jamaica. It included participants from four language areas in the Caribbean - Dutch, English, French and Spanish. This consult-ation helped to awaken Christians, not just to their responsi-bility in the spiritual life of the region, but also in the field of economics, politics and the total sphere of develop-ment.[19] The Caribbean Conference of Churches (CCC) itself was to hold its Inaugural Assembly in Jamaica two years later. The amazing thing about the CCC is its strong contingent of Catholics and Pentecostals. The support of these groups is a unique feature, when one considers that at the level of the

World Council of Churches (WCC), this type of ecumenical
co-operation is non-existent.

> "The eventual membership of the Roman Catholic Church in
> the World Council of Churches is still a wide open
> question,"[20] and

> "there are still many Pentecostal groups which remain
> suspicious of the official ecumenical movement."[21]

The study papers prepared for the 1971 Consultation helped to
highlight past weaknesses in Caribbean theologizing.

> "In the past the work of the churches had a 'conserving'
> character. Her role was the preservation of her flock
> from the world. The people were taught to come to terms
> with the misery and poverty in which they lived. In
> pursuing this kind of pastoral activity the churches
> were promoting acceptance of the subservient economic and
> social role assigned by the colonial authorities. Given
> the theological under-pinnings, which debated how many
> natures Christ possessed, angels, purgatory and sin, it
> is not surprising that the impact of the churches on the
> social life of the region was insignificant. In assuming
> this role, the churches were reacting to the closed,
> traditional world in which their membership lived and
> they did not see it as part of their mission to change
> it."[22]

Now the focus was on change. The Church, embarrassed by its
record in the past, was becoming more and more aware that
development would take place whether it contributed or not.
Without doubt, the experience of Cuba must have had some
influence upon the thinking of Caribbean Christians in the
1970s. This country approached misery and poverty from an
entirely different angle and achieved certain positive results
of which many other Caribbean nations were envious.

Castroism

Before the Revolution began in 1959, Cuba displayed all the

symptoms of under-development. Seventy-five percent of rural
dwellings were made from palm trees. The roads were in an
appalling condition. There was a shortage of medical facilities
Hunger, starvation and poor sanitation constituted the lot of
the masses. There were limited supplies of water and electri-
city, and the country folk suffered a rather high rate of
illiteracy. About sixty-one percent of children in the rural
areas were not attending school. Twenty-two percent of Cuba's
farm land was cultivated, sugar being the dominant crop.
Seventy-five percent of arable land was controlled by American
sugar companies, which meant that Americans virtually controlled
the country's destiny. An estimated twenty-five percent of the
labour force was chronically unemployed. It is no surprise
that this country had the reputation for being a den of
gambling and prostitution. Most Cubans remained poor. The
rich minority were corrupt politicians and military officers.

Fidel Castro, the man who led the Cuban revolution had been
thrown in prison on the 26th July, 1953 after he and his men
had launched an attack against General Batista. The Batista
government had been notorious for torturing and killing its
political prisoners. Castro, who in his defence speech on
16th October, 1953 quoted the famous words "history will
absolve me" was to remain imprisoned until 15th May 1955. The
26th of July Movement, formed by him and his followers after
their release from prison, sought help in Mexico and the United
States for the overthrow of the Batista regime. On the

1st January, 1959, General Batista fled the country. With Cuba at his feet, Fidel Castro began his revolution.

The Cuban revolution began as a movement for the liberation of the country from American control. As a means of emphasizing its anti-American feelings, it followed the principle of Marxist Socialism: from each according to his ability, to each according to his work. It was a Communistic ideology best described as Marxism-Leninism. The fact is that Communism was not the cause of the Revolution. It was a result. In 1960, for example, a trade agreement had been concluded with Communist countries. Russia had agreed to buy Cuban sugar for a period of five years, as well as grant military aid to the country. Cuba also became the first Latin American country to open diplomatic relations with Peking. Following the Bay of Pigs fiasco in 1961 when Cuban exiles from the United States had tried to overthrow his government, Castro willingly accepted an offer from Russia to boost the country's defence. President Nikita Kruschev was to send ships into Cuban waters and have his men install ballistic missiles and pads. However, through the strategy of the American President, John F. Kennedy, these plans had to be abandoned. Despite this Cuba did benefit militarily. However from then on, Caribbean and Latin American leaders began to mistrust Castro for being a stooge of Moscow. And yet, Castro was quite willing to pay the price of alienation occasioned by his country's becoming a satellite state of Russia. To revert to American influence would mean the loss of all that he had dreamed of doing for the people of Cuba. This was, for Castro, no choice at all.

During the early years of the Revolution, lots of technocrats and experts were lost to the country. The middle class did not like how Castro mingled freely with the working classes, how he cut cane with the farmers during harvesting season. Rather than stay behind and endure the novelty, they migrated. The Church, middle class as it had been, also lost quite a significant number of its leaders. The majority of Methodist pastors fled the country. There were fewer departures among the clergy of the Reformed Presbyterian Church[23] which stayed behind to identify with the people in their revolution. Before the revolution, blacks had been regarded as inferior. Now Castro helped them to assert their dignity, affording them equality in schools, jobs, apartment and clubs. Indeed, Cuba was

> "the first Caribbean country to have got rid of the legacy of slavery - the obsession with race and colour."[24]

One writer on the Cuban Revolution has said:

> "If Fidel Castro brought some tragedy to some families, I believe that it is demonstrable that he brought a better life to a majority of Cubans."[25]

Despite early setbacks, there had been successes to report. In the first six months of the revolution, six hundred miles of road had been constructed.[26] In thirty months, Castro had been able to open more classrooms than his predecessors had opened in thirty years. His literacy campaign reduced the illiteracy rate to four percent of the total population. Homes for the aged, institutes for the handicapped and children's nurseries were established. Castro's rate of house-building is estimated at twenty-seven per day and eight hundred and thirty-three a month.[27] It is claimed that prostitution virtually disappeared.

One of Castro's big successes was in the realm of health. He successfully constructed a water and sewage scheme. Rural medicine centres were built and mobile dispensaries introduced. Other glowing reports come to the fore:

> "Mortality from infectious diseases has been markedly reduced in the revolutionary period. The gastroenteritis mortality rate fell from 58.1 per 100000 persons in 1962 to 9.7 in 1973. The mortality rate for tuberculosis was 19.6 per 100000 in 1962 and 4.1 in 1973. The mortality rate for measles, which was 1 per 100000 population in the first years of the decade, is now 0.2 per 100000. Poliomyelitis has been practically eradicated; its incidence, which was 200 - 400 cases per year in the early 1960s, has fallen to only 3 cases in the last 9 years - all children who for some reason had not been vaccinated. The eradication of malaria was completed in June 1967. The incidence of diphtheria averages only 2 - 3 cases a year, and no case has appeared since 1971. The control programmes for leprosy and tuberculosis are now close to detecting and giving medical care for all cases estimated to exist in the country. The pattern of other diseases is changing more slowly but the trend is always towards a reduction, which serves as a stimulus to continue the work."[28]

Although by all appearances, Castro's home performance has been remarkable, his performance on the world scene has been much criticized. He, who once fought so desperately against imperialism is now accused of assuming the role of imperial aggressor. Cuban involvement in places like Ethiopia, Mozambique, Angola and Central America confirms this. Indeed, Cuba has grown to a position whereby her military might is

a talking-point around the world. There are training camps
set up around the countryside, within a radius of 100 km from
Havana, where recipients of training include people from
Equatorial Guinea, the People's Democratic Republic of Yemen
(PDRY), Cape Verde, Malawi and Kenya. People from the last
two countries are there without the approval or knowledge of
their respective governments.[29] The training camps themselves
had been set up after the first conference of the Organisation
for Solidarity of the Peoples of Asia, Africa and Latin America
held in Havana in 1966 (The Tricontinental Conference). Let
us look at the accusation of imperialism as it affects just one
of the above mentioned countries - Angola.

It is estimated that in Angola some 19,000 Cuban soldiers are
occupying parts of the south. In defence of this, it is claimed
that Castro did not impose his troops on Angola. He had been
invited by the ruling People's Movement for the Liberation of
Angola (MPLA) to contribute to the country's development when
they had secured their independence from Portugal in 1975. At
that time, the country desperately needed help to build up its
economy, and Cuba provided technicians, doctors, teachers and
other skilled personnel numbering an estimated 9,000 apart
from the soldiers who had been sent. The troops helped to
provide protection for the country's vital economic interests,
for example, oil as produced by Gulf and other companies. The
Cubans are supposed to be contributing greatly to stabilise the
economy of Angola which, apart from oil, is blessed with

diamonds, coffee, iron ore, timber, wheat and sugar. All along,
the country's rulers have encouraged Cubans to stay in Angola.
Testimony to this fact came out in a statement made in 1976
by Prime Minister Lopo do Nascimento during a visit to Italy
when he said that Cuban forces

> "would remain in Angola as long as was necessary to
> reorganize the Angolan forces."[30]

It is claimed too that Cuban presence in Angola is in keeping
with Castro's commitment to this ideal of liberation. Before
Angolan independence, there had been serious divisions within
the three major nationalist movements. The National Union for
the Total Independence of Angola (UNITA) and the National Front
for the Liberation of Angola (FNLA) had been waging a guerilla
war against the MPLA. These two movements received the
backing of African neighbours Zaire and Zambia as well as the
United States of America. The MPLA received aid from the Soviet
Union and eventually Cuba. Cuban involvement was claimed to
have justified itself all the more when South Africa, renowned
for its enmity of black liberation, invaded Angola in 1975/76.
According to journalists, South African troops had been aiding
the FNLA and the UNITA, and these two liberation movements could
not discern how they were being used by the oppressive white
South Africans to maintain black subordination.

Angola is but one example of Cuba adopting the style of the
imperial aggressor. But there are differences of opinion as
to the extent to which Castro must be condemned for his actions.

However, to return to Castro's glorious performance on the
home scene, the real benefit for theological thinking in the
Caribbean was how the regime forced people to appreciate
socialism. The Caribbean had for long revered the European
democratic model as the ideal. Any conceivable change within
society had to take place within the democratic framework
The Church had come to respect democracy as sacrosanct. Everything evil had to do with Communism. When, for example, Christians saw themselves as working towards the establishment of
God's kingdom upon earth, they were thinking in terms of
bringing about an end to poverty, hunger, malnutrition, disease,
exploitation and injustices of all sorts, but through democratic
means. The fact that Marxism-Leninism in Cuba could produce
the type of society after which Christians had been craving,
suggested that a system whose orientation was atheistic could
in fact help to create an atmosphere wherein one could better
appreciate the possibility of God's kingdom existing on earth.
This was a frightening thought to Caribbean Christians, that
God could employ non-Christian forces to accomplish his will,
that His Holy Spirit could be active through channels not
traditionally regarded as sacred. It was similar to the scare
which Israel had when they were told by the prophets that
countries such as Assyria and Babylon would be used by God to
discipline them, His chosen people. Indeed Cuba has demonstrated to Caribbean Christians that

> "in the movement towards a more human society, the churches
> must show solidarity with the new humanism and with the
> forces for change in the region. This means refraining
> from denigrating criticism of the non-Christian forces

> for change and from concentrating on the negative aspects
> of society. Solidarity means working with such forces
> and stressing the values in their work which are benefi-
> cial. This is the only way in which the authenticity
> and seriousness of the churches' conviction to work for
> change will be accepted."[31]

So that apart from being challenged to look at socialism as

a possible working model, Christians are now reflecting on the

theological implications for co-operating with non-Christian

religions. Now it is true to say that the Church continues

to learn that it must co-operate with Islam, Hinduism and

other non-Christian faiths whose doctrines may be different,

whose approaches to God may not be through Jesus, but whose

commitment to the development of the Caribbean people is almost

identical.

Liberation and Blackness

Just as Development is considered to be a major ingredient in

the bouillon of Caribbean theology, so too is the theme of

Liberation. In fact it is being realized more and more that

> "the basic problem facing the Caribbean today is not
> underdevelopment, but dependency, the solution to which
> is not development, but liberation."[32]

As the Church became more concerned about development in the

1970s it also learned this lesson about how too much dependence

could be counter-productive in so far as its theology was

concerned.

> "The larger religions of the region are still dependent
> on their European and North American bases for finance
> and personnel............................... These
> churches have generally conceived their role as being
> the incorporation of the Caribbean into the universal
> church rather than the integration of the Church into
> the Caribbean. With isolated exceptions, local clergy

have not shown a markedly different mentality in this regard than their expatriate brethren."[33]

The problem is that our tremendous concern for being part of the universal church has made us ignore the need for a united, ecumenical approach towards tackling our under-development.

Idris Hamid has expressed this problem quite adequately:

"The implication of this new community-mindedness for the ecumenical life and witness of the churches in the Carib-bean must be seriously taken. We cannot afford to conti-nue mirroring the religious differences originating in Europe and fight over other people's divisions. Even our religious denominationalism is an import. No one is proposing a giant united church, but calling for a serious view of the nature of the church vis-a-vis its given unity in Christ, and the meaning of this for our battered communities. Even theological dogma rooted long in the best of tradition must give way to the need for present redemptive work of God: Just as Jesus put aside the Sabbath to reveal the presence and activity of God, so too we must lay aside our inherited theological differences, which some have come to cherish, to give pre-eminence to the presence and activity of God in our society. For the strength of the church lies not in the purity of its doctrine or its faithfulness to its sectarian tradition, but in its responsiveness and faithfulness to the presence of Christ in the world."[34]

The Caribbean Conference of Churches is now helping our theology to mature, in that liberation is occupying a place on its agenda. Its ecumenical approach to Caribbean needs is a clear indication that the God whom we love and serve is personally interested in our problems as a people.

It must be said that the focus on liberation and development by Caribbean Christians in the 1970s was also the influence of Latin Americans. The Roman Catholic Church by this time had developed into a vibrant body. The revolutionary nature of theology was evidenced in the Conference of Latin American bishops in Medellin, Colombia in 1968 where the "liberacion" motto had been adopted. This Conference urged that there be no longer the separation between faith and life, that the Church must commit itself to participate in social justice, social change, relevant education systems, promotion of workers' professional organizations, encouragement of evangelization, renewal or creation of new structures in the Church, and ecumenism. The church was to fulfil the role of catalyst for change in Latin American society. The Latin American situation included oppressive military regimes; arbitrary arrest and detention; imprisonment without trial; repression by legal machinery; limitations imposed on political activity; denial of basic human rights; restrictions on trade union movements; control of press and communications media; cultural enslavement including the censorship of reading material. The depressing situation in Latin American countries such as El Salvador and Nicaragua, to mention just two, has forced the Latin Amercian Church to emphasize liberation theology. In a lecture delivered at a Conference on Third World Theologies held at the Ecumenical Institute, Bossey, in September 1978, it was stated that:

> "The theology of liberation does not pretend to be a new theology. It is simply a correct theology about the living God, present among men of today in the same way as he presented himself in the events as recorded in the Bible. It is the only valid theology for Latin America."[35]

Spurred on by the Latin Americans, the Church in the Caribbean soon became aware that it also must be involved in taking political decisions and that not to participate makes the

Christian answerable to God. , The Church felt compelled to expose the systems of exploitation and oppression which denied people their freedom and basic human rights, and to encourage people to agitate for justice, fairplay and moral integrity at all levels of the society. Whereas in the past the Church used to promote acceptance of the subservient economic and social role assigned by the colonial authorities, it became a significant factor in the call for control of Caribbean resource by indigenous people as a means towards development.

As the 1970s developed, liberation, as a theme for theological reflection, took root in South Africa, the United States of America and the Caribbean. Liberation theologians constantly refer to the God of the Exodus, ever concerned about liberating His people from all forms of enslavement, be they social, political or economic. An account given in Luke of Jesus' sermon in the synagogue, when He quoted from Isaiah 61, is seen as a key:

> "The Spirit of the Lord is upon me,
> because he has chosen me to bring good news to the poor.
> He has sent me to proclaim liberty to the captives
> and recovery of sight to the blind;
> to set free the oppressed
> and announce that the time has come
> when the Lord will save his people." (Luke 4: 16 - 21)

After reading this, Christ had said to the people,

> "This passage of scripture has come true today, as you
> heard it being read."

Liberation theologians affirm that Christ points the way first and foremost to freedom upon earth as a prerequisite to accepting and appreciating a spiritual freedom. Blacks in

America used to live in the hope of better days. Hence there are Negro spirituals which sing of the better days. But these days were not to be experienced in anybody's lifetime. They were for the life after death. For example:

> "I've got a shoes, you've got a shoes
> All of God's children got a shoes.
> When I get to heav'n, goin' to put on me shoes
> Goin' to walk all over God's heav'n, heav'n, heav'n
> Everybody talkin' 'bout heav'n ain't goin' there
> Heav'n, heav'n, goin' to shout all over God's heav'n."

The Latin American theologian sees liberation theology as one which

> "implies identification with oppressed human beings and
> social classes and solidarity with their interest and
> struggles. It involves immersion in the political process
> of revolution, so that from there we may proclaim and live
> Christ's gratuitous and liberative love. That love goes
> to the very root of all exploitation and injustice; the
> breakup of friendship with God and other people. That
> love enables human beings to see themselves as children
> of their Father and brothers and sisters to each other."[36]

Much has been written about liberation theology.[37] It is a theology which claims to interpret the Christian faith in the light of a practical response to human situations, what is often referred to as the theory of praxis of faith. Sometimes it is difficult to see how such a theology can penetrate to the grass roots' level, namely, to those for whom the liberation theologians pretend to write. A helpful book to appreciate how this is done has been written by Derek Winter. In Hope in Captivity he shows how many of the theologians, including well-known names as Gustavo Gutierrez, Helder Camera and Jose Miguez Bonino, are actively involved with the poor in their struggle for social justice and human dignity. For many of them,

> "acceptance of the Christian message means action, becoming
> aware of a new life and hope, of a task where we strive
> to build a better world with a sense of human rights and
> dignity, and an appreciation of the most humble person,
> a world in which there's justice not simply for the more
> able, lucid and strong, but justice within reach of the
> lowest people."[38]

In South Africa, the United States of America and the Caribbean,
the liberation theme has been expressed through Black Theology.
Writing about the expression of it in South Africa, Allan
Boesak says:

> "Black theology is a situational theology. It is the black
> people's attempt to come to terms theologically with their
> black situation. It seeks to interpret the gospel in
> such a way that the situation of black will begin to make
> sense. It seeks to take seriously the biblical emphasis
> on the wholeness of life, which has always had its
> counterpart in the African heritage, trying to transform
> the departmentalized theology blacks have inherited from
> the western world into a biblical, holistic theology.
> It is part of the black struggle toward liberation from
> religious, economic, psychological, and cultural
> dependency."[39]

For Boesak and other South Africans, black theology is a
theology of liberation which is concerned about the situation
of the poor and oppressed. Liberation is seen as the central
theme of the gospel of Jesus Christ:

> "Indeed, black theology is a theology of liberation in the
> situation of blackness. For blacks it is the only
> legitimate way of theologizing - but only within the
> framework of the theology of liberation. Black theology,
> therefore, finds itself in intention and theological
> methodology, and certainly in its passion for liberation,
> not only alongside African Theology, but also alongside
> the expression of liberation theology in Latin America
> and Asia. And it is indeed in these expressions of
> Christian theology that western theology will ultimately
> find its salvation."[40]

It is interesting to note how the South African brand of black theology calls for liberation without advocating violent revolution. Could it be that their interpretation of the gospel suggests peaceful methods as the ideal Christian manner of dealing with the problem? Or is it because there are severe penalties imposed within their society for advocating violence? Whatever the root cause, it is noticeable that in the American type of black theology, the language at any rate appears to be more violent. Dr. James H. Cone says:

> "Black theology is the story of the black people's struggle for liberation in an extreme situation of oppression. Consequently there is no sharp distinction between thought and practice, worship and theology, because black theological refelctions about God occurred in the black struggle for freedom."[41]

Cone sees it as

> "a theology whose sole purpose is to apply the freeing power of the gospel to black people under white oppression."[42]

The application of this freeing power must involve some form of rebellion:

> "In Christ, God enters human affairs and takes sides with the oppressed. Their suffering becomes his; their despair, divine despair. Through Christ the poor man is offered freedom now to rebel against that which makes him other than human."[43]

South African theologian, Boesak, seems concerned about some of the strong remarks made by Dr. Cone about liberation.[44]

For example, Cone says:

> "Black theology cannot accept a view of God which does not represent Him as being for blacks and thus against whites. Living in a world of white oppressors, black people have no time for a neutral God. The brutalities are too great and the pain too severe.................... There is no use for a God who loves whites same as blacks."[45]

Cone's language is indeed more violent, as in his situation,

he finds himself forced to say that black theology is necessary

because white theologians do not consider the oppresion of

black people as an important item on their theological agenda.

In the preface to the book which seems to disturb Boesak, Cone

has written:

> "It will be evident, therefore, that this book is written
> primarily for the black community and not for white
> people."[46]

And yet, Cone was not rejecting white people, for in the same

book he said:

> "A black man is anyone who says he is black, despite skin
> colour."[47]

This particular book, <u>A Black Theology of Liberation</u>, is

indeed helpful if one truly wants to understand Dr. Cone and

his concept of black theology. Hear, for example, what he has

to say about the necessity of black theology being violent.

It has to speak, he says,

> "with a passion which is in harmony with the revolutionary
> spirit of the oppressed.

> "The sin of American theology is that it has spoken without
> passion. It has failed miserably in relating its work to
> the oppressed in society by refusing to confront the
> structures of this nation with the evils of racism. When
> it has tried to speak for the poor, it has been so cool
> and calm in its analysis of human evil that it implicitly
> disclosed whose side it was on..........................

> "Black Theology rejects this approach and views theology
> as a participation in passion on behalf of the oppressed."[48]

The violence and passion of Cone's language is evident every-

where as he expounds his understanding of Black Theology. It

is noticeable that in <u>God of the Oppressed</u>[49] although he is

consistent, he seems less violent. This may be so because
he is critical of his own theology. He notes that Black
Theology could turn out to be nothing but the

> "ideological justification of radical black politics. While
> some black theologians may be content with the identifi-
> cation of Black Theology with current black politics, I
> maintain that the authenticity of black theological dis-
> course is dependent upon its pointing to the divine One
> whose presence is not restricted to any historical
> manifestation. Indeed, unless Black Theology seeks
> to bear witness to the divine Word who transcends the
> subjective musings of black theologians, then there is
> no difference between Black theology and White theology
> when viewed from the perspective of Feuerbach's critique
> that religion is nothing but human talk, nothing but
> human projections and illusions."[50]

Whereas in earlier works, Cone leaned heavily on physical
liberation - political, social, economic - now in this book he
spells out the spiritual side of liberation. For example, in
Chapter VII, "The Meaning of Liberation"[51] he talks about
faith, prayer, worship and the future hope in death. The overall impression, on reading God of the Oppressed is that herein
we are presented with a well-balanced treatment of a black
theology of liberation.

The tenor of God of the Oppressed could also have been due to
the fact that it contains his autobiographical references
about the Bearden experience and the Macedonia A.M.E. Church.
The book ends on a note of reconciliation, particularly that
between black and white. It must be stressed, though, that for
Cone,

> "liberation is the precondition of reconciliation" ....
>
> "only black people can define the terms on which our
> reconciliation with white people will become real."[52]

The other thing to be noticed about God of the Oppressed is
how Cone everywhere takes pains to elaborate his position, not
as the dogmatic, uncompromising theologian as some students of
theology have made him out to be, but rather as the humble
seeker after God's truth. To quote a typical example:

> "I realize that my theological limitations and my close
> identity with the social conditions of black people could
> blind me to the truth of the gospel. And maybe our white
> theologians are right when they insist that I have over-
> looked the universal significance of Jesus' message. But
> I contend that there is no universalism that is not
> particular. Indeed their insistence upon the universal
> note of the gospel arises out of their own particular
> political and social interest. As long as they can be
> sure that the gospel is for everybody, ignoring that God
> liberated a particular people from Egypt, came in a parti-
> cular man called Jesus, and for the particular purpose
> of liberating the oppressed, then they can continue to
> talk in theological abstractions, failing to recognize
> that such talk is not the gospel unless it is related to
> the concrete freedom of the little ones. My point is that
> God came, and continues to come, to those who are poor and
> helpless, for the purpose of setting them free. And since
> the people of color are his elected poor in America, any
> interpretation of God that ignores black oppression cannot
> be Christian theology. The 'blackness of Christ', there-
> fore, is not simply a statement about skin color, but
> rather, the transcendent affirmation that God has not ever,
> no not ever, left the oppressed alone in struggle. He was
> with them in Pharaoh's Egypt, is with them in America,
> Africa and Latin America, and will come in the end of time
> to consummate fully their human freedom."[53]

Let us turn now to see how the theologies of blackness and
liberation have featured in the bouillon of Caribbean theology.

Black culture suffered greatly under the oppression of slavery.
When Caribbean people became conscious of being black, there
were the accompanying feelings of self-hatred and self-
resentment. Black signified inferiority. Even after

Emancipation, there were forces which combatted against the black person, forces which precipitated an eventual loss of identity. Colonialism meant that blackness identified with powerlessness - no political or economic power. The hatred which blacks had for themselves was dramatized when a group of small children was once placed in a room with black and white dolls, and told to select a doll and leave the room. It appears that one boy, the last to leave the room, who had, like most other black children, selected a white doll, seized a black doll. Convinced that nobody was looking at him, he battered it until it was completely destroyed. Then satisfied, he left the room.

In the 1960s the sociologist Errol L. Miller carried out a survey with 475 secondary school pupils from three secondary schools in Kingston, Jamaica.[54] These pupils ranged between the ages of 11 and 15 years. The aim of the sociologist was to discover how maturing members of the society perceived their bodies and physical beauty in relation to their skin colour. He used the questionnaire method, asking sufficiently general questions, e.g. What do you like/dislike about your body? What parts of your body would you change if it were possible? What is your idea of the handsome boy/beautiful girl? To these questions there was no suggestion of desired responses. There was no ambiguity in them. From the survey it was clear that these adolescents, the majority of whom were black, regarded white and Caucasian features as highly desirable whereas black

or Negroid features, such as flat nose, thick lips, curly
hair caused tremendous dissatisfaction. The inference is
clear. Many young Caribbean blacks during the 1960s hated
their blackness. Even in the late sixties and early seventies,
with so much talk about black consciousness and "black is
beautiful" black people were still apologizing for their
skin colour. Even today some mothers say to their daughters,
"Don't marry him; he's too black. Think of the future of
your children!"

Black Theology, as it relates to the Caribbean situation, takes
very seriously the Biblical teaching on <u>love</u>. In 1 John 4:
19 - 20 we read:

> "We love because God first loved us. If someone says he
> loves God, but hates his brother, he is a liar. For he
> cannot love God, whom he has not seen, if he does not
> love his brother whom he has seen."

These words are crucial. To know and to love God begins with
self-love. Black Theology for the Caribbean begins when persons
learn to love themselves and their black culture. They can
then appreciate that God loves and accepts them as they are.
To quote Manas Buthelezi:

> "The black man must be enabled through the interpretation
> and application of the Gospel to realize that blackness,
> like whiteness, is a good natural face cream from God
> and not some cosmological curse."[55]

Or to quote Dr. James Cone:

> "In a world which has taught blacks to hate themselves,
> the new black man does not transcend blackness, but
> accepts it, loves it as a gift of the Creator. For he
> knows that until he accepts himself as a being of God in
> all of its physical blackness, he can love neither God
> nor neighbour."[56]

Cone further states:

> "The task of Black Theology is to make Christianity really
> Christian by moving black people with a spirit of black
> dignity and self determination so they can become what
> the Creator intended."[57]

Some people ask the question, "Is black theology a racist

ideology?" The answer is "No!" Allan Boesak says:

> "So it is not hatred of white people that blacks have. It
> is white oppression they hate. And hate it they must, with
> all their hearts."[58]

Black Theology is not a denial that "white is beautiful". It

merely upholds the worth of blackness which for centuries in

the Caribbean at any rate was denied. Cone has himself pointed

out that black theology is for whites as well:

> "Being black in America has very little to do with skin
> colour. To be black means that your heart, your soul,
> your mind, and your body are where the dispossessed are."[59]

It is in a similar vein that we understand the claim that Jesus

Christ, the Messiah is black:

> "The importance of the concept of the Black Messiah is that
> it expresses the concreteness of Christ's continued
> presence today. Jesus came and lived in this world as the
> Oppressed One who took upon himself all the suffering and
> humiliation of all oppressed peoples."[60]

The theme of liberation will continue to be the focus of

theological reflection in the Caribbean for quite some time.

This is so because of the continued growth of the Rastafarian

movement which began in Jamaica towards the close of the last

century but is now to be found in several Caribbean territories.

Liberation and Rastafarianism

After the abolition of slavery, Jamaica experienced a Great
Revival which reached its peak during the 1860s. This period
witnessed the upsurge of Zionism, Pocomania and other religious
movements which were partly African, partly European Christian.
The one which goes under the name of Rastafarianism is regarded
as having been conceived at this stage, but it was not until
the 1930s that it developed into the modern entity which it now
is. The 1930s was a time when Jamaica was suffering from severe
social and economic problems, the ideal time for new preachings
to be sympathetically listened to. With unemployment running
as high as twenty percent, and with the masses of blacks
existing in conditions of poverty and depression, many people
flocked to the capital, Kingston, in pusuit of the myth that
employment can easily be found in urban areas. This crucial
situation had been further aggravated by the fact that the
minority white population held the important jobs in the
country. Black people, at the lowest echelons of society, were
therefore searching desperately for a way out of their misery.

Guidance as to a possible course of action seemed to come from
the United States of America, where blacks were equally undergoing a period of oppression. Within that situation there arose
a number of religious leaders urging that the only means of
liberation for blacks would be for them to leave the virtual
hell of the New World and return to Africa from which they had
been cruelly seized during slavery. One such leader was the

Jamaican nationalist, Marcus Mosiah Garvey (1887-1940) whose leadership of the Universal Negro Improvement Association and whose preaching during the 1920s caused thousands to revere him as a prophet.

> "Garvey presented Africa as the true home of the black people to which they must all return if they were to be free and happy; he actually started the Black Star Shipping Line to take them home, and prophesied the crowning of a black king in Africa as a sign of deliverance. When the Ethiopian prince, Ras Tafari, was crowned emperor in 1930 biblical study convinced many in Jamaica that this was the black king and that their time had come. The idea appealed to a number of the poor and landless, and found expression in several independent leaders in the early 1930s who gathered a following under the banner of Ras Tafari beliefs."[61]

Although the name of Garvey is cited in the early history of the movement, there were many other leaders - Leonard Howell, Joseph Hibbert, Archibald Dunkley, Robert Hinds and Claudius Henry. Apart from Claudius Henry, whom we will mention later on, these remain just names because of the insufficient information about them.

Liberation, as a theme of the first Rastafarians, had to do with leaving Jamaica and journeying back to Africa. Black people were believed to be the reincarnations of the ancient Israelites. It was pointed out to these Rastafarians that the Israelites were a black nation (Lamentations 4: 8) and that Solomon was a black king (Song of Solomon 1: 5). They must therefore leave 'Babylon' and return to their homeland, no longer as captives but as a free people. There could be no real freedom in a society dominated by English laws, customs and education. 'Babylon' was everywhere, in governement, the legal system, the police, commerce and the Church.

> "Christianity is seen by the brethren as supporting and
> justifying colonialism, teaching people of a 'God in the
> sky' who doesn't exist, and helping to keep people ignor-
> ant and enslaved - resemblance is noted between the
> church bell and the slave bell. The Roman Catholic Church,
> led by the Pope in Rome, is seen as the epitome of a
> colonising wihite Church, attempting to impose an alien
> culture upon black people."[62]

Politics, or 'politricks' as some Rastas preferred to call it,
was 'not the black man's lot but the white man's plot.' Heaven
was in Africa, and more specifically, in Ethiopia, a country
well-spoken of in the Bible (Psalm 68) but also one which had
never been colonized by Europeans. When Rastas talk about
Ethiopia instead of Africa, this is not a contradiction in
terms.

> "This is religious language - a language aimed at inspir-
> ation, not information."[63]

Haile Selassie, "a symbol of black glory and ancient African
lineage dating back to Solomon and Queen of Sheba"[64] was
accepted as God incarnate. He became known as King of Kings,
Lord of Lords and the conquering Lion of the Tribe of Judah
(Revelation 5: 2 - 5, Ezekiel 30, 1 Timothy 6, Isaiah 43,
Revelation 17 and 19). This is not to deny the divinity of
Jesus. In fact, many Rastafarians believe that the real Jesus
was a black man, and that Selassie fulfils the prophecy of the
second coming of Jesus. Selassie therefore embodied two
important creeds of Rastafarianism. One is the humanity of
God, the other is the divinity of man. Many modern Rastafarians
still maintain the doctrine of Haile Selassie's divinity. This

belief has hardly been affected by his fall from power in 1974
and his death of August 28, 1975 at the age of 83. Many
believe that, like Jesus in Christianity, he is very much
alive. Not a few assert that he lives in the spirit and that
in the spiritual state he is even more powerful than ever
before. In some quarters, though, he is placed in the same
category as Marcus Garvey, namely that of a prophet. This all
goes to show that there is no uniformity of belief or of
theology within Rastafarianism.

Another important doctrine for Rastafarians is the terrestriality
of Salvation. The Caribbean, be it Jamaica, Dominica, Trinidad
and Tobago, St. Lucia, Antigua or Grenada, does not constitute
home. A return to the motherland, Africa, is essential for
complete liberation. Repatriation does not itself mean salvation. It is merely the condition to be fulfilled in order
that salvation may be realized. Of course 'Back to Africa' has
two interpretations. One is the actual physical return of all
the sons and daughters of Negus[65] to the African continent.
It was thought that this would be possible in the early days
following a rumour that the Emperor Haile Selassie had put
aside 500 acres of land in Ethiopia for blacks in the west who
wished to repatriate.

> "The Emperor himself had authorised the Ethiopian World
> Federation Inc, New York to organise black settlers to
> occupy lands which he had personally made available
> from his own estate in Ethiopia."[66]

However much frustration resulted from attempts by Rastafarians
to repatriate. Associated with one fiasco on repatriation is

the name of Rev. Claudius Henry. Self-styled "repairer of the breach" and founder of the African Reformed Church in Western Kingston, Claudius Henry had actually set the date, October 5, 1959, as the occasion when the promised repatriation scheme would materialize. In preparation for that day, some people even sold their houses. Unfortunately, no return to Africa was forthcoming, and Henry was arrested, found guilty of creating public mischief and bonded for one year.

In the 1960s more attempts were made to repatriate Rastafarians, but the numbers of those actually making the trip were very small. During 1963-5, three Rastafarian brethren[67] went on a fact-finding mission to Ethiopia, but no successful scheme of repatriation followed. On April 21, 1966, when Emperor Haile Selassie himself landed in Jamaica for an official visit thousands had been convinced that their hour of deliverance had come. But this proved not to be the case.

> "Over a period of then years only some 20 Rastafarians out of a 1960 estimate of 20,000 have been able to migrate to Ethiopia."[68]

The other interpretation of 'Back to Africa' is a purely cultural one. In order to dramatize their rejection of the dominant white culture, Rastas have developed a culture resembling parts of the African continent. Many Rasta men wear their hair long, giving it a matted texture, commonly referred to as <u>dreadlocks</u>. In so doing they bear striking likenesses to the Masai tribesmen of East Africa. They have

accepted to keep their hair long following the demands of the
Nazirite vow of the ancient Israelites to (i) refrain from
strong drink, (ii) let the locks of hair on the head grow long,
and (iii) avoid coming into contact with dead bodies.[69]   On
this last point, they maintain that the dead must be left to
bury their dead. Not all Rastafarians adhere rigidly to these
rules. Obviously in a Rastafarian commune, someone must have
the responsibility of disposing of the dead. So too, some
men keep a short cropped head of hair, and some are clean
shaven. Not all are able to fulfil the demands of wearing
beards (Ezek. 5). As far as the womenfolk are concerned, they
are expected to appear in public with their hair covered. They
must refrain from using cosmetics. Usually Rasta women are
very obedient to their menfolk and appear to accept their
subservient role.

> "Concubinage is prescribed in the monogamous form, the
> 'wife' being called a Queen and being treated with great
> respect."[70]

Men and women prefer to wear the colours popularly associated
with the movement, viz. red, yellow, green and black. The
original colours of the Garvey movement were red, black and
green. Red stood for the blood of the martyrs, black for the
African skin colour and green for vegetation. The colours
of the Ethiopian flag are red, yellow and green. The red
stands for blood and is symbolic of patriotism. The yellow
is a sign of the faith and hope of the people. Green represents
fertility.

In the field of health and wholeness, herbs are preferred to
Western medicines. There is a strong belief in divine healing.
Here again, the Rastafarians are not unlike some of the African
Independent churches. Where they differ, though, is in their
attitude to one particular herb which is outlawed by western
society - marijuana. The Rastas regard this herb as sacred,
for they claim that since it ranks among the 'good' created
by God (Genesis 1: 12), it must be regarded as a gift from
Him (Genesis 1: 29). Indeed, they associate it with the herb
mentioned in Revelation 22: 2,

> "and the leaves of the tree were for the healing of the
> nations."

It is not called 'ganga' but the "wisdom weed" or the "holy
herb". Because of its sacramental importance during religious
ceremonies, smoked as it is in a cow-horn pipe, it is also
given the names "the chalice" and "the cup". Some people
consider it to be an instrument of liberation, since its use
induces a trance-like state following which one is transported
away from the evils of society. Some Rastafarians are vege-
tarians, but all seem to be united in their refusal to eat
pork. This is in accordance with an ancient law given to the
Israelites that pigs are unclean and must therefore not be
eaten.[71] There are those who will not eat foods prepared with
animal fat. They prefer bread, for example, which has been
made with vegetable oils. In general they opt for natural
(or "Ital") food, since processed food is considered harmful
to the body. All in all, they are trying to fashion a culture
which, though not identifying completely with Africa, at any rate

emphasizes their total rejection of western culture.

Rastafarians are a religious people. During their religious ceremonies, music is accompanied by the beat of drums. They seek out from the Bible passages which either portray God as a great deliverer of His people, or which spell out behaviour patterns for the members. Preferred readings include the following chapters: Genesis 8, 18; Leviticus 11, 21; Numbers 6; Deuteronomy 16; Psalms 8, 18, 21, 29, 48, 68, 87, 137; Isaiah 11, 43, 48; Jeremiah 8; Daniel 7; 1 Corinthians 4; 1 Timothy 6; 1 John 4; Revelation 13, 15, 17, 18, 19, 22. Rastafarians feel that the Old and New Testaments must be read selectively, because of a suspicion that white translators may have distorted the original message. There is strong support of a move to include Apocryphal books in the Bible. A Rastafarian song says:

> "Bring back Maccabees version
> That God gave to the black man.
> Give back King James version
> It belongs to the white man."

The deeply religious Rastas are conversant with their Bibles and can quote chapter and verse. They demonstrate a familiarity with the sacred texts which many Christians are unable to claim for themselves. However, not all Rastafarians are religious, in the true sense of the word. There are some 'functional Rastafarians' which includes

> "those converts to the drug culture, with no real religious
> conviction, but who are mere followers of a segment of
> people who see liberty as their goal. A large segment of
> these will be escapees from the law using the anonymity of
> the Rastafarian as a disguise."[72]

Certain aspects of Rastafarianism may be regarded as having a definite word to say about a black theology of liberation. When for example, the movement's followers are asked to refrain from hair-straightening, this is in effect a call for people to accept their natural, God-given physical attributes rather than try to change them. If one is dissatisfied with the texture of one's hair, or the colour of one's skin, it may indicate a hatred of self. According to Rastafarians, one must learn to love self first, if indeed one is to love one's neighbour as oneself.

There are, though, weaknesses in the Rastafarian theology of black liberation. The trouble with the teaching concerning an actual physical repatriation for black people in the Caribbean, is that it has mistakenly equated Africa with a heaven on earth wherein all may dwell in 'peace and love'.[73] Africa today is still a place of great fragmentation, of skirmishes, where black people are still struggling to be free. All over the continent, there is the noise of battle, and it is obvious that the liberation of Africa is far from complete. For any successful repatriation scheme, participants must be prepared to identify fully with the current struggles for freedom, and this may result in suffering and death. They must also possess definite skills which would be to the advantage of the receiving nations, and not naively suppose that the sameness of skin colour would be passport enough to afford them the right of entry and settlement. Added to this is the fact that Caribbean people, no matter how they may try to detach themselves from western culture, are bound to experience terrible culture shocks upon arrival in Africa. Nothing positive can ever be achieved unless they are prepared to bide their time and ease gradually into the culture just like any European, American or western oriented individual.

With regards to the cultural return to Africa, this idea is less of an illusion. The Africanization of the Caribbean might quite likely provide a starting-point for the complete break with western cultural imperialism. But there are dangers. I think Rev. William Watty has put his finger on the problem:

> "The repatriation-theme of the Rastafarians is as delusory as is their deification of Haile Selassie. It is escapist, reactionary and alienating. Its only difference from the typical colonial mentality is that Africa is substituted for Europe. The fact that our forebears were forcibly extracted from Africa and transported to the Caribbean is hardly sufficient to make persons of African descent exiles in the Caribbean. History does not allow for such back-moves over such a lapse of time. The African in the New World is no longer in a diaspora situation. The blood, sweat and tears of his fore-parents have given him an inalienable right to the region. The movement of history is only forward because God acts in history, creating what is new out of human miscalculation and misconception. Africans in the Caribbean are no longer Africans abroad but Africans in a new homeland."[74]

The other note of caution to be sounded in reference to the cultural return to Africa is that it may well indicate a denial of the mixed nature of Caribbean heritage. Certain segments of Rastafarianism do acknoledge the mixture. In the past,

> "the members were almost all of African stock. At present, the overwhelming majority of members still are, but there are also Chinese, East Indians, Afro-Chinese, Afro-East Indians or Afro-Jews, mulattoes, and a few whites. Every ethnic minority is now represented in the Rastafarian

camps."[75]

However, it would be erroneous to pretend that all Rastafarians recognize this mixed nature of Caribbean cultural heritage. In this type of attitude, whereby some persons display little or no respect for other people's differences, we are presented with the pathetic spectacle of the liberators becoming imprisoned by their own shortsightedness. The Caribbean person may be of any origin - African, Indian, Chinese, Syrian, Lebanese, Jew, European. The people of Trinidad and Tobago and Guyana know this fact only too well, since their populations are more cosmopolitan than others. True liberation for the Caribbean must involve acceptance of this diversity of cultural roots. Theology within such a context acknowledges that God is interested in all people, regardless of colour, creed, class or race.[76]

Perhaps the real challenge presented by Rastafarianism is that it is forcing the Church to constantly review its presentation of Christ to Caribbean people. The Caribbeaness of the Son of God must be reflected at all levels of Christian Education, beginning with the visual aids used within the contexts of church schools. The new curriculum guide for Caribbean Sunday Schools[77] which has been written and produced by Caribbean Christian educators for the Caribbean people is an attempt to correct failings within the present system of transmitting the Christian faith to children and young people. It aims at giving a unique experience to young seekers after

truth. Its goal may be seen as helping to create an atmosphere
wherein the incarnation may become a local reality, wherein
Christ is no longer the European outsider, but an integral part
of Caribbean culture. Implicit in this idea of Christ's
complete identification with Caribbean people, is His identification with the poor, deprived masses. I agree with Barrett
when he says of the Rastafarians:

> "The movement is a symbol of religious neglect, exposing
> the established church which, for centuries, was the
> citadel of the status quo and the preservation of
> irrelevant religion. The church, therefore, failed
> significantly to reach out to the poor and needy and
> catered to the rich and the progressive in its liturgy
> and its teaching institutions."[78]

Now the Church is challenged to reformulate its theology so
that it is no longer imprisoned within a middle or an upper
class mould. If Rastafarianism is taken seriously, then this
might be the step needed to help Christians discharge better
the responsibility of proclaiming good news to the poor.

Part II - BOUILLON: The Flavour

Theology within the Caribbean has been influenced by the
experiences which people have lived through - conquest,
slavery, emancipation, colonialism, independence. In the
writings of indigenous theologians - William Watty, Ashley
Smith, Kortright Davis, Sehon Goodrige, the late Idris Hamid,
just to mention a few - there is a definite emphasis upon
the need for Caribbean culture to be reflected in Caribbean
theology. My contention is that the Haitian experience can
be of tremendous value here. More attempts should be made to
come to terms with the facets of Haitian folk culture, including the Vaudou religion, because therein lie deep spiritual
insights which have for long been overlooked, mainly
because they are the insights of the deprived masses,
rather than the influential, privileged minority. In order to
describe the flavour which the Haitian experience can give to
Caribbean theology, let us explore two themes: (i) Folk
Exegesis and (ii) Grass-Roots' Socialism.

Folk Exegesis

Let us, first of all remind ourselves what we mean by
"exegesis". This word may be rendered by three more familiar
English terms - exposition, explanation and interpretation.
Exegesis is taking a look at Holy Scripture with the intention
of having revealed to us the underlying truth of God. To
put it another way, exegesis is an exercise in God's revelation,
so that through it, God's Holy Spirit may be recognized to be

at work. Karl Barth's suggestion, with which I agree, is
that faithful exegesis will highlight the divine inspiration
of the Bible.[79] Indeed, when a passage of Scripture is
properly expounded, one ought to be in a position of knowing
more about the historical facts behind that passage, its context, but more important still, its meaning for us today.

In Chapter 2, when dealing with Revelation, we said that there
are certain material factors - cultural, social and economic -
which influence one's interpretation of Scripture. The culture
of the exegete influences the nature of the exegesis. European
exegesis is culturally conditioned and one noticeable feature
of it is its insistence upon demythologizing difficult passages
of Scripture. Modern European culture is goods-centred, not
person-centred or relation-centred. The spiritual realm as
exists in folk cuture is here treated as non-existent. In this
culture, there is hardly a belief in the continuous interaction
between physical and spiritual beings. When the European
exegete is confronted with passages of Scripture like the one
which mentions the elemental spirits of the universe (Colossians 2:8), the explanation he or she gives is that these
refer to the astronomical or astrological systems which are
familiar to most people. With the passage referring to the
principilties and powers in the heavenly places (Ephesians 6:
11-13), the tendency is usually to demythologize in order to
make sense of it. By contrast, the exegete in his or her
folk cultural setting is aware of the possibility of

interaction or communication between the living and the dead, between the material and the spiritual, the terrestrial and the celestial, and consequently is not unduly worried if certain Scriptural passages are not altogether clear.

Folk exegesis takes seriously the spiritual realm. It takes seriously the demonic order. Where there are passages of Scripture in which Jesus exorcises the demons, the folk exegete, though not unmindful of the possibility of psychiatric disorder, is not blind to the reality of demon possession. He or she is aware of the complex nature of the culture and that

> "illness is often attributed to the breaking of a taboo,
> or the machinations of malicious or sometimes displeased
> ancestral spirits. Other causes may be the evil eye,
> witchcraft, possession by an evil spirit and a curse by
> a sorcerer or an offended neighbour."[80]

Bishop Lesslie Newbigin often relates how, as an Englishman, he was once conducting Bible study in an Indian village, and when it came to sections about Jesus' ministry of exorcism, he would fumble, stutter and apologise. While he struggled to give, what to him seemed a reasoned scientific explanation, one of the village leaders interrupted him. Why was he making such heavy weather of the passage, and proceeded to rattle off a dozen or more exorcisms which had taken place in his village over the past weeks. The true folk exegete refuses to be sceptical of everything, allowing for the possibility that his or her understanding of God and the universe has yet to mature. As with the spiritual realm, so too with spiritual communication.

The folk exegete takes seriously the possibility of dreams and
visions being an authentic tool of divine communication in
this day and age. As we have already discussed in Chapter 3,
dreams and visions were commonplace in the era of the Old
Testament prophets.

Spirits, demons and supernatural forces which are accepted
as real within Haitian folk culture, are often dismissed as
sheer superstitions even by some Caribbean theologians.
It is worthwhile here to inject the view of Eugene A. Nida,
which we referred to in the Introduction to this study,
that

> "it is too easy to miss some important contrast or resem-
> blance by passing off other people's beliefs as 'super-
> stitions' and regarding one's own beliefs as 'doctrines'.
> In the same way we avoid 'savage' and 'native' when
> talking of social and material cuture, we do well to
> avoid the word 'superstition' in talking of religion."[81]

One has still to reckon with a certain amount of conservatism,
suspicion and in some instances direct opposition in any attempt
to give a theological appraisal of folk culture. I call to
mind the Ecumenical Consultation on Evangelism held in Trinidad
during September, 1975. At the time of this consultation,
there appeared in a local newspaper an article whose headline
ran as follows: "Clergymen Told Study Obeah". The fact that
'obeah' is the name for harmful magic within the Caribbean
meant that readers at a quick glance were successfully misled
to believe that the clergy were so faithless and disillusioned
that they were being advised to resort to nefarious practices
in order to evangelize people. In fact, members at the

consultation were acknowledging the error made by western
oriented theologians who shied away from the living issues
relating to the supernatural, classing every such thing, whether
good or bad, as being "out of place" on a theological agenda.
Whereas industrialized societies may ignore such phenomena,
theologians within folk cultures of the Caribbean dare not
follow suit.

For long, theological reflection in the Caribbean has been
heavily influenced by the West. This has meant that the
agnostic streak which had given rise to the Death of God
theology in the West, is making inroads into the thinking of
Caribbean theologians. However, not all Caribbean theologians
are adversely affected by the scepticism of the western
approach to theology:

> "When I was a student in Princeton, a group of people in
> my theology class wondered how I sat quietly at the back
> of the class during a heated discussion on the 'God is
> Dead' theology. They wanted to hear what I had to say
> about 'God is Dead' - and I told them that for us in the
> Caribbean that is the kind of luxury we cannot afford!
> We don't even talk about God being dead because we walk
> with him every day and know Jesus Christ as a risen
> reality and presence."[82]

Indeed, the anthem of the Caribbean Conference of Churches sound
a positive note of hope that God is alive and very active
throughout the region:

> "The right hand of God is writing in our land,
> Writing with power and with love.
> Our conflicts and our fears, our triumphs and our tears
> Are recorded by the right hand of God.
>
> "The right hand of God is pointing in our land,
> Pointing the way we must go.
> So clouded is the way, so easily we stray,

But we're guided by the right hand of God."[83]

The positive and hopeful note which folk exegetes bring to bear upon discussions about the nature of God may be said to be in keeping with the general character of folk culture. In Chapter 1 we described some of the obvious facets of Haitian folk culture - oral literature, Créole language, distinctive family patterns, grass roots' socialism, indigenous medicine, indigenous art forms, and popular beliefs. If one were to look at the stories which are told in this culture, or at the songs which are composed by the local people, immediately one can detect that the underlying motive is to excite laughter. People are encouraged to laugh at themselves, to smile even in the face of the most trying and difficult cirumstances. This

> "ability of black people to express the tragic side of social existence but also their refusal to be imprisoned by its limitations "[84]

is a liberating feature and may be regarded as one of the most distinctive contributions which exegetes from folk cultures across the world can bring to discussions on the nature of God. They can testify to a God who, though sometimes may appear to be dead and unconcerned about the trauma which His people undergo in everyday life, is in effect a Living God who walks with us "through all the changing scenes of life".[85]

With regards to methodology employed within folk exegesis, it must be said that narrative styles are preferred. Folk culture is largely oral in nature. Its heritage lies in oral tradition. In the next chapter we will look at the Bible's indebtedness to oral tradition.

As far as Haiti is concerned, the wealth of oral literature has been transmitted by word of mouth from one generation to the next. We already said in Chapter 1, that in the case of Haiti, the necessity of Africans from various tribes to communicate with one another gave rise to Créole, a new language. This language remained a purely oral vehicle of communication. It was not written down, hence few books have emerged in comparison to what has happened in other cultures which have for long been writing down their languages. It must be emphasized that it was not for want of ideas that Caribbean people did not write books. Preference was for the orally expressed, because the oral was cherished for its effectiveness. What this says to theology is that narrative exegesis will be preferred within this culture. Through the method of narrative exegesis, one is able to follow an excerpt from the Bible and enter into the possible thought patterns of narrator as well as the characters who present themselves. So that one has the advantage of looking at several points of view. Granted, the exegete who uses the narrative method is himself or herself limited in scope, selective, biased. Yet we are still able to derive from it that which we expect from any passage of Scripture - historical data, context, and the Word of God who now speaks through it. What is more, the narrative form tends to have a much wider appeal - not

merely to the academic, as does literary theology, but to
those who are not scholars, even to the illiterate. Indeed,
if God's story is to be told, then it must be told in the
language understood by all.

The liturgy, itself a powerful methodological tool, would in
a folk culture reflect the variety of oral expressions. In
Haitian vaudou, the liturgy makes use of folk music, drama and
dance. In this way, worshippers are helped to know that God
is directly involved in their situation and that He accepts
them as they truly are, products of the culture into which
He created them. Of course, although religious folk songs,
hymns and drama are gaining widespread acceptance in Caribbean
churches today, it must be recognized that such liturgical
changes are relatively new. I call to mind what happened
on the Bahamian island of Inagua during a month which I spent
there as a student pastor of the Matthew Town Methodist Church.
This was during September, 1972. An attempt was made to introduce a Folk Mass in the St. Philip's Anglican Church at Matthew
Town. The Anglican rector had scheduled such a service to take
place on the third Sunday of the month. On the Wednesday
preceding the service, the Church Council held an emergency
meeting because of protests within the Anglican community
that electric guitars and drums would be accompanying the
folk mass at the Church. One member at the meeting vehemently
denounced "calypso bands" playing during worship:
"We don't want to have any boom-boom-boom sound in the church!"

"Folk music is only for dance halls," said another Council member.

"As long as I live," declared a third, "I will never support that kind of music in church."

One lady member of the Council said that although a change ought to be made, "Inagua isn't ready for this." The Council voted against having guitars and drums play in church, so the folk mass never came off.

Further on the issue of folk liturgies, it must be said that dance has not yet been as fully exploited as religious songs. Many of the younger Christians of today are content to sing religious songs with local lyrics and bouncy rhythm, but as yet feel inhibited where dancing is concerned. This avenue has still to be explored, although it must be admitted that unconscious dancing usually accompanies singing and hand-clapping during liturgical expressions among indigenous religous groups. Perhaps people need to be reminded that the Hebrews, way back in Old Testament times, used dancing to express the joy which they felt in the presence of God.[86] What vaudou and other folk religions are doing is simply to continue a tradition which the Christian Church seems to have completely forgotten. Of course, there are a number of experiments carried out by churches in England[87] to recapture dancing as a bodily language of communication and to reinstate it in the life of Christian worship.

I am not now attempting to formulate a theology of dance. This has been done quite competently by Professor J.G. Davies, for whom

> "a theology of the dance is an attempt to explicate its meaning as a human activity in the light of the revelation of God in Christ."[88]

Professor Davies, in his work on the subject, has noted that the association of dancing with evil, carnal desires, has prevented the Church from exploiting to the full the potential of this art of communication. This prejudice needs to be overcome, and he cites the French Communist, Roger Garaudy, author of _Danser sa vie_, (Paris, 1973) as one for whom dance reveals that the sacred is also carnal.

Dance can help us to avoid the dichotomy which we so often create between the body and the soul:

> "So it is through dance that we come to recognize that the physical and the spiritual are not two separate domains but twin aspects of one and the same reality."[89]

It can also help us to understand and appreciate better the theological concept of God as liberator:

> "Dance is really only understandable in the light of this radical affirmation of freedom. Dance can be a medium of liberation and as such is a fitting response to the God who sets us free."[90]

Professor Davies also sees the use of dance within the context of the Eucharist. It can enhance the thanksgiving notion which is an integral part of the celebration of this feast. In fact "dancing itself is sacramental in character"[91] and this is something which the Church would do well to note.

It is almost certain that if a survey were to be taken today about the suitability of the various aspects of folk exegesis, many persons, indeed the majority, would say, "that's okay for a youth group, but not for mature Christians". At the back of their minds, story-telling, the singing of religious folk songs and calypsoes, dancing - these constitute working-class behaviour. They are not associated with the educated, the sophisticated, the academic. So that folk exegesis, before it can come into its own, has a long way to travel.

We turn now to the other theme which comes out of the Haitian experience.

Grass-Roots Socialism

Socialism is the form of social organization which is increasingly making an impact upon Caribbean people. This is so because socialism provides an alternative to the capitalist system which had been predominant during the historical periods of slavery, colonialism and even the present age of independence. Capitalism created gross inequalities in Caribbean societies, and people are looking to socialism for the solution to the region's social, political and economic inequalities. Christians, who in the past lent their full support to the 'status quo' because of a belief that all authority comes from God, are today entertaining thoughts that possibly socialism is a system which is more conducive to the creation of an earthly paradigm of the Kingdom of God.

In seeking after patterns of socialism, Caribbean politicians have hankered after imported models, chief among which is the Marxist-Leninist model of development. This we saw to be true in the case of Cuba. No attempt had been made to discover whether there had already existed indigenous forms of socialism, or "grass-roots' socialism". Rather, Castro, as a means of emphasizing his independence of American models of devleopment, chose the principle of Marxist Socialism - from each according to his ability, to each according to his work. It mattered little that when Marx had formulated his principles, he had been thinking of the Europe of his day and not the Caribbean of the twentieth century.

At least two other Caribbean territories have in some way been experimenting with socialism. In both cases, the models have been imported. Guyana, covering an area of 83,000 square miles, is not geographically speaking, a Caribbean country. But its history is bound up with that of the Caribbean islands. It is a country of the South American continent. With a population of 865,000 inhabitants, Guyana is well-known for its experiment as a 'co-operative people's republic'. It is an idea developed by Prime Minister Forbes Burnham and his ruling People's National Congress, who became alarmed at the socio-economic problems which plagued Guyana during the sixties. The country depended very much upon imported food, foreign investment, foreign capital, and the government was determined to make Guyana less dependent upon foreigners, and increasingly to rely upon its own resources.

The early 1970s saw the beginnings of a policy of intense nationalisation, when bauxite mining and export became the prerogative of the administration. The picture which obtains in the eighties is one of nationalization for the mass media (newspaper, radio, telecommunications), public transport, generation of power and the imports of particular items, all accounting for a figure of 80% of the country's economy being State-controlled. It must not be thought that there is no foreign private investment, for in reality, the economy is trisectoral, viz. the public sector, the co-operative sector and the private sector. Guyana cannot function without outside help, whether in the form of grants or loans from the IMF/World Bank Aid, in order to secure imports needed in agriculture or in the bauxite industry for alumina processing. The country relies heavily upon imported energy, in the form of oil, and to offset this, its hydro-electricity plant[92] which will take about six years to construct, is expected to make the county self-sufficient in so far as energy is concerned. In order to bring about a measure of self-sufficiency in basic food-stuffs, the government saw the need to develop land resources through a programmed approach to improved methods of farming, agriculture, forestry and fisheries.

It is difficult to say how far the co-operative people's
republic has succeeded as an experiment, or how far has Guyana
moved along the path of self-reliance. The country still
faces unemployment, estimated at 18% of the labour force.[93]
The rate of inflation in 1980 had been put at 14.1%. Strikes
and other forms of industrial action (or "industrial inaction"
to use Professor Hollenweger's terminology) are quite common.
Added to this are problems caused by the weather, chiefly floods
or drought.

Jamaica, covering an area of 4411 square miles, with a population
of 2.1 million inhabitants, made an experiment with the idea
of democratic socialism. This had been introduced in 1972
by Prime Minister Michael Manley and the then ruling People's
National Party. The government had been faced with severe
social and economic problems, viz, unemployment, a high rate of
crime, inequalities between rich and poor. All these had
been attributed to one root cause - the capitalist dominated
economy. Hence Jamaica had been ushered along the path of
'democratic socialism', which stressed 'democracy' as a system
geared towards the interests of all. The religious implications
of democratic socialism had been voiced from the very beginning
by Prime Minister Manley who himself assumed the role of
divine leader, even adopting the name 'Joshua'. He taught
that democratic socialism, rather than capitalism, would be
the Christian way of expressing the ideal of the equality of
all God's children. The programme which he and his government

planned emphasized free education for <u>all</u>, housing for <u>all</u>, the availability of health services to <u>all</u>, greater opportunities for employment, better working conditions, an end to class-distinctions between manual and mental workers, and an end to discrimination against women. Natural resources such as bauxite and sugar would be owned by the government on behalf of the people. Workers would be allowed to share in the ownership and management of business. With regards to agriculture, there would be the setting up of farm co-operatives where the workers would also be the owners and managers.

Although there had been some successes to emerge from the democratic socialist model, the attempt largely failed. The fact that in the October 1980 General Elections, Mr. Edward Seaga and his Jamaica Labour Party ousted the People's National Party by winning 51 out of 60 seats, is indicative of the fact that Jamaicans had grown weary of Manley's socialist experiment. There were other factors. In 1980, inflation was estimated at the rate of 29.1. Unemployment was officially put at 23% but the unofficial estimate is 30%. The economy had stagnated, through no fault of the socialist experiment, but due to extremes of drought and food, crop disease and declining world prices. There are balance of payment deficits and a shortage of foreign exchange. Even during his regime, Michael Manley had seen the failure of the democratic socialist model for Jamaica. For one thing, he realized that his country would not, at that stage in its development, survive without foreign financing. When in March 1980 he had broken off IMF loan negotiations, and that following this, several other international organizations refused to give loans, and foreign banks refused to extend credit, it meant that the end was in sight.

It is true to say that more people were suspicious of the democratic socialist model than those who had been unquestionably committed to it. Not only did foreign capitalists leave the country during the experiment. Many nationals departed too. It is not surprising that the newly elected government committed itself to free enterprise, seeking aid from the United States, Canada, the United Kingdom, Sweden and West Germany. The Jamaican people, steeped as they are in the Christian tradition, are at any rate reluctant to vote overwhelmingly in favour of socialism because of its atheistic orientation, or rather the godless slant of the Marxist-Leninist brand when it is put into operation.

Apart from Cuba, Guyana and Jamaica, which have coped with socialism to varying degrees of success, there is Grenada. When the regime of Eric Gairy had been overthrown on March 13, 1979 by the New Jewel Movement, Grenada found herself faced with a revolutionary government whose ideological orientation was Marxist-Leninist.[94] The NJM committed itself to the non-capitalist path to development.

> "To be sure, this commitment received its impetus with the Russian Revolution of 1917 and its adherence to scientific

socialism."[95]

The Grenada revolution therefore aimed at a socialist model
which had been tried outside the Caribbean region, though it
must be said that the leaders were not unmindful that before
such an imported model could work, they must win the confidence
of the people:

> "The decision to pursue a non-capitalist path rather then
> seek to move to scientific socialism in one leap, was
> governed by the need to maintain the neutrality, if not
> the support, of the middle strata. Plus, the clear
> understanding that this intermediate stage in the process
> of the development of societal socialist consciousness
> would have been acceptable, and comprehensible, to the
> relatively ideologically underdeveloped working class."[96]

It is difficult, at this stage, to say how far socialism has
worked in Grenada. The untimely death of Prime Minister Maurice
Bishop during the October 1983 crisis will take its toll upon
the country's development programme.

The Caribbean region is undoubtedly moving more and more
along the path towards socialism. But the model has always
been the scientifically worked out ideologies. Hardly have
our politicians and economists given a thought to developing
some of the grass-roots' models which are natural to the
Caribbean environment. The disadvantage of following imported
models is that people have first of all to be convinced, or
even cajoled into believing in their efficacy. In any case,
people tend to be slow in accepting radical changes. If, on
the other hand one were to make use of the available local
models, these would perhaps stand a better chance of succeeding.
In Chapter 2, for example, we identified two major features

of grass-roots' socialism in Haiti. We spoke of the sou-sou,
which entails the pooling of financial resources by village
folk, in order to produce a rotating credit association. We
also referred to the coumbite, a system whereby human resources
of labour are pooled in order to realize specific work-
projects. The fact is that this model of socialism is well-
known, not only in Haiti, but in other Caribbean territories.
It is a model which dates back to the African ancestors, who
undoubtedly introduced it on Caribbean soil. Melville J.
Herskovits, for example, describes the dokpwe in Dahomey,
which is the forerunner to coumbite:

> "A large part of the heavy labor in Dahomey is done by means
> of the co-operative groups known by the term dokpwe.
> These associations not only clear the fields, but do the
> strenuous work of erecting walls for houses and compound
> enclosures and of thatching. When work is to be done,
> the one who is in need of the services of a dokpwe goes
> to the chief and arranges for the men to work for him on
> a given day. If he is wealthy and the task is a consider-
> able one, he may call two or three dokpwe. No fee is paid
> these men for their services. If a field is to be hoed,
> each worker takes responsibility for a row, and the line
> of men moves down the acreage to be prepared for planting
> to the rhythm of drums and gongs, and to the accompaniment
> of songs which are at once the most characteristic and
> the most joyous aspect of this communal labor. Yet the
> invasion even of this co-operative spirit by the compet-
> itive drive is not absent, for if two or more groups are
> employed, each strives to outdo the other, while if only
> one dokpwe is working, it is divided into two squads
> which contest to see which one can hoe the larger plot.
> The reward for victory is the privilege of singing songs
> of derision against the laggards. When the assigned task
> has been completed, recompense takes the sole form of a
> feast, whose lavishness varies with the resources of the
> host for whom the work has been performed."[97]

There are certain features inherent in grass-roots'
socialism which make it a model well worth developing.

Firstly, it <u>acknowledges the worth and dignity of every indivi-</u>
<u>dual</u>, for it is a system which depends upon <u>people</u> more than
upon any other factor. It is human good will, devotion to one
another, which will bring about the co-operative effort of a
sou-sou or coumbite. In the case of the latter, work is
performed despite the fact that no monetary rewards are
forthcoming. People in such a situation are not the ones who
crave after life's luxuries. They want simply to have some
basic necessities - food, shelter, clothing. Hence no one
stays idle while a coumbite is in operation. If a piece of
land is being prepared for planting, then both men and women
busy themselves cutting, hoeing or digging for the sheer joy
of it. For those who cannot undertake strenuous tasks, there
is the opportunity to look after the physical needs of the
labourers, either by cooking food or fetching drinking water.
Each person contributes to the project according to his or
her abilities. No one need feel left out. This element
of belongingness - that you need your neighbours just as
much as your neighbours need you - is sadly missing from highly
industrialized societies wherein life is an impersonal entity,
a mad rat race, with each person looking selfishly towards
individual interests. With coumbite and sou-sou we experience
the essence of a truly co-operative venture.

Secondly, it can be said that in grass-roots' socialism, <u>people</u>
<u>are not valued in relation to their financial means</u>. The
class structure which in modern societies is based upon

economics is non-existent here. What matters in a sou-sou is
that people make a corporate decision as to what sum of money
they will invest on a regular basis to facilitate the running
of the credit association. The fee decided upon is usually
within the means of every participating member. The money is
pooled and allotted to individuals on a rotation basis. In
this way people may obtain essential items which under normal
circumstances would be outside their purchasing power. Through
this system, too, people can be helped to understand that
shortage of maney need not be an obstacle to development,
provided that the co-operation of others is ensured.

Thirdly, grass-roots' socialism is a system in which <u>all feel
a sense of belonging</u>. The mere fact that people can engage in
a joyful activity, singing as work is performed - a feature
common to the coumbite - suggests that they do not consider
themselves to be engaged in slavish work. This is important
when one considers that in Caribbean economic history, indigenous
people have always been working slavishly, not to their own
benefit, but to the benefit of others. In grass-roots'
socialism, they work for the common good, since they belong to
one another. It is <u>their</u> project. <u>They</u> are the <u>workers</u> as
well as the <u>owners</u>. Part of the reason for industrial disputes
in industrialized nations today stems from the lack of a sense
of belonging. The workers are not the owners. Their main
purpose in working is to get as much money as they possibly
can out of the system. Hence the never-ending demand for shorter

working hours and more pay. However, if people could feel, as those who form part of a coumbite or sou-sou do, that what they are engaged in will ultimately be to their own benefit, then the level of productiveness would automatically be lifted.

Fourthly, grass-roots' socialism stresses the importance of the small unit of production. If we again look at the economic history of the Caribbean, we will notice that undue emphasis has been given to plantation agriculture, which involved huge acres of land being managed by multi-national companies. The productive small farms or manageable family holdings had not been given due encouragement. Yet it would be on these small estate holdings that people would feel a sense of pride in their work. Here cultivation would proceed with the utmost care and dedication.

This emphasis on the small unit of production is relevant not only to the poorer nations whose economies are agricultural-based. The "small is beautiful" concept[98] as popularized by Schumacher, applies equally to industrialized England. Sir Adrian Cadbury, Chairman of Cadbury-Schweppes Lts, has pointed out in relation to his own business enterprise[99] that the small firm tends to be the place where there is a greater degree of commitment. This is so because in large firms, there exists a degree of anonymity, whereas within the smaller family firms, there is a better climate for industrial and social affairs.

The value of the smaller production unit is ably supported by politician Shirley Williams.[100] She points out that there is the tendency in Britain, as in modern industrialized countries, to concentrate on larger units of production. Small firms gradually expand into larger entities. This is lamentable, particularly because of

> "the enterprising and innovative characteristics of small firms."[101]

Since government policies have neither discouraged big firms, nor encouraged small enterprise, the time has come for positive action. This action must be designed to protect the small firms which suffer the want of many things; want of adequate financial backing, want of "the means to be mobile"[102] or the inability to control "inflationary pressures".[103] Every effort must be made to encourage small enterprise. In the words of Shirley Williams:

> "Yet it is doubtful if people want to work in centralized, concentrated structures, and it is questionable whether these are the most efficient producers of wealth. There has been a growing hostility towards centralization and bureaucracy. Politicians should look at their policy proposals in terms of what people want, how the quality of people's lives can be enriched and made more satisfac-factory. Reversing the tide of concentration is the first necessary step towards a more decentralized, responsive society; it may also be a crucial step towards controlling the powerful forces of inflation."[104]

The significance of grass-roots' socialism is that it offers an alternative to the Marxist model of development, which while containing the potential for the creation of a more just social and economic order, is not, in practice, antagon-istic to the Christian or other religious faiths. This respect

for religious traditions is, in the Caribbean context at any
rate, of vital importance.

Perhaps the nearest example of a socialism which functions
along lines similar to what we have just described is the
east African state of Tanzania. When Dr. Nyerere launched
Tanzanians along the path of socialism, he rejected the socialist model of Marxism-Leninism. He considered Marx and Lenin
as useful in so far as they thought about the objective conditions of their time and tried to work out actions necessary
to achieve certain ends. They were helpful as reference points
and not, as so many socialists believe, the ultimate authority.
Nyerere therefore sought to work out a brand of socialism in
the light of the Tanzanian situation. The model which he
selected was that of ujamaa.[105] Ujamaa means family-hood.
The development of the country would be realized through
traditional patterns of social living. The nation would be
encouraged to live as one family. This would be achieved throug
the setting up of communal farm villages, wherein members are
bound by mutual respect, they work together to produce as a
team, and they hold all things in common. Enshrined in the
practice of ujamaa are many socialist goals. People would be
encouraged to continue sharing what they have with others. All
social activity would be geared towards human development.
The acceptance of the equality of all people, and the upholding
of human dignity would be constantly sought after. All people
would make a contribution to the development of the country's

resources. The only ones exempt from contributing would be the very young, the sick and the aged. All others would receive fair rewards in proportion to their contribution, with special care being taken to prevent too great a degree of inequality between the incomes of different members of the society. There would be no exploitation, no masters and labourers. The people would themselves be in firm control of the tools of production and the mechanisms of exchange. This would not preclude private ownership. Nationalization would only operate as a measure to prevent private individuals from holding the society to ransom. This is why, for example, among the first things to be done by Dr. Nyerere was the national-ization of the banks, flour mills and some privately owned factories.

Dr. Nyerere stressed the principle of self-reliance and warned that true socialism need not have capitalism as its starting point. One is not obliged to depend heavily upon money, whether through gifts or loans. Rather, there are four things that matter: (i) People (ii) Land and Agriculture (iii) Good Policies (of Socialism and self-reliance) (iv) Good Leadership.[106]

The success of Dr. Nyerere's experiment[107] has been affected by the country's military involvement in Uganda, by rising oil prices, since Tanzania relies heavily upon imported oil, and by severe floods and periods of drought in 1973 and 1974. All these factors indicated the necessity for Tanzania to develop

industries to supplement agriculture. Hence in the late
1970s, invitations were extended to foreign firms to re-
establish operations in the agro-industrial field. This is
not to be seen as a failure of the ujamaa experiment, since the
government's policy of self-reliance remains the same. The
fact that following the October 1980 elections, Dr. Nyerere
was sworn in, on November 5th, as President for a further five
years, must indicate that the majority of Tanzanians have
confidence in the ujamaa brand of socialism, and that through
it considerable progress must have been made.

The big question is whether Caribbean politicians will be
courageous enough to develop the model of grass-roots'
socialism on a larger scale. It seems to work well on a
small scale, the level of rural Haitians, and it is worth a
try as Caribbean societies seek ways and means of developing
themselves. If Caribbean people can see the good in coumbite
and sou-sou, emerging as they do from within the folk culture,
then this can be a further step along the road to complete
liberation. It would be a signal that no longer do Caribbean
people feel that their patterns of social, political and
economic organization have to be validated by foreign ideologies
Instead, they would have discovered something of what it
means to develop into the type of people that God has called
them to be, namely a people free to be themselves rather than
other people's shadows.

CHAPTER 6 - NOTES

1. Marx and Engels, _Basic Writings_, ed. Feuer, 4th thesis, p. 244.

2. Lukas Vischer, "Introduction", in ed. Choan-Seng Song, _Doing Theology Today_, Madras, The Christian Literature Society, 1976, p. x.

3. For discussion on these questions, see the following: Walter J. Hollenweger, _Erfahrungen der Leibhaftigkeit Interkulturelle Theologie I_, Munich, Kaiser, 1979. Also, by the same author, _Umgang mit Rythen Interkulturelle Theologie II_, Munich, Kaiser, 1982.

4. Las Casas, "An Account of the First Voyages and Discoveries made by the Spaniards in America, 1540", in _Sources of West Indian History_, F.R. Augier and S.C. Gordon, London, Longmans, Green and Co. Ltd, 1964, p. 3.

5. Thomas Coke, _A History of the West Indies_.

6. See, for example, Eric Williams, _Capitalism and Slavery_; Eric Williams, _From Columbus to Castro: The History of the Caribbean 1492-1969_; Edward Brathwaite, _Folk Culture of the Slaves in Jamaica_; Elsa V. Goveia, _Slave Society in the British Leeward Islands at the End of the Eighteenth Century_.

7. Phillip Potter, "Foreword", in David I. Mitchell, ed., _With Eyes Wide Open_, Bridgetown, CADEC, 1973, p. 5.

8. C.L.R. James, _The Black Jacobins_, New York, Vintage Books, 1963, p. 8. Some critics question whether James is right in suggesting that John Newton composed the hymn referred to in the context as described.

9. F.R. Augier and S.C. Gordon, op. cit., p. 143.

10. J.E. Hutton, _A History of Moravian Missions_, London: Moravian Publication Office, 1922, pp. 44, 45.

    The theology of Moravian missionaries is dealt with in the reasearch of Dr. Kingsley Lewis, _The Moravian Mission in Barbados 1816-1876_.

11. "Know Your Methodism Series", Antigua, MCCA publication, 1979.

12. George Eaton Simpson, _Black Religions in the New World_,

New York, Columbia University Press, 1978, p. 42.

13. F.R. Augier, S.C. Gordon, D. Hall and B. Reckford,
    The Making of the West Indies, Trinidad and Jamaica,
    Longman (Caribbean) Ltd, 1960, p. 140.

14. F.R. Augier and S.C. Gordon, op. cit., p. 152.

15. George Eaton Simpson, op. cit., p. 41.

16. Idris Hamid, In Search Of New Perspectives, Bridgetown,
    CADEC, 1971, p. 8.

17. Idris Hamid, Out of the Depths, San Fernando, Idris
    Hamid, 1977, p. vii.

18. William Watty, "The De-Colonization of Theology." in
    Idris Hamid, ed., Troubling of the Waters, San Fernando,
    Idris Hamid, 1973, p. 68.

19. A full treatment of the Caribbean Conference of Churches'
    contribution to the theology of development is given by
    D.H. Kortright Davis, Mission for Caribbean Change.

20. WCC, What in the World is the World Council of Churches?
    Geneva, The Risk Book Series, 1978, p. 29.

21. Ibid, p. 33.

22. Michael McCormack, Liberation Or Development - The Role
    Of the Church In the New Caribbean, Study Paper No. 5,
    CADEC, 1971, p. 16.

23. Jacinto Ordonez, "Social Ecumenism in Cuba", Ecumenical
    Press Service, No. 15, 22nd May 1975, p. 5.

24. Eric Williams, From Columbus to Castro: The History of
    the Caribbean 1492-1969, London: Andre Deutsch Ltd, 1970,
    p. 509.

25. Herbert L. Matthews, CASTRO, A Political Biography,
    London: The Penguin Press, 1967, p. 298.

26. Eric Willimas, op. cit., p. 487.

27. Ibid, p. 487.

28. Arnaldo F. Tejeiro Fernandez, "The National Health System
    in Cuba", in Kenneth W. Newell, ed., Health By the People,
    Geneva, WHO, 1975, p. 26.

29. Africa Confidential, Vol. 19, No. 6, March 17, 1978.

30. *Africa Confidential*, Vol. 17, No. 21, October 22, 1976.

31. Michael McCormack, op. cit., p. 18.

32. Ibid, p. 8.

33. Ibid, p. 10.

34. Idris Hamid, *In Search of New Perspectives*, Bridgetown, CADEC, 1971, p. 10.

35. Professor J. Severino Croatto, ISEDET, Buenos Aires.

36. Gustavo Gutierrez, "Liberation Praxis and Christian Faith", in Rosini Gibellini, ed., *Frontiers of Theology in Latin America*, London, SCM Press Ltd, 1980, p. 24.

37. cf. Enrique Dussel, *History and Theology of Liberation*; J. Andrew Kirk, *Liberation Theology*; Gustavo Gutierrez, *Theology of Liberation*; Juan Luis Segundo, *The Liberation of Theology*.

38. Derek Winter, *Hope in Captivity*, London, Epworth Press, 1977, p. 35.

39. Allan Aubrey Boesak, *Black Theology, Black Power*, London and Oxford, Mowbrays, 1978, p. 13.

40. Ibid, p. 144.

41. James H. Cone, *God of the Oppressed*, London, SPCK, 1977, p. 54.

42. James H. Cone, *Black Theology and Black Power*, New York, Seabury Press, 1969, p. 31.

43. Ibid, p. 36.

44. Allan Aubrey Boesak, op. cit., p. 126.

45. James H. Cone, *A Black Theology of Liberation*, Philadelphia and New York, J.B. Lippincott Company, 1970, pp. 131, 132.

46. Ibid, p. 12.

47. Ibid, p. 124.

48. Ibid, p. 46.

49. James H. Cone, (God of the Oppressed), op. cit.

364

50. Ibid, p. 84.

51. Ibid, pp. 138-162.

52. Ibid, p. 239.

53. Ibid, p. 137.

54. Errol L. Miller, "Body Image, Physical Beauty and Colour Among Jamaican Adolescents", in Social and Economic Studies, Vol. 18, no. 1, March 1969, pp. 72-89.

55. Manas Buthelezi, "An African Theology or a Black Theology" in Basil Moore, ed., Black Theology - The South African Voice, London, C. Hurst & Co., 1973, p. 35.

56. James H. Cone, (Black Theology and Black Power) op. cit., p. 53.

57. Ibid, p. 130.

58. Allan Aubrey Boesak, op. cit., p. 29.

59. James H. Cone, (Black Theology and Black Power) op. cit., p. 151.

60. Allan Aubrey Boesak, op. cit., p. 42.

61. Harold Turner, "New religious movements in the Caribbean", in Brian Gates, ed., Afro-Caribbean Religions, London, Ward Lock Educational, 1980, p. 53.

62. "Rastafarians in Jamaica and Britain", in Notes and Reports London, Catholic Commission for Racial Justice, Jan. 1982, p. 6.

63. Leonard E. Barrett, The Rastafarians - The Dreadlocks of Jamaica; Kingston and London, Sangster's Book Stores Ltd and Heinemann, 1979, p. 79.

64. Rex Nettleford, Mirror Mirror: Identity, Race and Protest in Jamaica - London and Kingston, Collins and Sangster, 1970, p. 108.

65. Negus and Jah are names for God commonly used by Rastafarians. Negus is Amharic for 'king' or 'ruler', Amharic being the language spoken by Ethiopians. Jah is a derivation from the Hebrew Javeh.

66. M.G. Smith, R. Augier, R. Nettleford, The Rastafari Movement in Kingston, Jamaica, Mona, Dep't of Extra Mural Studies, University of the West Indies, 1978, p. 13.

67. <u>Brethren</u>, because of its association with Biblical language, is appropriate for Rastafarians, who are basically a religious people.

68. Rex Nettleford, op. cit., p. 110.

69. For the Nazirite vow, see Numbers 6 and Leviticus 21.

70. M.G. Smith, R. Augier, R. Nettleford, op. cit., p. 22.

71. cf. Leviticus 11: 7 and Deuteronomy 14: 8. Rastas will not pay serious attention to the account of the conversion of Cornelius, wherein Peter is told, in reference to animals which he considered unclean, "What God has cleansed, you must not call common." (Acts 10: 14).

72. Leonard E. Barrett, op. cit., p. 220.

73. 'Peace and love' are used as a greeting or a blessing by Rastas.

74. William Watty, <u>From Shore to Shore</u>, Soundings in Caribbean Theology, <u>Kingston, William</u> Watty, 1981, p. 23.

75. Leonard E. Barrett, op.cit., p. 3.

76. The national anthems within the region reflect this idea. E.g. the national anthem of Trinidad and Tobago: "Here every creed and race find an equal place/And may God bless our nation." The Jamaican motto "Out of many one people" crystallizes a sound theological concept, viz. God has made one people out of the many nations of the earth.

77. <u>Fashion Me A People</u>, A Curriculum Guide for Caribbean Sunday Schools, Jamaica, Caribbean Conference of Churches, 1981. The advertisement brochure suggests that <u>Fashion Me A People</u> "seeks to unite Caribbean people in worship, allowing participants to come to terms with their faith and to grow in their knowledge of God's goodness and that of their Brothers and Sisters".

78. Leonard E. Barrett, op. cit., p. 110.

79. Karl Barth, <u>Church Dogmatics</u>, Vol. 1., Part 2, Edinburgh, T. & T. Clark, 1969, p. 534.

80. Kofi Appiah-Kubi, "The Church's Healing Ministry in Africa", in <u>Pastoral Studies Spring School Papers, 1976</u>, pub. Theology Department, University of Birmingham, p. 30.

81. Eugene A. Nida, <u>Customs and Cultures</u>, California, William Carey Library, 1976, p. 140.

82. Allan F. Kirton, "Everyday Hope" in NOW, London, The Methodist Church Overseas Division, February 1982, p. 19. Rev. Kirton is a former Chairman of the Methodist Church in Haiti, currently the General Secretary of the Caribbean Conference of Churches.

83. Patrick Prescod, ed., Sing A New Song, No. 3, Bridgetown, Cedar Press, 1981, p. 54.

84. James H. Cone, (God of the Oppressed) op. cit., p. 22.

85. The quoted phrase is from a hymn by Nahum Tate, 1652-1751 and Nicholas Brady, 1639-1726, in The Methodist Hymn Book, London, Methodist Conference Office, 35th edition, 1972, Hymn No. 427.

86. Cf. John H. Eaton, 'Dancing in the Old Testament" in J.G. Davies, ed., Worship and Dance, University of Birmingham, Institute for the Study of Worship and Religious Architecture, 1975, pp. 4-15.

87. Cf. Ronald C.D. Jasper, "Worship and Dance Today: A Survey" in J.G. Davies, op.cit., pp. 22-28.

88. J.G. Davies, New Perspectives on Worship Today, London, SCM Press Ltd, 1978, p. 18.

89. J.G. Davies, ed. Worship and Dance, University of Birmingham, Institute for the Study of Worship and Religious Architecture, 1975, p. 48.

90. Ibid, p. 50.

91. Ibid, p. 56.

92. This hydro-electric scheme is to be localized in the Upper Mazaruni region, an area populated by some 4,000 Akawaio Indians. With the full implementation of the project, these Amerindians' lands would be flooded out by the dam. This raises the question: Is the government sympathetic to their claims and therefore concerned about justice for them, or is the government insensitive to their needs and will treat them as 'savage natives'?

93. Figures and statistics quoted in this chapter for Guyana and Jamaica have been obtained from the Group Economics Department, 54 Lombard Street, London.

94. For a development of this, cf. W. Richard Jacobs and Ian Jacobs, Grenada The Route to Revolution, Havana, Casa de las Américas, 1980.

95. Ibid, p. 83.

96. Ibid, p. 82.

97. M.J. Herskovits, <u>Life in a Haitian Valley</u>, New York, Doubleday & Co., Inc, 1971, pp. 23, 24.

98. E.F. Schumacher, <u>Small Is Beautiful</u>.

99. Lecture on "The Family Firm" delivered to students of the Selly Oak Colleges, Birmingham, January 15, 1982.

100. Shirley Williams, <u>Politics is For People</u>, Middlesex, Penguin Books, 1981.

101. Ibid, p. 114.

102. Ibid, p. 120.

103. Ibid, p. 121.

104. Ibid, pp. 124, 125.

105. For a complete exposition of <u>ujamaa</u>, see Julius K. Nyerere, <u>Freedom and Socialism</u>.

106. These were spelt out in the Arusha Declaration of February 5, 1967.

107. For an analysis of Nyerere's policies, see Michaela Von Freyhold, <u>Ujamaa Villages in Tanzania</u>.

CHAPTER 7

THE WAY FORWARD

Taking Folk Religion and Culture Seriously

> ".....we must now begin to <u>learn</u> from the experiences of ordinary people and from other cultures, not just to satisfy scholarly curiosity but to discover ways of life that can enlarge and enliven the one we now live.

> "...........We turn to people's religion now not because we want to study it but because we want people to <u>teach</u> <u>us</u>. We want to learn from their lives."

>   -Harvey Cox, <u>The Seduction of the Spirit</u>,
> The Use and Misuse of People's Religion,
> London, Wildwood House, 1974, p. 145.

Amusement parks always seem to excite young children. Take the case of the little boy who, with his father, had visited one of them. He had been thrilled by the first stall that he had seen. He knew very well that there were hundreds of interesting things to behold in the other stalls around that park. Indeed, there was a world of pleasant experiences which lay in store for him. This is why, upon leaving the stall, he turned to his father and said, "That was very interesting. Now what shall we look at next?"

For some people, looking at Haitian Folk Religion may be like looking into a stall at an amusement park. For them, it may be a source of entertainment. The phenomenon of Vaudou, with its unfamiliar religious behaviour, may evoke from a casual

observer, the comment: "Oh, isn't that fascinating!" The
aftermath to this might quite likely be a mad search for
another seemingly weird religion which would stimulate amusement. So that in common with the little boy at the amusement
park, the casual observer may, at the end of the day, feel a
sense of satisfaction. That was good fun! Yet nothing of
serious consequence had been achieved through the experience.
The truth is that for the many people looking on from the outside at expressions of religion within folk cultures across
the world, there is nothing to be learned. Consequently they
have not been affected at any deep level of consciousness.

The true theologian seeks to discover more about God and
about how He reveals Himself, not only in his or her own setting,
but within the various cultures throughout the world. The
tragedy is that too many theologians hailing from the west
have dismissed Haitian Folk Religion as superstitious nonsense.
In so doing, they have denied themselves the opportunity of
adding a further dimension to their understanding of God.
This sort of superiority complex displayed all too often by
the west stems from the placing of too much emphasis upon
material wealth. Westerners by and large feel that they have
nothing to learn from the poor people of the Third World. They
have been so preoccupied with material wealth that they
have become either blinded by it or condemned by it to a
tunnel-vision, that no new insights may appear to them. We
recall that Jesus was highly critical of those who allow

wealth to dominate their lives:

> "How hard it is for those who have riches to enter the
> kingdom of God! For it is easier for a camel to go
> through the eye of a needle than for a rich man to enter
> the kingdom of God."[1]

Granted, Jesus was referring to the man who was so rich, that

he just could not bring himself to give to others. Yet His

critique is equally applicable to those who are so rich, that

they just cannot bring themselves to receive from others.

It it therefore of paramount importance that western theologians

in particular take Haitian Folk Religion and Culture more

seriously than they are inclined to do. They must seek to

explore beyond the surface. It is only when they penetrate

the superficial barrier that they may obtain fresh insights,

which would facilitate a truly intercultural approach to

theology.

Obviously, some would want, at all costs, to resist the inter-

cultural approach to theology. The fact is, we all need to fight

against a natural tendency to be conservative in our religious

views. Resistance to change often springs from fear of losing

part of our identity. We have grown to cherish our beliefs

and our individual ways of doing things. It is a threatening

proposition to be told that we must change our outlook and our

modus operandi. Yet in any sincere quest for truth about God,

we ought to be open to the possibility of fundamental changes

in our thinking. A willingness to be born again is not a

natural human trait. Still we ought constantly to be reminded
that our perceptions are incomplete without an awareness of
the perception of others. We can all be greatly enriched if
we are willing both to give as well as receive from others.
The good television producer knows that one camera alone cannot
capture the varying aspects of a particular scene. In order to
give the viewers a more complete picture, he employs three or
four cameras which in turn focus upon selective facets of the
scene. Without stretching the analogy too far, it may be said
that if we are to be helped to surmount our incomplete
understanding of God, we who "know in part"[2] must open ourselves to dialogue with other faiths and cultures, including the
one upon which we have concentrated throughout this research -
Haitian Folk Religion and Culture.

Being Open To Fresh Theological Insights

While pursuing this study, there have been a number of
theological insights which came afresh to me. I had to reason
my Christianity in the light of my contemporaries in Haiti who
are not Christian, but who profess one God. Let us acknowledge,
as we have said elsewhere, that our view of God is conditioned
by our experiences in life. We have duly argued, in Chapter 2,
the case for contextual theology. For many of us, that context
is a modern, scientific one, the result being that we tend to
believe only what we have proven to be materially true. Owing
to the spread of knowledge occasioned by numerous expeditions
into outer space, we believe that there is earth, and that there

are other planets within a huge galaxy. Those who believe in
God as the initiatory force behind the created order, speak
of Him as the Creator of the Universe. Because of scientific
certainty and an accompanying spiritual scepticism, it is
noticeable that people hardly mention, or they dare not mention
at all the spirit world. They prefer not to risk the scandal
of being regarded as outmoded, archaic, anachronistic beings.
And yet those steeped in vaudou culture are by no means
apologetic about their world view. For them, the world
which God brought into being is not limited to the physically
testable. It includes that which none can, with authority,
speak about. But even though an individual may be at a loss
to describe the spirit world, as the astronauts who have
voyaged into space may speak of the planets, there are instances
when it is believed that the unseen and incomprehensible spirit
world breaks into the present, material world. This occurs
when, for example, a person becomes spirit-possessed.

Vaudouisants believe that there are endless numbers of
spiritual beings from the spirit world, who maintain contact
with our world. As we have seen, this view is not confined to
Haitians. Rather it is the explicity held view of parts of
Africa, Asia and Latin America, and tacitly accepted by a
significant number of Europeans and North Americans. Hence,
these last two continents will have to engage in a serious
reappraisal of their material culture in order to receive
fresh theological insights.

The debate about spirits is more than just a claim for the reality of a spiritual realm. It is an affirmation that God reveals Himself to His people in ways which in twentieth century western thinking may appear to be unorthodox. As we have already argued in Chapter 2, sometimes God chooses methods other than Jesus Christ, His Supreme Revelation, or the Church, to testify to His existence. His Holy Spirit cannot be limited, for He is at work everywhere in the world. How God chooses to make His will known through a spirit may be inconceivable to the western mind. But to people within folk culture, this is quite normal. Apart from spirits, there are dreams and visions. These were commonly employed by God to communicate to people in Biblical times. Yet it would seem that God still uses them for purposes of making His will known, particularly to people in Haiti and on the African continent. Unfortunately, Christians have a somewhat narrow concept of how divine truth may be imparted. The tendency has been to stop at the sermon and the theological book commentary, as though there were no other possible ways for God to speak His message. Folk religions can serve as a grim reminder of the many and varied ways through which God has spoken in the past. Certainly God can be relied upon to be just as creative and varied in His approaches to men and women today.

It would help if at this point we remind ourselves of the criteria for determining whether it is God's Holy Spirit which is operating through any given experience.

In Chapter 3, we cited three criteria as gleaned from Paul's first letter to the Corinthians:

(i)   The experience will serve "for the common good" $\pi\rho\grave{o}s$ $\tau\grave{o}\ \sigma\upsilon\mu\phi\acute{e}\rho\upsilon$.[3] It will not have been motivated by any personal or selfish ends in view.

(ii)   It will testify that "Jesus is Lord" $I\eta\sigma\upsilon\hat{\upsilon}s\ K\acute{\upsilon}\rho\iota\upsilon s$.[4] It will in no way act contrary to the trend of the Incarnation.

(iii)   It will be validated by the edification of the "outsider" $\tau\upsilon\hat{\upsilon}\ \acute{\iota}\delta\iota\acute{\omega}\tau\upsilon\upsilon$.[5] The Amen of approval may come from outside the sphere of the Christian Church.

Yet another gateway to receiving fresh theological insights is through getting rid of past obsessions.

"The new is not created out of the old but the death of the old."[6]

One idea which needs to die is that which depicts the judgment of God as directed against non-western religions and cultures, because they have not received Christ. The truth is that western Christianity is also under judgment, even though it has received Christ. This fact had been overlooked by past missionaries who convinced themselves that

"O'er heathen lands afar
Thick darkness broodeth yet."[7]

Now the motives for conversion to Christianity may have been pure. But in the process of taking the Gospel to "heathen lands", the poor heathens whom the missionaries encountered lost their culture, even their lives. This we saw to have

been the fate of the original inhabitants of the Caribbean -
the Caribs and the Arawaks. Hardly a trace of them has been
left, and this had all been due to the approach of western
civilization. Annihilation, cultural imposition and economic
exploitation had accompanied Christian missions to the New
World. In other words, western Christianity failed to be a
proper "light to the nations"[8], hence it stands under God's
judgment:

> "Therefore I tell you, the Kingdom of God will be taken
> away from you and given to a nation producing the fruits
> of it."[9]

The knowledge that western Christianity, like the non-western
religions, is under God's judgment should bring about a change
in attitude to other faiths and cultures. Western Christians
must now accept that they are not the only people of God,
even though they occupy a special place, as did the ancient
Israelites. Dr. James H. Cone has expressed succinctly the
core of my thoughts:

> "Because the Christian gospel lays a claim upon us that
> pushes us into relation to others, we must also be open
> to stories not specifically of the biblical tradition, to
> the stories of other religions from Africa, Asia, and
> elsewhere. To listen to what another culture is saying
> about life does not mean that we have to relinquish the
> biblical faith. That is neither possible nor even
> desirable. Indeed if one's faith is true to life and thus
> the defender of life, as the biblical faith most certainly
> is, then the faith in itself forces one to remain open
> to life as it is lived anywhere. By listening to another
> who is not of my faith, I am affirming my own faith insofar
> as it is the defender of life. Through this process, I
> am permitted to learn from another and to share with him
> the struggles of life. Indeed it is when we refuse to
> listen to another story that our own story becomes
> ideological, that is, a closed system incapable of hearing
> the truth."[10]

Christians are now challenged to _listen_ to other faiths,
including vaudou, which we have been looking at throughout this
study. Listening hard enough may bring about an understanding
of how God is experienced by others. Such an understanding is
vitally important, for it constitutes a giant step forward
towards an intercultural approach to theology.

Acknowledging Indebtedness to Oral Tradition

The noticeable thing about western theology today is that it
lays undue emphasis upon written culture. There needs to be
a reminder that theology had originally been steeped in an
oral culture. A close look at the Bible will confirm this.
The Old Testament existed as oral literature until the exile.

> "That is to say, the Old Testament as _written_ literature
> may in all probability be ascribed to the period between
> the destruction of Jerusalem in 587 B.C. and the time of
> the Maccabees."[11]

Any survey of the Judaeo-Christian tradition must acknowledge
this long period of existence as oral religion. Professor
Hollenweger reminds us[12] that Judaism only became a literary
religion when the Massoretes fixed the Hebrew text. But for
two thousand years it existed orally and the ensuing process of
oral transmission involved reinterpretations, editing of
passages in the light of each new cultural and political
situation. Christianity, likewise, became a book religion
following a long process of redaction and editing of manuscript
with the resulting Textus Receptus being made available far
and wide, due to the introduction of the printing-press.

In pre-exilic Israel, as in ancient Egypt and Mesopotamia, writing was a highly specialized art. It was a skill engaged in by the craftsman, hardly by the common man. Writing for really literary purposes belongs to the exilic and post-exilic era. This fact is emphasized by Nielsen[13] who also outlines for us some of the uses to which writing was put in pre-exilic times. It was important for laws; for political annals, e.g. Chronicles; the administration of justice, e.g. decrees such as bills of divorce (Deut. 24: 1ff.); for correspondence either between private individuals or, as was customary in the ancient Near East, between neighbouring kingdoms. Nielsen mentions 'the Book of the Upright' and 'the Book of the Wars of YHWH' which are basically collections of songs and poems, the former relating to the Southern Kingdom of Judaea, the latter to the Northern Kingdom of Israel. Amos and Hosea, as pre-exilic prophets of the Northern kingdom and Isaiah of the Southern kingdom are unique in that they are numbered among the first of the written prophets. It is quite likely that these prophets wrote only small parts and that the bulk of what has been preserved in Scriptures represents the labours of students of theirs. Writing in their times was politically motivated, for according to what we know, historical records suggest

"a feeling of political crisis as a motive for the increase of literary activity."[14]

Archaeological records merely attest that writing was a specialized job and not one engaged in by the ordinary lay-person.

Dr. R.C. Culley[15] has remarked that scholars[16] have often used the term 'oral tradition' without fully clarifying what is meant by it. He seeks to spell out his understanding of the term and suggests that in one method of oral tradition there may be a fixed form in which strict memorization is used, and in another there may be a freer form involving improvisation. He qualifies this further by saying that the fixed form may emerge (i) where a written text exists, and (ii) where one does not exist.

> "It is clear that oral tradition is a very complex process. So far three possible phases have been discussed: a period of oral composition in which there can be no fixed text, a period of oral composition in which the text is stable but not yet written, and a period of fixed trans- mission with a fixed written text in existence."[17]

Dr. Culley suggests that the Old Testament would include

(1) the written texts of literate authors

(2) texts taken down in dictation from an oral performer

(3) written texts which have been created through the copying of what was already fixed in oral tradition

(4) 'transitional' texts emerging from a period between oral composition and literary composition in which, for example newly acquired literary skills are employed to polish an originally oral composition

(5) the possibility that a person in the oral period might produce a work in a fixed form and take pains to see that it was passed on to others in a fixed form.

The Biblical world remained an oral cultural entity throughout. One has only to look at the book of Deuteronomy to see the

evidence of its oral origins. The laws were transmitted
orally, hence the words "Hear, O Israel" are common introduc-
tions to the statutes and the ordinances of Yahweh to His
people. They were to be recited orally, hence the suggestion
that they must be talked about in the context of home and family
life.[18] Oral tradition was never rejected, but always prized
for what it was worth.

> "The change from oral to written literature does not take
> place because cultural summits have been reached, nor
> because the ability to read and write has become common
> property, but because the culture itself is felt to be
> threatened - from within by syncretism, and from without
> by political events."[19]

It is no surprise that oral transmission continued into the
exilic and post exilic times. On the one hand, oral tradition
continues in any culture because living conditions change, and
in order to ensure that the fixed, written forms do not become
absolute, the oral is crucial. But the real value of oral
tradition is that it enhances memory. Just as oral cultures
are a stimulus to remembering, so too the literary cultures
encourage loss of memory.

The mnemonic devices used everywhere in the Bible indeed stem
from oral tradition. Professor W.J. Hollenweger has listed[20]
several of these oral forms: parables; proverbs; the words of
institution in the liturgical acts of Baptism and the Eucharist;
the traditional structural outline of a miracle (viz. the
seriousness of the illness, the healing, the gratitude - or
ingratitude - of the person healed); the traditional stuctural
outline of credal statements (e.g. in the Apostles Creed -

belief in God the Father, belief in Jesus Christ the Son,
belief in the Holy Spirit); the memorable structure of
prayers.

The oral culture of Haiti can serve as a reminder of the
original culture in which theology had been cradled. The
practice of learning by rote means that people in an oral culture are in a better position to have words of Scripture
literally inscribed on their hearts, as did the Israelites,
whereas those who are the products of literary cultures are
ignorant of the contents of the Holy Book. Another aspect
of oral culture is the approach to evangelism. Here, it must
be done on a personal basis, through dialogue or personal encounter. In literary cultures, where there is so much opportunity to produce written evangelistic material, so that people
can read for themselves, the personal encounter is lost.
Granted, the written word can reach millions of people in a
relatively short space of time. But there can be no substitute
for the enthusiasm of a live individual, with a message to
share.

As we said in the Introduction to this study, the western
Church has lost contact with the oral people of this age.
Western Christianity identifies mainly with written culture.
This is unfortunate, for it means that the Church is sectarian
in its outlook, alienating as it does, a significant percentage
of the people of God. Encountering folk religions and cultures

from Haiti and other parts of the world is crucial to the
survival of the western Church. The only way for such a Church to
continue bearing the title "Body of Christ" is through serious
dialogue with the guardians of oral tradition, and a willingness
to learn from them.

Making Use of Indigenous Idioms

Much of what has been said throughout this study points to a
failure on the part of the Church to distinguish between the
essential Christian Gospel and the trappings of western
culture. In Chapter 2, we mentioned the tendency within
Protestantism to reject, expel or excommunicate anything which
could not readily be reconciled with western Christianity. In
Chapter 5, we referred to the condemnatory attitude of the
church towards indigenous medicine and the necessity for a
serious re-appraisal of approaches to health and wholeness
which are commonly adopted in the West. "In the Church's
attempt to bring salvation to the whole man through her healing
ministry, she must emphasize the mystical, spiritual and
physical understanding of health and disease."[21] It must
be admitted that there is, in indigenous therapeutic methods,
a profundity of insight which it would be a pity to lose.

When we looked at folk exegesis in Chapter 6, we made a plea
for the implementation of songs, music, narrative forms,
drama and dance within folk liturgies, in order that we may
understand that God accepts His people just as they are, namely,

products of the culture into which they have been born. Also
in the last chapter, reference was made to the almost
sacrosanct status of Marxism-Leninism as the model for
socialism, and the glaring neglect of the indigenous expressions
of grass-roots' socialism, which can produce much the same
results as would Marxism-Leninism.

The struggle to make Christianity relevant to indigenous
culture must not be thought of as an issue which is faced only
in the Caribbean. In Halmahera, Indonesia, the Church is also
seeking to transmit truth through the use of indigenous idioms.
In the Halmaheran culture, there is the belief in the gòmànga,
who are the living dead (not to be confused with Haitian
zombies) or spirits of the dead. In this situation, Christians
base their Christology on the concept of a senior Gòmànga, an
unseen, great leader. According to Dr. James Haire,

> "this tended not to result in a systematised understanding
> of Christ such as the 'vere deus, vere homo' of Chalcedon;
> for the gòmànga-influence in Halmaheran thinking rendered
> a clear distinction between the divine and the human both
> impossible and incomprehensible in Halmaheran terms.......
> ..... In any case, the gòmànga-concept explained and
> integrated for the Halmaherans what was the Christological
> problem in Latin terms."[22]

The need to use local cultural idioms to expound truths of the
Christian faith is not confined to concepts, but extends to
practices as well. One practice which missionaries from the
west had found in Africa and had vehemently denounced was
rainmaking. According to Dr. John Rutherford,[23] the tabooed
subject of rainmaking ought to be re-opened for discussion.

It is unfortunate that through pressure from the Church and from modern technology, rain-makers had been made to suffer much humiliation. But in spite of persecution, they have not disappeared, but persist in several parts of Africa. Dr. Rutherford's argument is that rain-making could well be an integral part of the ministry of Christian priests and pastors in Africa. He is in agreement that the undesirable elements associated with rain-making practices must be cast aside. But the positive elements must not be sacrificed. For example, he makes out a strong case for taking out the liturgy associated rain-making, Christianizing it, and using it to good effect within the worship life of the Christian Church. I am in agreement with Dr. Rutherford, for such a rite can be very effective in dealing with the enormous social tensions which are usually built up during a time of drought.

Naturally much of what is being suggested in this whole area of indigenization will depend upon the type of leadership which churches within folk cultures receive. Implicit in this is the nature and content of theological training which is being offered to aspiring priests and pastors. Can the United Theological College of the West Indies in Jamaica, the Roman Catholic seminaries of St. John's Vianney, Trinidad and St. Michael's, Jamaica, and the Anglican seminary at Codrington College, Barbados, be relied upon to ensure that all graduates are well-equipped to function as Christ's ministers in the setting of folk culture? We can only hope that if the answer is in the negative, there will be positive efforts made to correct the deficiency. I am myself the product of a theological education which was largely designed to equip for a general ministry. When at the end of my days in seminary I had been sent to minister to God's people in the French and Créole speaking Republic of Haiti, I realized there and then how inadequate had been my theological training. I had been ill-equipped for proclaiming the Good News in Haiti. It was not simply the question of casting aside the English language in exhange for French and Créole as my media of thought and expression. But there in Haiti I was faced with a culture which I had not reflected upon seriously. I soon realized that my theological bag would be of greater use within western industrialized societies, but for Haiti I would again have to formulate my theological ideas in the light of the cultural environment. Of course, this is what any student of theology is expected to do, namely to try and relate academic ideology to practical reality. If theology within the Caribbean is to relate fully to the realities with which the people of God are living day by day, then the approach to folk culture and folk religion must be seriously reflected upon in our theological training institutions.

Let us recognize that the task entrusted to theological training institutions is an uphill one. For one thing, the seminaries themselves are sponsored by those churches which have been established by foreign missions, not by the

inidigenous churches. The former view theology as an intellectual exercise, to be engaged in by academics and philosophers. The latter see theology as a practical exercise in
which they relate to God through the use of their own
cultural idioms. The theologians of the established churches
believe that they are theologizing at best when their sermons
and prayers in public bear the marks of academic excellence.
By contrast, listen to how the average person in rural Haiti
prays to God, and you recognize how intimate a relationship
he or she has with Him. It is as though God is as real to the
believer as the person sitting, standing or kneeling nearby.
The style adopted is 'down to earth', no high-flown literary
style which can cover up a multitude of sins. Faulty grammar
is not a cause for distraction. The priorities are different.
What matters is that in prayer, the believer communicates with
God from the very depth of being.

The task of theological training institutions must be to make
people aware that theology must be engaged in by all God's
people, ordained as well as lay.

> "Theology is characteristically a lay discipline - the word
> laos being used in its rounded sense, so that it includes,
> in modest proportion, the ordained and specialists (the
> problem has been keeping that proportion modest)."[24]

One way of ensuring a modest proportion is achieved is if
seminarians would from time to time be allowed to live and
work in rural communities, particularly where the only
religious presence is a folk religion. They can learn a tremendous amount from such an experience. Similarly, seminarians

ought, as part of their training, to be exposed to areas where
the only healing agency is the obeah-man, native herbalist
or vaudou priest. Such an exposure would greatly enrich the
level of theological discussions in seminaries. As we mentioned
in Chapter 5, seminary life tends to alienate people from their
roots. This is certainly true of the priest who, at the
completion of seven years' institutional life, discovers to
his horror, that he has forgotten the art of living and working
alongside men and women in communities. Furthermore, because
he has been out of touch with their way of life, their language,
their idioms, their joys, their frustrations, he also discovers
that the staid liturgies which he had been taught to conduct
during his days in seminary, do not even whet their spiritual
appetites. Too long a period of separation from one's roots
can render the individual ineffective. Theological institutions
must therefore devise various ways and means whereby continuous
contact between the two is maintained.

Remembering the Commitment to the Poor

Since we have been reflecting upon theological training, let
us also say that many young men and women graduate from
seminary with the intention of serving Christ's Church. But
that Church is not the complete "Body of Christ", for the poor
are markedly absent. Bishop Lesslie Newbigin notes that

> "the standard type of seminary training tends to create a
> professional elite separated from the ordinary membership."

He further states :

> "it aligns the leadership of the Church with the privileged

387

elements in society instead of with the poor and marginal. It thus serves to perpetuate an improper alliance between the churches and the ruling classes in society."[25]

In Chapter 5, when examining the content of membership of the Methodist Church of Haiti, we observed that the number of adherents, or those who are attached to the Church, but do not yet receive the sacrament of Holy Communion, is greater than the number of persons who are full communicant members. The noticeable thing about these adherents is that the majority of them are illiterate. Why? Because the church's policy is to accept as communicant members only those who satisfy an appointed group of examiners that they can orally express the tenets of the Christian faith. Now, it is all well and good for a Church Council to think that it is raising standards when it admits to full member status only those persons who are articulate, and can mouth explicitly the doctrines of the particular denomination. But the not-so-articulate who are excluded are usually the poor. The tragedy of it is that as long as such a system persists, the poor will always be left outside the Church.

This calls for a sympathetic view. Many of the early Christians could not read or write. They would probably have failed miserably if an examination in Christian Doctrine had been required of them. The most important thing was that they had had an experience of the risen Christ, and could testify publicly, or privately, to the Lordship of Jesus. Testimony,

more than anything else, needs to be taken into account when
church councils are trying to make up their minds as to what
criteria ought to be followed in accepting men and women
into full membership of the Church. It matters not if, to all
intents and purposes, a person is illiterate and cannot articulate the faith. If he or she sets a good example of Christian
discipleship within the local community, and if through that
witness others are inspired to learn more about God and of
His Son Jesus Christ, then there should be no hesitation in
enlisting that individual among the ranks of the Church.

The other way in which the poor are placed at a disadvantage
is in the matter of church discipline. For long, the attitude
of the Church towards persons engaging in sexual unions,
without first of all soliciting the blessing of the Church
and the legal approval of the State, had been to exclude such
"sinners" from the Lord's Table. Usually, the condemnatory
attitude adopted by the Church meant that those couples who
had entered into common-law marriage relationships, opted to
stay away from the Church. The current approach which some
churches are adopting and which is well worth a try by others
which persist in their rigid attitudes, involves respect and
understanding for the poor in their situation. The fact is
that most people who have chosen common-law unions are finan-
cially incapable of getting married in the traditional way.
Certainly in the folk culture of the Caribbean, people
associate weddings with completely new outfits, lots of food

and drink, music and dancing. The Church, which is aware of
these social pressures, will do all in its power to extend
its continual pastoral care to such people. In some instances,
as often happens in Haiti, the Church helps persons so affected
to make their marriage acceptable in the eyes of both Church
and State.

The Church has a moral responsibility to protect the poor from
being discriminated against. It must constantly review its
policies to ensure that they are treated just as equally as
are the rich, educated middle and upper classes which predomin-
ate most congregations across the world. The implication of
this concerted effort to keep the Church open to the poor, is
that the Church will no longer suffer from the absence of
the people of oral culture. As we said elsewhere in this
study, the Church in the west, in particular, has lost its
contact with these oral people, the result being that it has
become too narrow, too sectarian in outlook. And such sectarianism can have a most devastating effect on the mission
which it has been called upon to execute in today's world.

Epilogue

Throughout this study, we have affirmed that God has given a
unique revelation of Himself to people in the folk culture
of Haiti. Their understanding of Him, and how He communicates
with His people may differ vastly from how westerners understand
Him. However, we have maintained that western theologians

ought to make a concerted effort to listen to the shared
insights of that culture, just as people from the folk cultures
across the world have been listening to and benefitting from
the theological perspective of western culture.

This inter-cultural approach to theology, whereby we broaden our
understanding of the God who is, and who reveals Himself in all
the cultures of the world, is something which ought to be
encouraged. The theologian who heeds no other voice apart from
the one which speaks out of his or her own culture, is missing
a glorious opportunity for inter-cultural growth. However the
theologian who, apart from hearing sounds from his or her own
culture, can listen sympathetically to voices speaking out of
other cultures, is likely to develop a mature understanding
of God. And such an individual cannot be far from the Kingdom
of Heaven!

CHAPTER 7 - NOTES

1. Luke 18: 25.

2. 1 Corinthians 13: 12.

3. 1 Corinthians 12: 7.

4. 1 Cornithians 12: 3.

5. 1 Corinthians 14: 16.

6. Colin Morris, Poster of the Methodist Church Overseas Division, 25 Marylebone Road, London, NW1.

7. Lewis Hensley, 1824-1905, in the Methodist Hymn Book, London, Methodist Conference Office, 1972, Hymn No. 811.

8. Isaiah 49: 6.

9. Matthew 21: 43.

10. James H. Cone, God of the Oppressed, London, SPCK, 1977, p. 104.

11. Eduard Nielsen, Oral Tradition, London, SCM Press Ltd, 1954, p. 39.

12. W.J. Hollenweger, "Le livre oral. Portées sociale, politique et theologique des religions orales" in G. Poujol et R. Labourie, Les Cultures Populaires, Toulouse, Edouard Privat, Institut National d'Education Populaire, 1979, pp. 123_134.

13. Eduard Nielsen, op. cit., pp. 39-62.

14. Ibid, p. 52.

15. R.C. Culley, "An Approach to the Problem of Oral Tradition" in Vetus Testamentum, Vol. XIII No. 2, Leiden, E.J. Brill, 1963, pp. 113-125.

16. These include Nyberg, H. Birkeland, I. Engnell, J. Van Der Pleog, G. Widengren, H. Gunkel, E. Nielsen.

17. R.C. Cully, op. cit., p. 122.

18. Deuteronomy 6: 6, 7.

19. Eduard Nielsen, op. cit., p. 60.

20.   Walter J. Hollenweger, op. cit., pp. 123-134.

21.   Kofi Appiah-Kubi, "The Church's Healing Ministry in
      Africa", in Pastoral Studies Spring School Papers,
      pub. Theology Department, University of Birmingham,
      1976, p. 29.

22.   James Haire, The Character and Theological Struggle of
      the Church in Halmahera, Indonesia, 1941-1979,
      Frankfurt Am Main, Verlag, Peter D. Lang, 1981, p. 258.

23.   John Rutherford, W.C. Willoughby - Missionary Practi-
      tioner and Scholar.

24.   Ian M. Fraser, Reinventing Theology as the People's Work,
      London, I.M. Fraser, 1981, p. 5.

25.   Lesslie Newbigin, "Theological Education in a World
      Perspective", in Ministerial Formation 4, Geneva,
      WCC, October 1978, p. 4.

BIBLIOGRAPHY

Abbott-Smithm <u>A Manual Greek Lexicon of the New Testament</u>,
    Edinburgh, T & T. Clark, 1964.

Alexander, Hartley Burr, <u>The Mythology of All Races</u>, Vol. XI,
    Latin America-Boston, Marshall Jones & Co., 1920.

Appiah-Kubi, Kofi, "The Church's Healing Ministry in Africa",
    in <u>Pastoral Studies Spring School Papers</u>, University of
    Birmingham, Theology Department, 1976, pp. 29-37.

Assmann, Hugo, "The Power of Christ in History: Conflicting
    Christologies and Discernment" in Rosino Gibellini, ed.
    <u>Frontiers of Theology in Latin America</u>, London, SCM Press
    Ltd. 1980, pp. 133-150.

Augier, F.R., Gordon, S.C., Hall, D. and Reckord, B., <u>The
    Making of the West Indies</u>, Trinidad and Jamaica, Longman
    (Caribbean) Ltd. 1962.

Augier, F.R. and Gordon, S.C., <u>Sources of West Indian History</u>,
    London, Longmans, Green and Co. Ltd. 1962.

Barrett, C.K., <u>A Commentary on the Epistle to the Romans</u>,
    London, Adam & Charles Black, 1967.

Barrett, Leonard E., <u>The Rastafarians - The Dreadlocks of
    Jamaica</u>, Kingston, Sangster's Book Stores Ltd., in
    association with Heinemann, London, 1979.

Barth, Karl, <u>Church Dogmatics</u>, Vol. 1, Edinburgh, T & T.
    Clark, 1969.

Bastide, Roger, <u>The African Religions of Brazil</u>, Baltimore
    and London, The John Hopkins University Press, 1978.

Bastien, Rémy, "Vodoun and Politics in Haiti", in Harold
    Courlander and Rémy Bastien, <u>Religion and Politics in
    Haiti</u>, Washington, D.C., Institute for Cross-Cultural
    Research, 1966.

Bennett, Louise, <u>Anancy and Miss Lou</u>, Kingston, Sangster's
    Book Stores Ltd., 1979.

Blatty, William Peter, <u>The Exorcist</u>, New York, Bantam Books,
    1971.

Boesak, Allan Aubrey, <u>Black Theology, Black Power</u>, London and
    Oxford, Mowbrays 1978.

Brathwaite, Edward, Folk Culture of the Slaves in Jamaica, London and Port-of-Spain, New Beacon Books, 1970.

Brown, Francis, Driver, S.R., Briggs, C.A., Hebrew and English Lexicon of the Old Testament, Oxford, Clarendon Press, 1906.

Brown, Karen McCarthy, The Vévé of Haitian Vodou: A Structural Analysis of Visual Imagery, Pennsylvania, Temple University, PhD, 1976.

Brown, Peter, The Cult of the Saints, London, SCM Press Ltd., 1981.

Bruce, F.F., Commentary on the Epistle to the Hebrews, London Marshall, Morgan & Scott, 1977.

Bryant, John H., Five Challenges to the Churches in Health Work, Geneva, Contact 42, CMC, World Council of Churches, December 1977.

Bultmann, Rudolf, Theology in the New Testament, I, II, New York, Charles Scribner's Sons, 1951 & 1955.

Burns, Sir Alan, History of the British West Indies, London, George Allen and Unwin Ltd., 1965.

Buthelezi, Manas, "An African Theology or a Black Theology" in Basil Moore, ed., Black Theology - The South African Voice, London, C. Hurst & Co., 1973.

Campbell, Horace, "The Rastafari Intervention: An Enquiry into the Culture of Rastafari - from Garvey to Rodney", paper for the Society of Caribbean Studies Conference, School of Social Sciences, University of Sussex, Falmer, Brighton, February 1979.

Caribbean Conference of Churches, Fashion Me A People, A Curriculum Guide for Caribbean Sunday Schools, Jamaica, CCC, 1981.

Catholic Commission for Racial Justice, "Rastafarians in Jamaica and Britain" in Notes and Reports, London, January 1982.

Clarke, Edith, My Mother Who Fathered Me, London, George Allen & Unwin, 1957 & 1966.

Clines, David J.A., "Story and Poem: The Old Testament as LIterature and as Scripture" in Interpretation, Virginia, Union Theological Seminary, April 1980, pp. 115-127.

Coke, Thomas, A History of the West Indies, in 3 vols, London, Clarendon Press, 1810.

Cone, James H., Black Theology and Black Power, New York, Seabury Press, 1969.

Cone, James H., A Black Theology of Liberation, Philadelphia & New York, J.B. Lippincott Company, 1970.

Cone, Hames H., God of the Oppressed, London, SPCK, 1977.

Courlander, Harold and Bastien, Rémy, Religion and Politics in Haiti, Washington D.C., Institute for Cross-Cultural Research, 1966.

Croatto, J. Severino, "Hermeneutique Biblique Pour La Théologie de La Libération", Buenos Aires, ISEDET, 1978.

Crowley, Paul, "The Ministry in Africa", in Ministerial Formation - Programme on Theological Education, Geneva, WCC, 1978, pp. 11§17.

Culley, R.C., "An approach to the problem of oral tradition" in Vetus Testamentum, Vol. XIII, no. 2, Leiden, E.J. Brill, 1963.

Cupitt, Don, Explorations in Theology 6, London, SCM Press Ltd., 1979.

Daly, Mary, Beyond God the Father, Boston, Beacon Press, 1977.

Davies, J.G., Christians, Politics and Violent Revolution, London, SCM Press Ltd., 1976.

Davies, J.G., Worship and Dance, University of Birmingham, Institute for the Study of Worship and Religious Architecture, 1975.

Davies, J.G., New Perspectives on Worship Today, London, SCM Press Ltd., 1978.

Davis, Kortright, Mission for Caribbean Change, Frankfurt Am Main, Lang., 1982.

Davis, John D., The Westminster Dictionary of the Bible, revised and rewritten by Henry Snyder Gehman, London and New York, Collins Clear-Type Press, 1944.

Deren, Maya, Divine Horsemen: The Living Gods of Haiti, London, Thames & Hudson, 1953.

Dickson, Kwesi and Ellingworth, Paul, Biblical Revelation and African Beliefs, London, Lutterworth Press, 1969.

Diedrich, Bernard and Burt, Al, Papa Doc: Haiti and Its Dictator, England, Penguin Books Ltd., 1972.

Djukanovic, V. and Mach, E.P., eds, Alternative approaches to meeting basic health needs in developing countries, Geneva, A joint UNICEF/WHO Study, 1975.

Dorsainvil, J.C., Vaudou et Névrose, Port-au-Prince, Imprimerie La Presse, 1931.

Douyon, Emerson, "Research Model on Trance and Possession States in the Haitian Vodoo" in Richard P. Schaedel, ed., Research and Resources of Haiti, New York, Research Institute for the Study of Man, 1969.

Driver, S.J., The Books of Joel and Amos, Cambridge University Press, 1901.

Drot, Jean-Marie, Journal de Voyage chez les Peintres de la Fête et du Vaudou en Haiti, Genève, Editions d'Art, 1974.

Dussel, Enrique, History and Theology of Liberation, New York, Orbis Books, 1976.

Edwards, P.A., Education for Development in the Caribbean, Bridgetown, CADEC, 1971.

Eliade, Mircea, Patterns in Comparative Religion, London and New York, Sheed and Ward, 1958.

Eliade, Mircea, "The Three Cosmic Zones and the World Pillar" in M. Eliade, Shamanism, London, Routledge & Kegan Paul, 1970, pp. 259-266.

Eyre, Ronald, Ronald Eyre on the Long Search, Great Britain, Collins Fount Paperbacks, 1979.

Ezeanya, Stephen N., "God, Spirits and the Spirit World" in Kwesi Dickson and Paul Ellingworth, Biblical Revelation and African Beliefs, London, Lutterworth Press, 1969.

Fasholé-Luke, Edward W. et al., eds, Christianity in Independent Africa, London, Rex Collins Ltd., 1978.

Favret-Saada, Jeanne, Les Mots, La Mort, Les Sorts, Paris, Editions Gallimard, 1977.

Fohrer, Georg, ed., Hebrew and Aramaic Dictionary of The Old Testament, London, SCM Press Ltd., 1973.

Fraser, Ian M., Reinventing Theology as the People's Work, London, Ian M. Fraser, 1981.

Freire, Paulo, <u>Pedagogy of the Oppressed</u>, Great Britain, Penguin Books, 1977.

Freyhold, Michaela Von, <u>Ujamaa Villages in Tanzania</u>, London, Heinemann, Ltd., 1979.

Garcia, A., <u>History of the West Indies</u>, London, George G. Harrap & Co. Ltd., 1965.

Garrison, Len, <u>Black Youth, Rastafarianism and the Identity Crisis in Britain</u>, London, ACER Project, 1979.

Gates, Brian, ed., <u>Afro-Caribbean Religions</u>, London, Ward Lock Educational, 1980.

Gayot, François, "Evangelisation and Development in Haiti", Trinidad, Study Document, Consultation on Evangelism, CCC, 1975.

Gibellini, Rosino, ed., <u>Frontiers of Theology in Latin America</u>, London, SCM Press, 1980.

Glasswell, Mark E. and Fasholé-Luke, Edward W., eds, <u>New Testament Christianity for Africa and the World</u>, London, SPCK, 1974.

Goodridge, Sehon, <u>Politics and the Caribbean Church</u> - A Confession of Guilt, Bridgetown, CADEC, 1971.

Goveia, Elsa V., <u>Slave Society in the British Leeward Islands at the End of the Eighteenth Century</u>, New Haven and London, Yale University Press, 1965.

Guillaume, Alfred, <u>Prophecy and Divination</u> among the Hebrews and Other Semites: The Bampton Lectures 1938, London, Hodder and Stoughton Ltd., 1938.

Guthrie, G. Malcolm, ed., <u>Lingala Grammar and Dictionary</u>, Conseil Protestant Du Congo, 1935.

Gutierrez, Gustavo, <u>Theology of Liberation</u>, New York, Orbis Books, 1973.

Gutierrez, Gustavo, "Liberation Praxis and Christian Faith" in Rosino Gibellini, ed., <u>Frontiers of Theology in Latin America</u>, London, SCM Press Ltd., 1980.

Haire, James, <u>The Chracter and Theological Struggle of the Church in Halmahera, Indonesia, 1941-1979</u>, Frankfurt Am Main, Verlag, Peter D. Lang, 1981.

Haley, Alex, <u>Roots</u>, London, Picador, 1977.

Hamid, Idris, In Search of New Perspectives, Bridgetown, CADEC, 1971.

Hamid, Idris, ed., Troubling of the Waters, Trinidad, Idris Hamid, 1973.

Hamid, Idris, "Evangelism and Practice", Trinidad, Study Document, CCC, 1975.

Hamid, Idris, ed., Out of the Depths, Trinidad, Idris Hamid, 1977.

Hasted, John, The Metal-Benders, London, Routledge & Kegan Paul, 1981.

Henry, F. and Wilson, P., The Status of Women in Caribbean Societies - An Overview of their Social, Economic and Sexual Roles, Social and Economic Studies, Vol. 24, No. 2, June 1975.

Herskovits, Melville, J., Life in a Haitian Valley, New York, Doubleday & Co., 1971.

Herzel, Susannah, A Voice for Women, Geneva, WCC, 1981.

Hick, John, God Has Many Names, London, Macmillan Press Ltd., 1980.

Hollenweger, Walter J., "Ethical Standards in World Religions" in Expository Times, 85/10, July 1974, pp. 292-298.

Hollenweger, Walter J., Pentecost Between Black and White, Belfast, Christian Journals Limited, 1974.

Hollenweger, Walter J., Evangelism Today, Belfast, Christian Journals Limited, 1976.

Hollenweger, Walter J., The Pentecostals, London, SCM, 1976.

Hollenweger, Walter J., "The Religion of the Poor is not a Poor Religion" in Expository Times, 87/8, May 1976, pp. 228-232.

Hollenweger, Walter J., "Le livre oral. Portées sociales, politique et théologique des religions orales" in G. Poujol et R. Labourie, Les Cultures Populaires, Toulouse, Edouard Privat, Institut National d'Education Populaire, 1979.

Hughes, Langston and Bontemps, Arna, eds, Book of Negro Folklore, New York, Dodd, Mead & Co., 1958.

Hull, John M., _Hellenistic Magic and the Synoptic Tradition_, London, SCM Press Ltd., 1974.

Hurbon, Laënnec, _Dieu dans le Vaudou Haitien_, Paris, Payot, 1972.

Hutton, J.E., _A History of Moravian Missions_, London, Moravian Publication Office, 1922.

Hyppolite, Michelson Paul, _La Mentalité Haitienne et le Domaine du Rêve_, Haiti, Imprimerie de l'Etat, 1965.

Idowu, E. Bolaji, _Olodumare - God in Yoruba Belief_, London, Longmans, 1962.

Ilogu, Edmond, _Christianity and Ibo Culture_, Leiden, E.J. Brill, 1974.

Jacob, Edmond, _Theology of the Old Testament_, London, Hodder & Stoughton, 1958.

Jacobs, W. Richard and Jacobs, Ian, _Grenada the Route To Revolution_, Havana, Casa de las Américas, 1980.

James, C.L.R., _The Black Jacobins_, New York, Vintage Books, 1963.

Jean-Baptiste, Pauris, _Kout Flach Sou 250 Proveb Dayiti_, Port-au-Prince, Bon Nouvel et Boukan, 1974.

Johnston, Sir Harry H., _A Comparative Study of the Bantu and Semi-Bantu Languages_, Vols I and II, Oxford University Press, 1919 & 1922.

Jones, Hugh, "The Concept of Story and Theological Discourse" in _Scottish Journal of Theology_, Vol. 29, no. 5, 1976.

Jung, Carl G., _Memories, Dreams, Reflections_, London & New York, Collins, The Fontana Library - Theology & Philosophy, 1974.

Kane, Margaret, _Theology in an Industrial Society_, London, SCM 1975.

Kelsey, Morton T., _Healing & Christianity - In Ancient Thought and Modern Times_, London, SCM Press Ltd., 1973.

Kerboull, Jean, _Vaudou et pratiques magiques - Initiation et Connaissance_, Paris, Pierre Belfond, 1977.

Kerr, John Stevens, _The Mystery and Magic of the Occult_, London, SCM Press Ltd., 1971.

Kilson, Martin L. and Rotberg, Robert I., eds, The African Diaspora - Interpretive Essays, Cambridge, Massachusetts and London, Harvard University Press, 1976.

Kirk, J. Andrew, Liberation Theology, Marshall, Morgan and Scott, 1979.

Lambourne, R.A., Community, Church and Healing, London, Darton, Longman & Todd, 1963.

Lampe, G.W.H., God as Spirit, The Bampton Lectures 1976, Clarendon Press, 1977.

Lanternari, Vittorio, The Religions of the Oppressed, New York Macgibbon and Kee, 1963.

Lawrence, Roy, Christian Healing Rediscovered, Eastbourne, Kingsway Publications, 1976.

Lecale, Errol, Zombie, London, New English Library, 1974.

Lewis, Kingsley, The Moravian Mission in Barbados 1816-1876, University of Birmingham, PhD, 1983.

Leyburn, James G., The Haitian People, New Haven, Yale University Press, 1941.

Lovell, George, The Church and Community Development, An Introduction, London, Grail/Chester House Publications, 1972.

Macquarrie, John, Principles of Christian Theology, London, SCM, 1971.

Malinowski, The Dynamics of Culture Change, New Haven, Yale University Press, 1961.

Ma Mpolo, Masamba, La Libération des Envoutés, Yaoundé, Edition Clé, 1976.

Marwick, Max, ed., Witchcraft and Sorcery, England, Penguin Modern Sociology Readings, 1970.

Marx and Engels, Basic Writings, ed. Feuer, 4th thesis.

Matthews, Herbert L., Castro, A Political Biography, London, The Penguin Press, 1967.

Maximilien, Louis, Le Vodou Haitien, Port-au-Prince, Imprimerie de l'Etat, 1945.

Mbiti, John S., "Eschatology" in Kwesi Dickson and Paul Ellingworth, eds, Biblical Revelation and African Beliefs, London, Lutterworth Press, 1969.

Mbiti, John S., Concepts of God in Africa, London, SPCK, 1971.

Mbiti, John S., Introduction to African Religion, London, Heinemann, 1977.

McConnell, H. Ormonde and Swan, Eugen, Jr., You Can Learn Créole, Port-au-Prince, 1960.

McConnell, H. Ormonde, Haiti Diary, 1933-1970, Cincinnati, UMCOR, 1977.

McCormack, Michael, Liberation Or Development - The Role of the Church in the New Caribbean, Bridgetown, CADEC, 1971.

McGilvray, J.C., ed., The Quest for Health - An Interim Report of a Study Process, Cleator Moor, England, Bethwaites Printers, 1979.

Methodist Church, A Methodist Statement on Exorcism, London, Division of Social Responsibility, 1976.

Methodist Church, The Church and the Ministry of Healing, London, Division of Social Responsibility, 1977.

Métraux, Alfred, Le Vaudou Haitien, Paris, Gallimard, 1958.

Miller, Errol, "Body Image, Physical Beauty and Colour Among Jamaican Adolescents" in Social and Economic Studies, Vol. 18, no. 1, March 1969, pp. 72-89.

Millspaugh, Arthur Chester, Haiti Under American Control, 1915-1930, Boston, World Peace Foundation, 1931.

Mitchell, David I., ed., With Eyes Wide Open, Bridgetown, CADEC, 1973.

Moltmann, Jürgen, The Experiment Hope, London, SCM Press Ltd., 1975.

Montague, Ludwell Lee, Haiti and the United States 1714-1938, Durham, N.C., Duke University Press, 1940.

Montilus, Guérin, "Initiation à La Théologie de La Religion Traditionnelle Africaine", Cotonou, 1972.

Montilus, Guérin, "La Naissance Dans la Pensée Traditionnelle Fon", Cotonou, 1972.

Montilus, Guérin, "Le Vodou Fon - Ses Images et Ses Symboles", Cotonou, 1972.

Moore, Basin, ed., Black Theology - The South African Voice, London, C. Hurst & Co., 1973.

Morris, L., Women Without Men, The British Journal of Sociology, vol. XXX, no. 3, September 1979.

Nemec, Jeanne, "Rediscovering an Ancient Resource - A New Look at Traditional Medicine", in Contact 58, Geneva, C.M.C., WCC, October, 1980.

Nettleford, Rex, Mirror Mirror: Identity, Race and Protest in Jamaica, Kingston, William Collins and Sangster Ltd., 1970.

Nevius, J.L., Demon Possession and Allied Themes, Chicago, Fleming H. Revell Company, 1896.

Newbigin, Lesslie, "Theological Education in a World Perspective", in Ministerial Formation - Programme of Theological Education, Geneva, WCC, October 1978, pp. 3-10.

Newell, Kenneth, W., Health by the People, Geneva, WHO, 1975.

Nicholls, David, From Dessalines to Duvalier, Cambridge University Press, 1979.

Nida, Eugene, A., Customs and Cultures, California, William Carey Library, 1976.

Niebuhr, H. Richard, Christ and Culture, New York, Harper and Row, 1975.

Nielsen, Eduard, Oral Tradition, London, SCM Press Ltd., 1954.

Nyerere, Julius K., Freedom and Socialism - A Selection from Writings and Speeches, 1965-1967, London, Oxford University Press, 1969.

Nygren, Anders, Commentary on Romans, Philadelphia, Fortress Press, 1974.

Ordonez, Jacinto, "Social Ecumenism in Cuba", in Ecumenical Press Service, no. 15, May 22, 1975.

Parrinder, Geoffrey, West African Psychology, London, Lutterworth Press, 1951.

Parrinder, Geoffrey, _West African Religion_, London, Epworth Press, 1969.

Parry, J.H. and Sherlock, P.M., _A Short History of the West Indies_, London, Macmillan & Co. Ltd., 1963.

Parvey, Constance F., ed., _Ordination of Women in Ecumenical Perspective_, Geneva, WCC, 1980.

Paul, Emmanuel C., _Panorama du Folklore Haitien: présence africaine en Haiti_, Port-au-Prince, Imprimerie de l'Etat, 1962.

Paynter, William H., ed., _Primitive Physic_, A Book of Old Fashioned Cures and Remedies, Plymouth, Parade Printing Works Ltd., 1970.

Pearn, Julie, "West Indian Popular Culture: 'Is Fe We Own'", Study Paper for the Society of Caribbean Studies Conference, Falmer, Brighton, February 1979.

Peddie, J. Cameron, _The Forgotten Talent - God's Ministry of Healing_, Collins, Fontana Books, 1975.

Pegis, Jessie Corrigan, _A Practical Catholic Dictionary_, New York, All Saints Press, 1965.

Potter, Philip, "Healing and Salvation", in _The Ecumenical Review_, Vol. 33, no. 4, Geneva, WCC, October 1981, pp. 330-340.

Poujol, G. et Labourie, R., eds, _Les Cultes Populaires_, Toulouse, Edouard Privat, Institut National d'Education Populaire, 1979.

Prescod, Patrick, ed., _Sing a New Song_, No. 3, Bridgetown, Cedar Press, 1981.

Pressoir, C., _Le Protestantisme Haitien_, Vols I & II, Port-au-Prince, Maurice Vilaire, 1976 & 1977.

Price-Mars, Jean, _Ainsi Parla L'Oncle_, Ottawa, LEMEAC, Collection Caraibes, 1973.

Richards, John, _But Deliver Us From Evil_, London, Darton, Longman and Todd, 1978.

Richardson, Alan, _An Introduction to the Theology of the New Testament_, London, SCM, 1966.

Ringgren, Helmer, _Israelite Religion_, London, SPCK, 1966.

Roberts, Robert Campbell, Rudolf Bultmann's Theology: A Critical Interpretation, London, SPCK, 1977.

Rocourt, D. Alain, "The Challenge of Development in Haiti" in David I. Mitchell, ed., With Eyes Wide Open, Bridgetown CADEC, 1973, pp. 71-81.

Rodman, Selden, The Miracle of Haitian Art, New York, Doubleday & Co. Inc., 1974.

Roumain, Jacques, Gouverneurs de la Rosée, Paris, Les Editeurs français réunis, 1946.

Ruether, Rosemary, Liberation Theology, New York, Paramus, Toronto, Paulist Press, 1972.

Rutherford, John, W.C. Willoughby - Missionary Practitioner and Scholar, University of Birmingham, PhD, 1983.

Salgado, Jean-Marie, Le Culte Africain Du Vodou et Les Baptisés en Haiti, Rome, Université Pontificiale " De Propaganda Fide", Editiones Urbanianae, 1963.

Sawyerr, Harry, God: Ancestor or Creator, London, Longman, 1970.

Schmidt, Hans, The United States Occupation of Haiti 1915-34, New Brunswick, New Jersey, Rutgers University Press, 1971.

Schumacher, E.F., Small Is Beautiful - A Study of Economics as if People Mattered, London, Blond & Briggs Ltd., 1975.

Schweizer, Eduard, Spirit of God (Bible Key Words from Gerhard Kittel's Theological Dictionary of the New Testament), London, Adam & Charles Black, 1960.

Seal-Coon, F.W., An Historical Account of Jamaican Freemasonry, Kingston, 1976.

Segundo, Juan Luis, The Liberation of Theology, Dublin, Gill & Macmillan Ltd., 1977.

Sherlock, Philip, West Indies, London, Thames and Hudson, 1966.

Simpson, George Eaton, "The Vodun Cult in Haiti" in Religious Cults of the Caribbean - Trinidad, Jamaica and Haiti, Rio Piedras, University of Puerto Rico, 1970.

Simpson, George Eaton, "Religions of the Caribbean" in Martin L. Kilson and Robert I. Rotberg, eds, The African Diaspora - Interpretive Essays, Cambridge, Massachusetts and London, Harvard University Press, 1976.

Simpson, George Eaton, Black Religions in the New World, New York, Columbia University Press, 1978.

Skinner, John, ed., The Century Bible - Kings, Edinburgh, T.C. & E.C. Jack, 1910.

Smith, M.G., Augier, Roy, and Nettleford, Rex, The Ras Tafari Movement in Kingston, Jamaica, Kingston, University of West Indies, 1960.

Smith, M.G., West Indian Family Structure, Seattle, University of Washington Press, 1962.

Song, Choan-Seng, Doing Theology Today, Madras, The Christian Literature Society, 1976.

Stapleton, Ruth Carter, The Gift of Inner Healing, London, Hodder & Stoughton, 1979.

Taylor, A.J.W., "Possession or Dispossession" in Expository Times 86/12, Septe ber 1975, pp. 359-363.

Taylor, John V., The Go-Between God, London, SCM Press Ltd., 1972.

Telemaque, Reuben, Redemptive Healing, Barbados, Cedar Press, 1976.

Tillich, Paul, Systematic Theology, Combined Volume, Digswell Place, James Nisbet and Co. Ltd., 1968.

Titus, Harold H., Living Issues in Philosophy, New York, Van Nostrand Reinhold Company, 1970.

Toffler, Alvin, The Third Wave, London, Pan Books Ltd. in association with Collins, 1981.

Trible, Phyllis, "Feminist Hermeneutics and Biblical Studies" in The Christian Century, Vol. 99, no. 4, Chicago, Illinois, February 3-10, 1982, pp. 116-118.

Turner, Adam, Voodoo Queen, London, New English Library, 1972.

Turner, Harold, "New Religious movements in the Caribbean" in Brian Gates, ed., Afro-Caribbean Religions, London, Ward Lock Educational, 1981.

Turner, John, The Healing Church, Belfast, Dublin and Ottawa, Christian Journals Limited, 1978.

Turner, Mark, Holy Spirit and the Sacraments, post-graduate thesis (in progress), University of Birmingham.

Turner, Victor, The Forest of Symbols - Aspects of Ndemba Ritual, Ithaca and London, Cornell University Press, 1970.

Vandercook, John V., Black Majesty, New York, Harper, 1928.

Vilaire, Maurice ed., 4 Causeries, Haiti, Imprimerie du Séminaire Adventiste, 1974.

Watty, William, "Man and Healing - a Biblical and Theological View", in Contact 54, Geneva, CMC, World Council of Churches, December 1979, pp. 1-8.

Watty, William, From Shore to Shore, Soundings in Caribbean Theology, Kingston, William Watty, 1981.

Webb, Pauline, Where are the Women?, London, Epworth Press, 1979.

Werner, David, Health Care and Human Dignity - A Subjective Look at Community-Based Rural Health Programmes in Latin America, Contact 57, Geneva, CMC, World Council of Churches, August 1980.

Werner, David, Where There Is No Doctor, London, Macmillan Press Ltd., 1981.

Wesley, John, Forty-Four Sermons, London, Epworth Press, 1946.

Williams, Eric, Capitalism and Slavery, Chapel Hill, N.C., University of North Carolina Press, 1944.

Williams, Eric, From Columbus to Castro: The History of the Caribbean 1492-1969, London, André Deutsch, 1970.

Williams, Paul V.A., Primitive Religion and Healing, A Study of Folk Medicine in N.E. Brazil, Cambridge and New Jersey, D.S. Brwer, 1979.

Williams, Shirley, Politics is For People, England, Penguin Books, 1981.

Willoughby, W.C., The Soul of the Bantu, London, SCM, 1928.

Wilson, Michael, Health is for People, London, Darton, Longman & Todd Ltd., 1977.

Wilson, Michael, "The Hospital in Society - Health, Attitudes and Values", in Contact 27, Geneva, CMC, World Council of Churches, June 1975, pp. 3-8.

Wilson, Michael, "Violence and Non-Violence in the Care of Disease", in Christian Century 87/24, June 1970, pp. 756-758.

Wilson, Michael, The Church Is Healing, London, SCM Press Ltd., 1966.

Winter, Derek, Hope in Captivity, The Prophetic Church in Latin America, London, Epworth Press, 1977.

Wolff, Hans Walter, Anthropology of the Old Testament, London, SCM Press Ltd., 1974.

World Council of Churches, What in the World is the World Council of Churches?, Geneva, The Risk Book Series, 1978.

Young, Frances, Can These Dry Bones Live?, London, SCM Press Ltd., 1982.

Zain, C.C., Ancient Masonry, Los Angeles, Elbert Benjamine, The Church of Light, 1938.

GLOSSARY

Anansi. An Ashanti spider-god who possesses magical powers.
He appears in many folk tales of Jamaica and other parts of
the Caribbean.

Asson. The sacred rattle of a vaudou priest.

Assen. A serpent in cast iron, symbol of the Spirit Damballah.

Bocor, Bokor. A magician and healer who may act either for
good or for evil. He is sometimes referred to as a sorcerer.

Bouillon. A kind of soup, well-flavoured with meats, vegetables and ground provisions.

Brûler-zin. A ceremony performed during rites of initiation,
consecration and funerals, where fire is used to animate
the spirits.

Clairin. Haitian native rum.

Coumbite. A system whereby members of a community pool
themselves to provide the labour force needed for some
specific project.

Créole. A French-based language spoken in parts of the

Caribbean. Its grammar and syntax often bear resemblances to the structure of certain Bantu languages.

Damballah. A powerful spirit, whose symbol is the snake.

Dessounin. A rite which involves the removal of the spirit from the dead vaudou worshipper's body.

Erzulie. A female spirit, often associated with the Virgin Mary.

Fidèles. The community of the faithful, or the believers in vaudou.

Gourde. Haitian unit of currency, valued at twenty American cents.

Govi. A clay or earthenware jar in which are stored the spirits of the dead.

Gran-Mèt-la. The Créole equivalent of the French, "le Grande Maître" the Great Master or Grand Master. This is the name by which God is known in Vaudou.

Gros-bon-ange. One of the two spiritual principles of the individual, which directs his intellectual life.

Guédés. The spirits of death, worshipped on November 2nd.

Hougenikon. The choir director during a vaudou ceremony.

Houmfort. The hut or 'temple' where vaudou worship takes place.

Houngan. A priest in Haitian vaudou.

Hounsil. A person who assists the priest or priestess during a vaudou ceremony.

La-place. The one who looks after the physical arrangements for a vaudou ceremony.

Legba. The spirit who, in Haitian vaudou, guards the crossroads or keeps the gates.

Loa. The term for a 'spirit' in Haitian vaudou. Loas are also calle mystères, anges and saints.

Loa-protecteur. The protective spirit, similar in function the the guardian angel.

Loup-garou. A sort of vampire; werewolf.

Lutin. The ghost of a child who had died without having been baptized.

Macumba. A spirit religion in Brazil.

Mambo. A priestess in Haitian vaudou.

Marassa. The divine twins, regarded as the first children of God.

Mystère. Another name for 'spirit'.

Obeah. A term used to describe harmful magic.

Ouanga. An evil spell. (Sometimes spelt **wanga**.)

Peristyle. The defined area within a vaudou temple where the ritual dances take place.

Petro. A name reserved for the spirits who are of Haitian origin.

Plaçage. A common-law marriage, or a sexual union which corresponds to a state of faithful concubinage.

Poteau-mitan. The sacred centre-pole in a vaudou temple. It is sometimes called the **pilier central**.

Rada. A name reserved for the spirits who are of Dahomean and Yoruba origins.

Râ-Râ. Bands which parade, blowing bamboos, particularly during the period of time nearing the end of Lent.

Rastafarians. A group which began in Jamaica, acknowledging the Ethiopian Emperor Haile Selassie, the former Ras Tafari, as the Messiah, the Living God.

Serviteur. A person who becomes possessed by a spirit during vaudou worship.

Shango. (1) The Yoruba god of thunder. (2) A spirit religion in Trinidad, based on Yoruba traditional religion.

Sou-sou. A rotating credit association, common among the working classes in the Caribbean.

Tap-tap. A Créole term meaning 'very quickly' which is used to denote the locally built buses and lorries in Haiti.

Ti-bon-ange. One of the two spiritual principles of the individual, which supports the spirit (loa) in a person's head.

Umbanda. An African form of spiritism encountered in Brazil.

Vaudou. A religion based upon the worship of 'loas' or spirits. (Also spelt **voodoo**.)

Vaudouisant. An adherent or worshipper within the vaudou religion.

Vévé, **Vêver**. A symbolic drawing on the ground used in the context of vaudou ritual.

Voyé mort. A ceremony held in the cemetery to send into a living person the spirit of a deceased individual.

Wanga. See **Ouanga**.

Zombie. A person who, having been raised from the grave soon after burial, now exists as a sorcerer's slave.

STUDIEN ZUR INTERKULTURELLEN GESCHICHTE DES CHRISTENTUMS
ETUDES D'HISTOIRE INTERCULTURELLE DU CHRISTIANISME
STUDIES IN THE INTERCULTURAL HISTORY OF CHRISTIANITY

Herausgegeben von/edité par/edited by

Richard Friedli
Université de Fribourg

Walter J. Hollenweger
University of Birmingham

Hans-Jochen Margull
Universität Hamburg

Band 1 Wolfram Weiße: Südafrika und das Antirassismusprogramm. Kirchen im Spannungsfeld einer Rassengesellschaft.

Band 2 Ingo Lembke: Christentum unter den Bedingungen Lateinamerikas. Die katholische Kirche vor den Problemen der Abhängigkeit und Unterentwicklung.

Band 3 Gerd Uwe Kliewer: Das neue Volk der Pfingstler. Religion, Unterentwicklung und sozialer Wandel in Lateinamerika.

Band 4 Joachim Wietzke: Theologie im modernen Indien - Paul David Devanandan.

Band 5 Werner Ustorf: Afrikanische Initiative. Das aktive Leiden des Propheten Simon Kimbangu.

Band 6 Erhard Kamphausen: Anfänge der kirchlichen Unabhängigkeitsbewegung in Südafrika. Geschichte und Theologie der äthiopischen Bewegung. 1880-1910.

Band 7 Lothar Engel: Kolonialismus und Nationalismus im deutschen Protestantismus in Namibia 1907-1945. Beiträge zur Geschichte der deutschen evangelischen Mission und Kirche im ehemaligen Kolonial- und Mandatsgebiet Südwestafrika.

Band 8 Pamela M. Binyon: The Concepts of „Spirit" and „Demon". A Study in the use of different languages describing the same phenomena.

Band 9 Neville Richardson: The World Council of Churches and Race Relations: 1960 to 1969.

Band 10 Jörg Müller: Uppsala II. Erneuerung in der Mission. Eine redaktionsgeschichtliche Studie und Dokumentation zu Sektion II der 4. Vollversammlung des Ökumenischen Rates der Kirchen, Uppsala 1968.

Band 11 Hans Schoepfer: Theologie der Gesellschaft. Interdisziplinäre Grundlagenbibliographie zur Einführung in die befreiungs- und polittheologische Problematik: 1960-1975.

Band 12 Werner Hoerschelmann: Christliche Gurus. Darstellung von Selbstverständnis und Funktion indigenen Christseins durch unabhängige charismatisch geführte Gruppen in Südindien.

Band 13 Claude Schaller: L'Eglise en quête de dialogue.

Band 14 Theo Tschuy: Hundert Jahre kubanischer Protestantismus (1868-1961). Versuch einer kirchengeschichtlichen Darstellung.

Band 15 Werner Korte: Wir sind die Kirchen der unteren Klassen. Entstehung, Organisation und gesellschaftliche Funktionen unabhängiger Kirchen in Afrika.

Band 16 Arnold Bittlinger: Papst und Pfingstler. Der römisch katholisch - pfingstliche Dialog und seine ökumenische Relevanz.

Band 17 Ingemar Lindén: The Last Trump. An historico-genetical study of some important chapters in the making and development of the Seventh-day Adventist Church.

Band 18 Zwinglio Dias: Krisen und Aufgaben im brasilianischen Protestantismus. Eine Studie zu den sozialgeschichtlichen Bedingungen und volkspädagogischen Möglichkeiten der Evangelisation.

Haire, James

THE CHARACTER AND THEOLOGICAL STRUGGLE OF THE CHURCH IN HALMAHERA, INDONESIA, 1941-1979

Frankfurt/M., Berne, Las Vegas, 1981. XII, 382 pp.
Studies in the Intercultural History of Christianity. Bd. 26
ISBN 3-8204-5888-3   pb. sFr. 74.–

This study looks at the expression of Christianity in the Eastern Indonesian Island of Halmahera in the years 1941 to 1979. Against the historical, theological and missiological backgrounds, it examines the interactions between pre-literary religion, Islam and Christianity. From this it tries to evaluate the nature of the Gospel in relation to its cultural expressions, and the implications for the Church.

Contents: Halmahera Church Independence Movements, 1941-47 – Church Development, 1947-79 – Historical Background – Dutch Theological Antecedents – Missionary Experience, 1865-1941 – Pre-Literary Religious Beliefs, and interactions of these, Islam and Christianity – Gospel and Cultures.

Davis, Kortright

MISSION FOR CARIBBEAN CHANGE
Caribbean Development As Theological Enterprise

Frankfurt/M., Berne, 1982. 259 pp.
Studies in the intercultural History of Christianity. Vol. 28
ISBN 3-8204-5732-1   pb. sFr. 61.–

Caribbean society has constantly been characterized by poverty, dependence, and alienation. The Caribbean Conference of Churches, during the 1970's, promoted extensive development programmes to meet these challenges. Was this development activity recognizable as theological praxis? This study provides a framework for such a recognition by exploring a theological hermeneutic appropriate to the Caribbean, and by suggesting a theologically illuminating way of understanding why liberation praxis and Church proclamation are inseparable for Christian witness in the Caribbean.

Contents: Poverty, Dependence and Alienation in the Caribbean – Ecumenical Action For Caribbean Development – For Full Human Development – Theology For Change – Theological Paths For The Caribbean – Caribbean Theological Explorations – The Caribbean Conference of Churches And Theological Praxis – Towards Greater Christian Maturity – Appendices, Bibliography.

Verlag Peter Lang Bern · Frankfurt a.M. · New York
Auslieferung: Verlag Peter Lang AG, Jupiterstr. 15, CH-3000 Bern 15
Telefon (0041/31) 32 11 22, Telex verl ch 32 420

Ford, David

BARTH AND GOD'S STORY

Biblical Narrative and the Theological Method of Karl Barth in the «Church Dogmatics»

Frankfurt/M., Berne, 1981. 194 pp.
Studien zur Interkulturellen Geschichte des Christentums. Vol. 27
ISBN 3-8204-5967-7   pb. sFr. 49.–

Karl Barth interpreted the Bible in a creative and controversial way. One key to his method is his handling of biblical narratives. He argues from them to his theological conclusions in ways that have many parallels with the literary criticism of realistic novels. The role of the resurrection of Jesus in the Gospel story is perhaps the most fascinating question, and Barth produces an original and, in literary terms, extremely sensitive understanding of it. The biblical narratives are also vital for his doctrine of God. Overall, there is in the «Church Dogmatics» a Christian spirituality that is based on reading the Bible in a certain manner.
Contents: Barth's exegetical method up to C.D.I.2 – Realistic Narrative – Election and Rejection – The Saga of Creation – The Two Natures of Jesus Christ – God and Time – The Spirituality of the «Church Dogmatics».

MacDonald, Charles

CHURCH AND WORLD IN THE PLAN OF GOD

Aspects of History and Eschatology in the Thought of Père Yves Congar o.p.

Frankfurt/M., Berne, 1981. XIII, 165 pp.
Regensburger Studien zur Theologie. Vol. 27
ISBN 3-8204-5945-6   pb. sFr. 40.–

Yves Congar's work is most often associated with ecclesiology and ecumenism. Here his copious writings are examined for his thought on history and eschatology. The historical situation of the Church «between the synagogue and the Kingdom» is found to be a central concern for Congar, just as it has been a recurring theme for French theologians since more than half a century. Each stage of Congar's development is recounted and critically examined. There emerges an account that sheds light on neglected aspects of Congar's theology. The work also adds to the chronicle of the development of modern theology.
Contents: The influences on Congar – Mystical Body theology – The Church in God's Plan – Congar's Christology – The Church, the World, and the Kingdom – Theology of Tradition – Preface by Yves Congar – Index of names.

Verlag Peter Lang Bern · Frankfurt a.M. · New York

Auslieferung: Verlag Peter Lang AG, Jupiterstr. 15, CH-3000 Bern 15
Telefon (0041/31) 32 11 22, Telex verl ch 32 420

Lindén, Ingemar

THE LAST TRUMP

An historico-genetical study of some important chapters in the making and development of the Seventh-day Adventist Church

Berne, Frankfurt/M., Las Vegas, 1978. 372 pp.
Studies in the Intercultural History of Christianity. Vol. 17
ISBN 3-261-02370-8   pb. sFr. 54.–

This study is the first serious scholarly presentation of Adventism. The author discusses the world-wide Adventist denomination from its origin in Miller's spectacular apocalyptic revival in the 1840s. The main concern in the work is devoted to the talented visionary Ellen G. White. Her development and importance is analysed, also in psychological terms. The book is based on an impressive share of formerly not consulted primary material. The author is sympathetic towards the S.D.A. Church, but aims hard at an unprejudiced presentation.

Pfeiffer, Baldur Ed.

THE EUROPEAN SEVENTH-DAY ADVENTISTS MISSION IN THE MIDDLE EAST 1879-1939

Frankfurt/M., Berne, Las Vegas, 1981. 124 pp.
European University Papers: Series 23, Theology. Vol. 161
ISBN 3-8204-5918-9   pb. sFr. 29.–

The history of the European S.D.A. Mission in the Middle East presents itself as a complete chapter of mission history. It demonstrates the strength and weaknesses of a western mission encountering the complexity of the Middle Eastern people, their religions and cultures. It analyses the theological and sociological changes brought about to the mission itself and to the people it served. The problems presented may be helpful in the search of a modern mission theology.
Contents: The development of Seventh-day Adventism in the United States of America – Transplantation to Europe – The mission among foreigners in Egypt – Indigenous beginnings at the Upper Nile – The development in Mesopotamia, Palestine and Syria – Problems of adaptations – The impact of World War I on the mission – Theological aftermath – The mission studies of Erich W. Bethmann and Wilhelm H. Lesovsky.

Verlag Peter Lang Bern · Frankfurt a.M. · New York
Auslieferung: Verlag Peter Lang AG, Jupiterstr. 15, CH-3000 Bern 15
Telefon (0041/31) 32 11 22, Telex verl ch 32 420